**Masculinity and Femininity
in the MMPI-2 and MMPI-A**

Masculinity and Femininity
in the MMPI-2 and MMPI-A

Hale Martin and Stephen E. Finn

 University of Minnesota Press

Minneapolis

London

Published by the University of Minnesota Press
111 Third Avenue South, Suite 290
Minneapolis, MN 55401-2520
http://www.upress.umn.edu

Library of Congress Cataloging-in-Publication Data
Martin, Hale.
 Masculinity and femininity in the MMPI-2 and MMPI-A / Hale Martin and Stephen E. Finn.
    p. cm.
 Includes bibliographical references and index.
 ISBN 978-0-8166-2444-7 (hc : alk. paper) — ISBN 978-0-8166-2445-4
 (pb : alk. paper)
 1. Sex (Psychology) 2. Masculinity. 3. Femininity. 4. Minnesota Multiphasic Personality
 Inventory. I. Finn, Stephen Edward. II. Title.
 BF692.M334 2010
 155.3'30287—dc22

                         2010019708

Printed in the United States of America on acid-free paper

The University of Minnesota is an equal-opportunity educator and employer.

16 15 14 13 12 11 10   10 9 8 7 6 5 4 3 2 1

We dedicate this book to our clients, whose varied expressions of sexual orientation, gender identity, and masculinity-femininity have helped us expand our view of what it means to be human.

Contents

Tables

Figures

Acknowledgments

We are grateful to Beverly Kaemmer for her patience and encouragement, to Auke Tellegen for his sage advice, and to Jim Durkel, who cooked for us on numerous occasions and offered general moral support.

Hale Martin received a grant from the University of Minnesota Press to support a portion of this research.

Chapter 1

Issues in Masculinity and Femininity

What Are Masculinity and Femininity?

When someone describes a person as "masculine," what comes into your mind? When you use the word "feminine" to characterize a person, what do you mean? How do you understand these two concepts? *Masculine* and *feminine* are words that most of us use confidently in everyday conversation, and we generally feel comfortable that our message has been conveyed when we describe someone or something as masculine or feminine. In fact, it seems clear that these two terms have helped people organize and express their experience of the world, and this is true of their equivalents in most if not all languages today as well as in past ages.

We can look in the dictionary and find that the word *masculine* is derived from the Latin word *mas*, which means "male." In current popular usage, masculine refers to qualities characteristic of a man. *Feminine* is a derivative of the Latin *femina*, which means "woman," and in modern English it refers to characteristics typical of women (Merriam-Webster Collegiate Dictionary, 1993). Thus, by their etymology and usage, the terms *masculine* and *feminine* are clearly integrally tied to our conceptions of gender.

There is an abundance of humor circulating on the Internet these days that revolves around differences between men and women. The humor generally presents stereotypical conceptions of masculinity and femininity. One drawing pokes fun at the purported complexity of women and the simplicity of men, showing a single on/off switch on man's control panel but over fifty knobs, dials, and lights on the control panel labeled "woman."

Another figure, entitled "The Comparative Anatomy of Brains," shows fictional cross-sections of male and female brains, labeling parts of the brains differently for males and females. The female brain shows areas dedicated to romance, jealousy, phone skills, emotional thoughts, arguing and debating, shopping, chocolate, babies, business, indecision, grudges and vengeance, and dancing. There is a full lobe labeled "need for commitment," but only miniscule areas labeled "directions nugget," "logic chip," and "sex particle (grows with age)." On the other hand, the male brain shows a very large sex area ("shrinks with age") and a tiny commitment molecule. It also has areas devoted to cars and machinery, sports, remote control addiction, interruption, computer fixation, dirty jokes, blood and guts movies, farting and belching, map stuff, lame excuses, and ability to drive a stick shift as well as a Miche-lobe. There are very small areas labeled "listening particle" and "personal hygiene atom."

The popular theater production *Defending the Caveman* depicts with humor the differences between males and females; it has been playing to sold-out crowds for a number of years. There is a Web site that promises to tell you with 100 percent accuracy whether you are male or female by simply answering some seemingly unrelated questions not involving one's "clothes, grooming, or chest" (http://community.sparknotes.com/gender/). One of the more popular self-help books in the past twenty years is *Men Are from Mars and Women Are from Venus* (Gray, 1992). As the title implies, the book advances the notion that males and females seem to be from different planets, particularly in the way they participate in relationships. In short, there are many popular avenues in which Americans consider the differences between the sexes, often with humor, and generally seek insight into this often problematic area of life experience.

There is also an abundance of more serious debate about male and female differences. Two recent books take different stances on the nature versus nurture issue of sex/gender differences and highlight the intensity of the arguments that have boiled for the past thirty years. In *Taking Sex Differences Seriously*, Steven Rhoads (2004), professor of public policy at the University of Virginia, argues strongly that the culture of the United States has lost sight of the clear biological underpinnings of sex differences. Rhoads maintains that since the sexual revolution, the feminist movement, in support of political correctness, has insisted that sex differences are largely socially constructed, often ignoring the facts. Moreover, he claims that feminist notions have even inhibited research and open discourse that might suggest that the sexes are fundamentally different. Rhoads argues that basic sex differences—including attitudes and preferences around sexuality, nurturing tendencies, aggression, and competition—are biologically determined. He contends that these disparities are determined prenatally because the "impact of testosterone on the developing brain [has] a permanent organizational effect" (p. 3). Testosterone (which has higher levels in most males than females) increases sex drive and aggression and diminishes nurturing behaviors, whereas oxytocin (for which females have more neural receptors than do males) increases nurturing behaviors. Rhoads cites an impressive volume of evidence to support his position.

Rhoads also discusses the effect of the feminist "misperceptions" about sex differences on various social issues. He asserts that feminist ideology puts many women in a conflicted position in that they may wish to be home with their children rather than follow the politically correct pressure to continue a full-time job. Another issue he raises concerns the impact that Title IX has had on sports. (Title IX is the federal legislation from the 1970s that requires colleges to spend equal amounts of money on men's and women's sports.) Rhoads argues that this law effectively decreases the avenues that young males have to channel aggression into socially acceptable athletic behaviors. Thus, he contends, policies founded on a political ideology that denies facts promulgates poor public policy.

Same Difference: How Gender Myths Are Hurting Our Relationships, Our Children, and Our Jobs by Rosalind Barnett and Caryl Rivers (2004) makes the case for the power of nurture in creating and fostering sex differences, although they use the term *gender differences* (see Table 1.1 for the distinction). They too cite an impressive array of evidence to support their conclusions. They acknowledge that nature clearly plays a role in people's behavior, but that experience is a powerful force in development: everything children see and touch "stimulates neural activity, which in turn transforms the brain, which in turn changes the way they see and interact with the world." They urge us not to overlook the immense power of learning and its consequences.

Barnett and Rivers contend that "personality and talent are individual, not gender based" (p. 6). They acknowledge gender differences but argue that these differences do not determine a person's behavior to the extent that many assume. They also point out that the vast differences among women and among men must be considered, as well as the differences between men and women. Otherwise, they say, we are at great risk of preventing men and women from realizing their full human potential. Barnett and Rivers acknowledge the growth in recent years of "gender difference" theories but express concern about the harm that these ideas do to women's opportunities and to those who do not fit the traditional gender-role beliefs. The conclusions one draws in this debate have "real, practical consequences for the lives and health of men, women, and children" (p. 7). The gender difference theories "hurt male-female relationships, undermine equality in schools and the workplace, adversely affect the division of labor in the home, and deprive our children of the opportunity to develop their full human potential" (p. 8). They suggest that the ideas that women are "less aggressive, less logical, emotionally weaker, and more naturally dependent than men" are myths (p. 247).

Harvard University president Lawrence Summers stumbled into this debate in a speech he gave at a diversity conference in January 2005. After observing that more top scientists, by far, are male than are female, he offered three explanations for this phenomena in order of probability: that women are not as interested as men are in making enormous sacrifices to become renowned experts; that men may have more intrinsic aptitude for complex science than women have; and that women may be discriminated against in vying for such high-powered positions. It was Summers' suggestion that males and females may differ in basic aptitude for math and science that fueled a firestorm of criticism. He apologized numerous times, but some critics still called for him to lose his job. Summers eventually resigned from the position, apparently partly because of this conflict. To us, the incident demonstrates how polarized the discussion of gender differences has become in recent years and how strong the feelings run on both sides of the issue. As Dr. Summers can attest, for those in public positions, beliefs about gender differences are a political hot potato.

Another force in the debate about male-female differences comes from the religious arena. For example, on May 31, 2004, the Vatican released a "Letter to the Bishops of the Catholic Church on the Collaboration of Men and Women in the Church and the World" (Vatican Information Services, 2004). This letter was penned by then-Cardinal Ratzinger, who subsequently became Pope Benedict XVI, and Angelo Amato, Titular Archbishop. It likely was written in response to modern debates about women's roles in society and in the Catholic church. This letter develops, from Christian works and tradition, the notion that male-female differences are rooted in nature and are complementary rather than in competition. Women exemplify a "capacity for the other," and this "capacity is a reality that structures the female personality in a profound way." Femininity is characterized as "the fundamental human capacity to live for the other and because of the other." The "dispositions of listening, welcoming, humility, faithfulness, praise and waiting" are exemplified in the Virgin Mary and thus in women. Interestingly, the letter suggests that passivity is an outdated notion of femininity. The letter argues that although women have a unique role to play in the family, including inculcating unconditional love and respect for others, they may also make valuable contributions in the workplace and in government. However, their role in the

Catholic church does not include that of priest. The letter further advises that women who freely choose to devote full time to the household should not be stigmatized or penalized. Thus, conceptualizations of femininity and the role of women emerge from long-standing religious traditions as well as from social and scientific quarters.

It is clear that differences between men and women are a hot topic, one with important consequences for society as well as for individuals. These differences are also exceedingly complex. At least to some extent, controversies about gender differences are reflected in research on the topic of masculinity-femininity. Despite commonplace usage of the terms *masculine* and *feminine* by the lay public and despite the prominent place of masculinity-femininity scales on personality inventories, the scientific community has reached little agreement about what masculinity and femininity are, at least in terms useful to science. There is a long history of efforts to operationalize and measure these constructs, but no gauge has been acceptable to the scientific community for long, if at all. And inevitably, scientific efforts have been influenced by social and political opinions about sex/gender differences and masculinity-femininity, which has only added to the confusion. Without reasonably acceptable measures of a construct, it remains virtually impossible to study it scientifically. This has led some researchers to question the very existence of masculinity-femininity, if not its relevance (e.g., Constantinople, 1973; Spence, 1985).

From another perspective, the feminist movement has generally eschewed the study of masculinity and femininity because it is believed that these concepts reify socially constructed stereotypes, hinder the equality of opportunity for men and women, and inhibit changes in the social milieu. Feminists and those in the "male liberation" movement argue that the concepts tend to polarize sex roles and preserve gender inequality in society. Some have suggested that the terms *masculinity* and *femininity* be replaced with the concept of "gender-related" characteristics. Modern feminist philosophy argues that concepts as contextual and individualistic as masculinity-femininity cannot be measured by objective methods. Hare-Mustin and Marecek (1990) contend that an idiographic approach is the only way to do justice to the complex realities around these concepts. This stance certainly raises excellent points that must be considered in the evaluation of any personal characteristic, especially characteristics as complex and controversial as masculinity and femininity.

However, the terms *masculinity* and *femininity* are still common in the lexicon. Furthermore, there continue to be many scientific studies published in this general topic area that seem to reflect an irrepressible, underlying curiosity and interest in masculinity-femininity. The concepts of masculinity and femininity seem to be integral to the way people make sense of their world. We believe there may be enough commonality and stability in these characteristics, when they are accurately conceived, to allow some nomothetic evaluation. Of course, it is always important to keep in mind the dangers and necessary safeguards when applying nomothetic methods to individuals

What Are the Goals of This Book?

The purpose of this book is to explore objectively the domain of masculinity and femininity as it is represented in the Minnesota Multiphasic Personality Inventory (MMPI), the mostly widely used personality inventory in the world for the past half century. Our hope is that by looking in detail at masculinity and femininity in the MMPI, MMPI-2, and MMPI-A, we can facilitate greater understanding of the concepts and make recommendations about how they could be optimally measured. And although our focus is on the MMPI, we situate our investigation in the context of (1) other efforts to measure masculinity and femininity, and (2) current theory and research related to gender differences.

In this chapter, we briefly examine the underpinnings of masculinity and femininity and several theories that attempt to explain their genesis. This effort is necessarily cursory because the research involving these underpinnings is vast and complex, and our focus in this book is on the empirical studies we present. However, it seems important to acknowledge both social and biological perspectives that provide important grounding and insight into the constructs. In chapter 2, we discuss the history of masculinity and femininity in science, as well as how efforts to measure the constructs as conceptualizations have changed. Chapter 3 is a focused history of the development of Scale 5 (masculinity-femininity scale) of the MMPI, MMPI-2, and MMPI-A, and a review of existing research on this scale. The main portion of this book, in chapters 4, 5, 6, and 7, is a careful examination of masculinity-femininity in both the adult and adolescent versions of the MMPI. Our main question is whether masculinity and femininity are valid constructs that can be sufficiently defined to prove useful in personality assessment. In chapter 8, we summarize the findings of our extensive research to answer the questions posed in this opening chapter.

What Is Meant by Sex, Gender, Gender Identity, and Sex Role Identity?

We recognize that the terminology in this area can be confusing. Let us first define in Table 1.1 a number of terms that are used throughout the book.

Table 1.1. Definition of Gender-Related Terms

Sex	One's genetic heritage of being male (XY) or female (XX) typically reflected in physical primary and secondary sexual characteristics. This can become more complicated, as with intersex people (i.e., those with chromosomal or genital anomalies)
Gender	Often used interchangeably with *sex,* but more accurately how one presents one's sex to others in society.
Gender identity	A fundamental sense of one's maleness or femaleness, as reflected in thoughts about oneself and one's sense of membership in the larger classes of "male" or "female." *Cross-gender identity* is a gender identity that is primarily opposite of that expected for one's sex.
Sexual orientation	Determined by the gender to which one is generally sexually attracted: heterosexual, homosexual, bisexual.
Sex role (identity) or Gender role (identity)	One's acceptance of and identification with "normative expectations about the duties, responsibilities, and rules for behavior in specific situations that men and women in a given society should assume" (Spence, Helmreich, & Sawin, 1980, pp. 3–4).
Gender constancy	Developmental realization that one's sex is tied to biological characteristics and is permanent; includes developmental stages of gender identity, gender stability, and gender constancy (Slaby & Frey, 1975).
Gender dysphoria	Distress about one's gender, usually but not exclusively because of cross-gender identity.
Transsexualism	A condition characterized by gender dysphoria and a desire to live as the other gender.

What Are the Biological Underpinnings of Masculinity and Femininity?

In most instances, whether one is considered male or female is biologically determined. There are certain apparent anatomical and physiological features that determine one's sex; these are generally clear and unambiguous at birth. Human males have XY sex chromosomes and are more influenced by testosterone than are females. Females have XX sex chromosomes and are more influenced by estrogen than are males. Both sexes have unique sexual organs. In early fetal development, the chromosomes are central in determining gender differentiation. When the gonads differentiate, their hormonal secretions become the guiding factor of sex development. Under hormonal influence, the external genitalia and the pattern of organization in the brain become sexually dimorphic.

Some argue that the sexually dimorphic genitalia and central nervous system are the basis for some behavioral traits that further reinforce gender differentiation. At birth, adult caretakers take their cue from the genitalia as to how to treat the child, and the socialization process then becomes central to gender differentiation (Money & Ehrhardt, 1972). Later, the individual's self-perception of his or her genitalia further influences gender development, but pubertal hormonal changes typically solidify the gender identity and characteristics that have evolved. Thus, although it is premature to draw clear conclusions about the determinants of gender identity, it seems likely that both biological and social influences are involved. The relative importance of these influences is yet to be determined and may even vary from person to person.

There are a growing number of studies that suggest that masculinity-femininity is at least partly biologically determined. To quote Swaab et al. (2001):

> There are now quite a number of structural and functional sex differences known in the human brain that may be related not only to reproduction, sexual orientation, and gender identity, but also to the often pronounced sex differences in prevalence of psychiatric and neurological diseases. (p. 97)

Later, we discuss possible social/environmental influences on masculinity-femininity, but for now let us review three possible avenues of biological influence: hormonal, genetic, and evolutionary.

Hormonal Influences on Masculinity-Femininity

Wilson (2000) reviewed the importance of androgens in determining gender role. She cited research that supports the idea that androgens, primarily testosterone, are central in determining gender identity and gender-related behavior. Although testosterone is present in females, males have as much as ten times more of it than females (Udry, 2000). Androgens seem to be a powerful influence in the dimorphic development of males and females. Rhoads (2004) concludes from his reading of the literature that "men's higher testosterone levels explain in large part their greater desire to dominate" (p. 28).

Udry (2000) followed 163 biologically normal women (from an original sample of 470) from before birth to their thirties. Along with prenatal androgen levels from each of the three trimesters and adult androgen levels, he assessed how mothers encouraged feminine behaviors. Udry concluded that:

> mother's prenatal hormones have an effect on the gendered behavior of the daughters three decades later . . . prenatal androgen exposures from

the second trimester affect gendered behavior . . . The second trimester is the period of greatest sensitivity to the effects of androgens, and is also the period during which male and female fetuses have the biggest difference in prenatal exposure to androgens. (p. 449)

He also found that prenatal levels of androgens explain adult gender preferences and behaviors better than do adult levels. This study provides strong evidence of the powerful effects of androgens on development and the potential limits of female gender socialization.

Women with congenital adrenal hyperplasia (CAH) experience a high level of androgen prenatally. The condition can be treated after birth, but the effect of that exposure during critical periods of physical development is profound. These women typically have masculine interests, behaviors, and skills (e.g., visuospatial skills) through life. Conversely, females who do not produce testosterone are typically extremely feminine. Wilson (2000) acknowledges that although androgen action plays an important part in gender role behavior and gender identity, it likely is not the only determinant. We refer you to her work for a more detailed discussion of hormonal influences on development.

Defective virilization of the male embryo is referred to as male pseudohermaphroditism, which results from problems with androgen synthesis or androgen action, as well as defects in müllerian duct regression, during development. These defects result in a number of physical abnormalities, including ambiguous genitalia. The metabolic blocks involved in these cases are largely genetically determined (Braunwald et al., 1987), so we discuss pseudohermaphrodites in the section covering genetic influences.

Genetic Influences on Masculinity-Femininity

Genetic influences on masculinity and femininity largely operate through the effects of hormones that the genes orchestrate. Therefore, we refer you to the prior section to understand the importance of genes in masculinity-femininity through the actions of hormones that they create. One's genetic makeup determines the type of hormones that bathe the developing body and the timing of the release of those hormones. There is some belief that variance in the timing of those baths can have significant consequences for the developing fetuses, for example, that incomplete masculinization of the brain may underlie homosexuality in males (Bailey, 2003).

There are genetic disorders that clearly demonstrate the importance of genes and their associated hormones in development. The most frequent disorder of sexual differentiation is Klinefelter syndrome, with an incidence of one in five hundred males. These males have an extra X chromosome (XXY, although there are variations). After puberty, they typically show low levels of androgens, have breast development, and are infertile. They tend to be tall as a result of an increase in leg length. Other associated features include obesity, varicose veins, decreased facial and axillary hair, mild mental deficiency, and social maladjustment. They are generally heterosexual, although they have decreased sexual function (Braunwald et al., 1987).

Another relevant genetic disorder is Turner syndrome (gonadal dysgenesis). The karyotype of these females is typically X (although there are variations). The genitalia are female but remain immature (including primary amenorrhea), and breasts do not develop at puberty. These individuals tend to be short and to have a webbed neck, a shield-like chest, and a low hairline. Associated features include a low set of deformed ears, ptosis, and other physical abnormalities (Braunwald et al., 1987).

These two examples demonstrate the role of genes in determining sexual physical differences as well as more widespread physical development. It is not unreasonable to expect less visible differences as well.

Lippa & Hershberger (1999) investigated the contribution of genes and environment to gender-related individual differences. Their behavior genetic modeling analysis, which they completed post hoc on a large twin data set (Plomin, Willerman, & Loehlin, 1976), suggested that both genetic and non-shared environmental factors contribute to individual differences on gender-related measures. Although the measures they used are suspect and cannot be equated with masculinity or femininity, the results suggest a significant genetic component to gender-related characteristics. More recently, Loehlin et al. (2005) discovered, through behavior genetic modeling with twin studies, that gender diagnosticity (a novel approach to the measurement of masculinity-femininity that we discuss in the next chapter) "behaved as a fairly typical personality trait, with about 40% of its within-sex variability associated with the genes and little or none with shared environment" (p. 1315).

You may be familiar with the famous case reported by John Money (Money & Ehrhardt, 1972). It involved an accident during the circumcision of one infant of male monozygotic twins that severely damaged the boy's penis. At twenty-one months of age, the boy underwent surgery that removed his penis and testicles and constructed female external genitalia. Money, a respected psychologist and sexologist, believed that gender identity was socially constructed and advised that the child be raised as a female. At puberty, the child, named Brenda, was given female hormones to further facilitate "feminization." Money reported that the child and her family adjusted well. The story caused some stir in the media because the case was reported as an example of the mutability of gender identity in the face of social influences. However, not everyone was convinced. Diamond (1982) argued that the jury was still out.

Years later, investigators located Brenda (then called David) and a very different story emerged. Evidently, Brenda/David had behaved and felt like a male from the very beginning. As a child, she/he "hated to wear girls' clothes, had little interest in dolls, bought herself a toy gun, and insisted on going to the toilet standing up" (Murphy, 1997). At age fifteen, beset with growing problems being a female, she/he was told of her/his conversion to a female. She/he subsequently sought and received a mastectomy, male hormones, and a surgically constructed penis. In the early 1990s, David was married to a woman and was father to three adopted children (Murphy, 1997).

Other investigations have documented that many of the genetic boys who were surgically "reassigned" to be females during this same era had similar difficulty with the transition. In a sample of eighteen pseudohermaphrodites with male chromosomes but 5-alpha-reductase deficiency, who were raised unambiguously as girls, seventeen developed a male gender identity at or after puberty, and sixteen of the eighteen accepted the male gender role (Imperato-McGinley et al., 1979).

Thus, we see that genetics and hormonal action are closely intertwined and that the study of cases in which abnormalities in either exist are instructive. Rare genetic abnormalities can cause an individual who is a genetic male to have a female phenotype and consequently be raised as a female (sometimes with difficulties). However, upon reaching puberty and experiencing the genetically programmed testosterone associated with male adolescence, these individuals frequently change their gender behavior to male.

Although fictional, the Pulitzer Prize–winning novel *Middlesex* (Eugenides, 2002) offers an astute portrayal of the power of biology. The story traces the development over three generations of the previously mentioned autosomal recessive genetic condition called 5-alpha-reductase deficiency. This disorder causes the body not to produce dihydrotestosterone, which causes early external genitalia development of a genetic male to follow a primarily female path. However, during puberty, testosterone, which is not affected by the disorder, acts in the direction of masculine development. Thus, the central character and narrator of the novel is raised as a female until adolescence, at which point significant conflicts arise. The expert the family consulted recommended surgery and hormone treatments to keep her a female. However, the young person decided that she/he felt more male than female, particularly in being sexually attracted to females, and elected not to have the surgery or treatments. This seems to be a typical story for those who are genetic males but are raised as females, and it supports the power of nature over nurture, at least in this realm. The novel portrays the long difficult adjustment that the central character endures.

Evolutionary Influences on Masculinity-Femininity

Another source of information supporting the potential biological underpinnings of masculinity-femininity is found in the relatively new area of evolutionary psychology. Of course, evolutionary progression is effected through genetic mechanisms, which determine hormonal actions in individuals, both of which we have discussed previously. Central to the mechanisms of evolution is sexual selection.

Sexual selection is a complicated area, but a key concept is *anisogamy*, which is when there are two versions of haploids or gametes with different characteristics, as in humans (as opposed to *isogamy*, in which the haploids that join to produce a zygote are identical, as is true of many algae and some fungi). In these conditions, there are two sexes (interestingly, never three or more). One sex produces eggs, and the other produces sperm. The differences between the two gametes and between the circumstances created by those differences are integral to sexual selection. Eggs are fewer than sperm and involve more resources to produce than sperm. Evolutionary scientists believe this fact promulgates an imbalance between the sexes in the investment that they make in reproduction.

Trivers (1972) developed the theory of parental investment, which explains mating systems as a function of the relative disparity in the reproductive efforts contributed by each sex, including both mating efforts and parenting efforts. If one sex invests more time and energy in reproduction than the other sex, the sex with a greater investment is available to reproduce less frequently than the other sex and thus becomes a limited resource to the sex that invests less time and energy. Thus, the sex with low investment is pressured to compete with other low investors for the scarce resource. The more fit the competitors are in whatever characteristics determine their mating success, the more offspring they produce, which in turn favors those "fitness" characteristics in the gene pool. For example, if aggressiveness is an advantage in the competition for access to the limited female resource, it increases in the gene pool

The implication is that, over time, these different evolutionary pressures have led to a divergence in characteristics of the sexes. Buss (1995, 1989) basically explored the behavioral divergence that is a consequence of differing mating pressures promulgated by anisogamy. He examined mate selection in diverse cultures and found commonalities among women and among men, but differences between the two. He found that females tend to seek mates who are reliable, stable, and good providers. He reasoned that women make an enormous investment with their sexual encounters because they face the possibility of becoming pregnant and providing for a child for many years. Hence they prefer males who will be good partners in this potential venture. Thus Buss concluded that women have been hardwired through evolutionary time to be attracted to certain characteristics: those associated with being a dependable, good provider.

Men, in contrast, have less long-term investment in sexual encounters than women. Buss argues that they compete to spread their genes as widely as possible in places where they are likely to perpetuate their genes through offspring. One might also see this drive rooted in simply competing for a limited resource. Thus, males seek attractive females (i.e., those with healthy bodies, healthy skin, etc.) because their being attractive is a sign of general fitness as well as of fecundity. A healthy caretaker with a nurturing nature increases the chances of the offspring's being cared for sufficiently to survive. Also, aggressiveness serves to help males be more successful in their efforts to mate. Buss thus explains the observed sex differences in mate selection as a result of evolutionary pressures. Sex differences, such as criteria for mate selection, desired quantity of sexual partners, dominance, aggression, jealousy, and sex roles—as well as other personality characteristics—may have evolved out of their correlation with these core pressures (Buss & Schmidt, 1993).

The evolutionary theory of sex role differences has been criticized on many fronts (see Bussey & Bandura, 1999). One criticism focuses on the emphasis on purposeful strategies over blind natural selection processes. "Survival of the fittest" does not neatly explain males' attempts to maximize their sexual opportunities. The ideas are also viewed as descriptive, post hoc explanations that lack scientific rigor. Bussey and Bandura (p. 680) claim:

Psychological evolutionism does not provide the mechanisms responsible for social patterns of behavior, nor does it specify the nature of the interactional relationship between genetic and environmental influences for disentangling their impact. Contrary to the claims of its adherents, predictions from psychological evolutionism are not consistently supported in comparative tests of evolutionary and sociostructural theories or by the attributes males and females prefer in their mates. Some theorists even question the evolutionary validity of some of the predictions made from evolutionary biology by psychological evolutionists. Others challenge universalized predictions that are evolutionally relevant but portray organisms as disembodied from variant ecological conditions under which they live that present quite different selection pressures.

Eagly and Wood (1999) conclude from their metatheory investigation that the evidence supports the social structural model rather than an evolutionary explanation of mate preference, although they see compatibility between the two explanations. Both evolutionary and social structural theory consider biology and environment, but they differ in how they reconcile these forces. The social structural model argues that there is wide diversity across societies in the situations that males and females face and that "a society's division of labor between the sexes is the engine of sex-differentiated behavior, because it summarizes the social constraints under which men and women carry out their lives" (p. 409). Sex differences in behavior are the result of current social conditions that allow men and women to maximize positive outcomes for themselves. Thus, from a social structural perspective, mate selection "reflects people's efforts to maximize their utilities with respect to mating choices in an environment in which these utilities are constrained by societal gender roles as well as by the more specific expectations associated with marital roles" (Eagly & Wood, 1999, p. 415).

In the area of sex differences, it is difficult to separate biological from environmental effects. In general, adherents of a biological basis of gender-related characteristics agree that social and psychological influences are also important. We now turn to this area of research.

What Are the Possible Social Underpinnings of Masculinity and Femininity?

As mentioned previously, feminists have attempted to move away from the concepts of masculinity and femininity. Consequently, much work in the area of social influences on masculinity-femininity has taken on different terminology. Spence (1985) supports the idea that gender identity is a more useful construct when considering male-female differences than the concept of masculinity-femininity and that gender identity is at the core of what people mean by the term *masculinity-femininity*. She argues that gender is a critical influence on the developing psyche of males and females by "setting external constraints on what they are permitted to do or to become and shaping their values, aspirations, and expectations for themselves" (Spence, 1985, p. 81).

Echoing Spence, Martin (1999) contends that "The puzzle of gender development has many pieces: People carry a biological message about gender in their chromosomes, develop gender identities, develop friendships and interests based on gender, and use gender stereotypes" (p. 45). She later posits that gender might be better thought of as "many puzzles each with many pieces" (p. 65). At any rate, the multifaceted role of gender and of the socialization processes in gender development is evident.

Gender Schema Theory

Gender identity begins to develop at an early age, perhaps as early as two years. This developing self-image organizes much experience. Gender schema theory contends that this capacity to assign gender to self and others is all that is necessary for gender stereotyping to emerge. These stereotypes are important mechanisms in parsing the world into manageable components. They operate as organizing principles that help us make sense of an otherwise overwhelmingly complex world. Once established, gender stereotypes provide a framework for processing gender-related information. Interestingly, however, Huston (1984a) and others have noted that gender stereotypes are not clearly related to gender-linked behavior.

From the vast amount of information to which they are exposed, children thus gradually abstract the essentials of masculine and feminine characteristics. To earn approval, they adopt gender-congruent interests, attitudes, and behaviors, and, to avoid disapproval, they avoid gender-incongruent characteristics. The stereotypes they incorporate are more extreme and less flexible in the earlier stages (Huston, 1984b). The numerous and diverse models abstracted by children result in variation in how masculinity and femininity are expressed, but the sense of gender identity is set. Individuals seek out gender-confirming activities, beginning in early childhood, in order to protect their self-image vis-à-vis gender identity. From the point of view of a developmental perspective, a child progressively develops gender identity, gender stability, and gender constancy (Slaby & Frey, 1975).

Social Learning Theory

Bussey and Bandura (1999) contend through social cognitive theory that gender conceptions and competencies largely develop from observational learning of modeled behaviors. They also posit that the tools with which one constructs her/his gender role conceptions include evaluation of one's experiences and direct tutoring. The maintenance of gender roles and styles is further accomplished by social sanctions, self-sanctions, and self-efficacy beliefs. Parents, peers, and the media, as well as educational and occupational practices, are all seen as influences on gender development. Thus, a complex array of reciprocal influences gradually hones one's sense of gender roles.

However, Lueptow, Garovich-Szabo, and Lueptow (2001) reason that if social environment is central in determining gender differences, there should be changes in those differences as the social context changes. They examined sex-typed role assignments and attitudes in over four thousand subjects in seven studies since 1974 and found little change. They argue that given the substantial social changes during this period, the fact that sex roles and attitudes have not changed provides more support for the biological model than for the social model. Later, we discuss similar evidence that arises from the Strong Vocational Interest Blank, first used in 1943, which shows little change in stereotypical male and female vocational interests over many years (Willerman, 1991).

When gender conceptions, schemata, and stereotypes are embedded as the road maps to male and female differences, it is a small step to begin to apply the same constructs within gender as well. Because there are various models and thus numerous expressions of gender-related behavior, there is variance within gender as well as between males and females in those conceptions, schemata, and stereotypes. It is a natural extension of the stereotypes to apply them to those of the same sex, and to one's self. Usually, one's characteristics and behaviors are sufficiently correlated with one's gender identity to present no conflicts.

However, some people may face disturbing gender-incongruent situations. Homosexuals, people with gender atypical occupations (e.g., female soldiers, male nurses), and people with cross-gender roles (e.g., females providing for the family or males staying home with the children) may or may not learn to consider these characteristics or behaviors as irrelevant to their gender identity. Thus, gender identity "provides some kind of psychological glue holding together gender-related characteristics and behaviors, the latter acting primarily to protect a person's sense of masculinity and femininity" (Spence, 1985, p. 89).

A Complexity of Influences

Social and cognitive factors represent mechanisms beyond biology through which gender identity or masculinity-femininity is potentially formed and shaped. In conjunction with biological influences, these forces create a pervasive context for development of one's sense of self and of the world. Evidence that gender identity may develop as early as two years of age supports the contention that biological factors are involved. Bailey (2003) summarizes intriguing evidence that hormonal influences may be important in determining sexual orientation and that these or similar biological influences may affect the development of gender identity. The work of McCormick and Witelson (1994) suggests that the brains of homosexuals show neuroanatomical and neurochemical differences from those of heterosexuals. Witelson (1991) suggests that the brains of homosexuals may be a mosaic of male and female parts. Bailey (2003) contends that male homosexuality is likely caused by incomplete masculinization of the brain during sexual differentiation. Thus, a complexity of vectors apparently lead boys or girls to a relationship with their sense of gender and to their place in the world.

Insights from the Study of Transsexuals

Most experts believe that biological factors are involved in transsexualism (i.e., when gender identity is incongruent with gender). Although biological males usually have a male gender identity and biological females have a female gender identity, biologic sex and gender identity do not always align in this way. "Transgendered" individuals are those whose gender identities are different than their biologic sex/gender. They may express their variant gender identities through cross-dressing, by taking the role of the other gender in their sexual relationships, and in other ways. "Transsexuals" are a subset of transgendered individuals, who persistently desire to get rid of their primary and secondary sex characteristics and acquire the sex characteristics of the other gender. Transgendered individuals offer a unique opportunity to observe naturally occurring variations in gender identity and in other constructs related to masculinity-femininity. For example, even among transsexuals, there is some variance in gender identity, with some having extreme and others having more moderate cross-gender identities (cf. Freund et al., 1974; Lutz, Roback, & Hart, 1984).

Also, just as gender identity and sexual orientation are correlated but distinct constructs among nontransgendered individuals, so they are not perfectly correlated among the transgendered. Even among those individuals who define themselves as transsexual, some are homosexual, some are heterosexual, and still others are bisexual or asexual. Bailey (2003) advances the theory put forth by Blanchard (1991) that male-to-female "homosexual" transsexuals (who are erotically attracted to men) are a distinct subtype from those who are heterosexual, bisexual, or asexual. This theory is currently highly controversial, and Bailey's book has been excoriated by the transgendered community.

Another current controversy is whether cross-gender identity per se should be considered a mental disorder. Just as most scientists and clinicians no longer consider homosexuality to be a form of psychopathology, some now argue that transgender phenomena represent rare but "normal" variations in gender identity (cf. Cole, Denny, Eyler, & Samons, 2000). From this perspective, emotional difficulties faced by "gender variant" individuals result exclusively from their lack of acceptance by society and are not inherently connected to their cross-gender identities. Also, there are instances in which various cultures appear to accept transgendered individuals as "normal" or even as valued members of society. Other experts fail to see how any condition that leads an individual to feel discomfort with his/her primary sex characteristics could ever be considered "normal." This debate obviously touches upon issues of politics and values, but it is also one in which science could play a major role. As such, it should benefit from increased understanding of the relationships between gender, gender orientation, sexual orientation, and other gender-related characteristics.

Issues in the Study of Masculinity-Femininity

Beyond the debate over the underpinnings of masculinity and femininity are other important questions that arise in the study of these concepts. First, are gender differences viable criteria for establishing the definition of masculinity-femininity? Second, are there gender differences in the structure of masculinity and femininity (i.e., gender differences in the characteristics that compose masculinity-femininity, the relative importance of those characteristics, and the relationships among them)? Third, are there differences in masculinity and femininity that are due to the effects of different cultures, different times in the life span, and different generations? Finally, are the concepts of masculinity and femininity useful; that is, do they explain important aspects of personality that are not accounted for by other dimensions of personality?

Criteria for Establishing Masculinity and Femininity

Many efforts to measure masculinity and femininity have taken as their criteria differential endorsement of test items by males and females (Baucom, 1976, 1980; Gough, 1966; Terman & Miles, 1936). Thus, gender differences in item response frequency, whatever their basis, were translated into the definition of masculinity and femininity. However, this criterion does not recognize possible differences between males and females that would not be considered masculinity-femininity. For example, women's superior verbal fluency and perceptual speed are psychological gender differences, but these might not be considered integral to femininity. Likewise, males' superior mathematical and spatial reasoning might not be integral to masculinity. Thus, mere gender differences on a characteristic do not seem to be sufficient to label it masculine or feminine.

Helgeson (1994) argued that the "use of gender differences as the only criteria for MF [masculinity-femininity] is more than just questionable" (p. 655). In her overview of research on gender focused on the contributions of Janet Taylor Spence, Deaux (1999) discussed the problems inherent in using only gender differences in evaluating male and female characteristics. She advocates attention to more proximal explanations of gender differences as opposed to theoretical psychological differences. She believes that the movement to cross disciplinary lines into areas such as sociology, business, and education is important to an accurate understanding of gender differences. Thus, issues of construction and content become central to gender differences.

Differences between "normals" and "deviates" within one gender have also been used to define masculinity-femininity. The developers of the Minnesota Multiphasic Personality Inventory (MMPI) compared homosexual men to "normal" men as one step in establishing its operational definition of masculinity-femininity. As with gender differences, this criterion does not consider that psychological differences between homosexual and heterosexual individuals exist outside the realm of masculinity-femininity, nor does it consider that similarities between homosexual and heterosexual persons exist within the realm of masculinity-femininity. Thus, using heterosexual-homosexual differences carte blanche as the criteria of masculinity-femininity seems to us to only confuse the constructs.

The constructs of masculinity-femininity are further confounded when defined by both male-female differences (i.e., between-group differences) and homosexual versus heterosexual differences (i.e., within-group differences), as was done in the development of Scale 5 of the MMPI. It is unlikely that descriptions of masculinity-femininity derived from between-group comparisons would be synonymous with descriptions derived from within-group comparisons, especially given the substantial complications apparent in equating females with gay males. Consider all the possible differences between homosexual males and heterosexual females, who are considered as exemplars of a singular femininity. For example, it is likely that homosexual men in the 1940s would be inordinately anxious because of the prejudice to which they would be subjected if exposed. We see no good reason why the same would be true of women at the time. Thus, it seems clear that using gender differences as the sole criterion to define masculinity-femininity presents many problems and that using an additional criterion (homosexual-heterosexual differences) that contradicts the first criterion compounds the problems.

Other efforts to define masculinity-femininity have used different criteria. Measures such as the Bem Sex Role Inventory (BSRI; Bem, 1974), the Personal Attributes Questionnaire (PAQ; Spence, Helmreich, & Stapp, 1974), and the Sex Role Behavior Scale (SRBS; Orlofsky, 1981) were based on judges' intuitive decisions about what traits are masculine and feminine. These measures were subsequently validated by their ability to discriminate males from females. Although these measures may tap into a gender difference, they may only encompass a portion of the domain of such differences. In fact, Spence and Helmreich eventually recognized that the two dimensions measured by their PAQ were expressivity and instrumentality, which represent only components of the multidimensional, global concepts of masculinity and femininity (Spence, 1984; Spence & Helmreich, 1986). (As we discuss later, we doubt whether expressivity and instrumentality are even core aspects of masculinity-femininity.) Similar criticisms may be leveled at the BSRI; however, Bem (1981a) initially defended it as a "tool for identifying sex-typed individuals" (p. 369) and apparently has not retracted that assertion. It is disheartening that even today much research treats these measures as valid operational definitions of the global concepts of masculinity and femininity.

The Sex Role Interest Scale (Storms, 1979) used a self-rating method in which respondents rate how masculine or feminine they perceive themselves. This task seems like a parsimonious approach to assessing gender identity, but again, it may miss the larger construct of masculinity and femininity. Thus, the use of numerous, nonequivalent, and sometimes questionable criteria in defining masculinity-femininity casts confusion over the basic constructs.

Gender Differences in Psychological Characteristics

Although gender differences alone may not be sufficient in defining masculinity-femininity, they are clearly necessary to consider when grappling with the constructs, especially when one remembers that *masculine* refers to qualities appropriate to a man and *feminine* refers to characteristics appropriate to a woman. Willerman's (1991) review of psychological gender differences included differences in gender identity, sexual orientation, interests, personality, cognitive abilities, and rates of psychopathology. The largest psychological gender differences are in gender identity and sexual orientation. Most but not all males have a male gender identity and prefer a female as a sexual partner, whereas most but not all females have a female gender identity and prefer a male sexual partner.

There are also significant gender differences in interest patterns. For example, women are traditionally more interested in sewing, flowers, and romance novels; men are traditionally more interested in hunting, competition, and cars. Willerman (1991) claims, "sex differences in interest patterns are among the largest and most stable sex differences known" (p. 857). He points out that the re-standardization in the 1970s of the Strong Vocational Interest Blank, which was initially constructed in the 1930s by compiling the likes and dislikes of those in various occupations, shows little change in differential interest patterns between men and women. This result is surprising when one considers all the social changes that have occurred during the intervening forty years that reasonably would be expected to have altered the socialization differentials between men and women. One explanation for the finding is that greater social changes have been more recent, so that the re-standardization respondents, already adults in their occupations, may have missed the impact of these social changes in their formative years. Thus, changes in differences in interests between males and females might not be captured in this study but may be seen in the future. Another possible explanation is that interests are not as dependent on social influence as one might expect; perhaps they are more biologically influenced. In any event, current evidence points to stability of gender differences in occupation-related interests.

Willerman (1991) noted that, excluding the masculinity-femininity scales, there are few gender differences on self-report personality inventories, including no gender differences on the Dominance, Empathy, and Sociability scales of the California Psychological Inventory (CPI), scales that one might expect to display gender differences. However, men typically score higher than women on dominance scales. Gender differences appear on the Social Potency scale of the Multidimensional Personality Questionnaire (Tellegen, 1982), the Dominance scale of the Personality Research Form (Jackson, 1967), and Factor E of the Sixteen Personality Factor Questionnaire (Cattell, 1950). Factor E is described variously as submissive/deferential vs. dominant and humble vs. assertive (Craig, 1999). Females have characteristically scored higher on neuroticism and nurturance measures, although many researchers have suggested that the higher neuroticism scores are due to women's greater willingness to admit to distress.

Feingold's (1994) meta-analyses of gender differences found that females scored somewhat higher on measures of extraversion, general anxiety, trust, and nurturance, whereas males scored higher on assertiveness and self-esteem. He found no differences in social anxiety, impulsiveness, activity, reflectiveness, locus of control, or orderliness. Furthermore, his findings supported the idea that these differences are "generally constant across ages, years of data collection, educational levels, and nations" (p. 429). These studies suggest that there may be some gender differences in personality dimensions and that some of these may be relatively constant, but these differences are often not large, and there may be moderating factors involved.

Willerman (1991) reported that there are no gender differences in general intelligence but that there are differences in specific cognitive abilities. As mentioned previously, women appear to be superior in verbal fluency and perceptual speed, whereas males appear to be superior in mathematical reasoning, spatial visualization, written language, grammar, and arithmetic computation (Willerman, 1991). Some of these performance differences may relate to sex differences in brain anatomy that have been documented in recent years, such as Kimura's (1999) finding that women have more neurons in the corpus callosum (connecting the right and left hemispheres) than do men.

There are differences between the genders in the rates of various psychopathologies. It has been well established that men are more likely than women to be diagnosed with antisocial personality disorder, alcohol abuse or dependence, and paraphilias, whereas women are more likely than men to suffer from depression, phobias, and somatization disorders.

Although many of these differences are fairly reliable, it is important to keep them in perspective. Hyde (2005) reviewed forty-six meta-analyses of gender differences in cognitive abilities, communication, social and personality variables, psychological well-being, and motor behaviors. She argued that the genders are more similar than different and that the size of various gender differences varies widely at different ages. Interestingly, Hyde did not review gender differences in interests, sexual orientation, or gender identity.

In summary, regardless of the biological and social contributions, gender differences appear to exist in a broad range of areas, not all of which are clearly related to masculinity and femininity. The question that remains is this: how does one understand gender differences in relation to masculinity-femininity? Jackson (1971) argued that the construct validity of a personality measure is enhanced when the measure is derived from explicit, theory-based trait definitions. This type of clear-cut definition is not yet firmly established for masculinity-femininity.

Observer Ratings of Masculinity and Femininity

A different and intriguing approach to defining masculinity-femininity uses observer ratings rather than self-report ratings. Let us examine the intricacies of observer reports before we consider their potential application to the assessment of masculinity-femininity. Campbell and Fiske (1959) advanced the idea that convergent validity is most convincing when it involves correlations using measures derived from multiple methods of assessment. Thus, methods using observer ratings, as opposed to the common method of self-report, offer a potentially powerful source for establishing the validity of measures. However, Ozer (1989) argued that multimethod assessment is not necessarily superior to single-method assessment, but rather depends on the construct being assessed. Thus, possibly, traits vary on which method is best suited to capture that trait.

Tellegen (1991) furthers this view by proposing that each trait has its own "behavioral penetrance," that is, its own propensity to be expressed behaviorally, which can vary from context to context. Some traits may be manifested behaviorally more than other traits, and some behaviors may be manifested more in some contexts than in others. Harkness, Tellegen, and Waller (1995) observed this differential behavioral penetrance in their comparison of self-report data (S-data) and observer report data (O-data) within traits measured in the Multidimensional Personality Questionnaire (MPQ). They found that S and O ratings of some traits did not converge as highly as they did with other traits. They used Brunswik's (1956) lens model of perception to understand that this difference may exist because a certain trait is not strongly behaviorally expressed (i.e., "externally detectable") or because the observer does not sensitively register the behavior or fails to report the behavior.

Harkness et al. (1995) observe several parameters that bear on the degree of congruity of S-data and O-data. Important considerations include the nature of the trait, the context of observation, the favorability of the behavior, the "superfactor cross-over effect," and the category of observer. Some traits (e.g., Stress Reaction, Alienation) are more internal variables and thus generally less behaviorally penetrant than others that are more likely to be observed (e.g., Aggression). Some traits may be more behaviorally penetrant in one setting or context than in another (i.e., in a clinic versus in a social situation). "Favorability" of a trait (i.e., the social desirability) may influence its report. They note that level of favorability could result in increased or decreased expression of a trait that is controllable by force of will (especially in some contexts); it could lead to more or less "cue utilization" by the observer (i.e., traits that have an impact on the observer might be utilized and reported more than traits that would have less meaning for the observer); or favorability might cause a trait that was accurately perceived to be misreported. The superfactor cross-over effect is when a rater uses cues to a related trait to judge the original trait. For example, a rater might use observations about one's positive emotionality to rate one's negative emotionality, assuming incorrectly that one determines the other.

To control for some of these influences, Harkness et al. (1995) generally recommend the aggregation of ratings. However, they report one exception in their data that is instructive. In rating aggression, "the rater's relative status in any dominance hierarchies with the target may be highly pertinent" (p. 201). This exception illustrates what Ozer (1989) concluded: the usefulness of O-data may depend on the specific trait being measured. Harkness et al. also observed in their analyses that some classes of observers (i.e., peers, mothers, fathers) were more congruent with self-report data than others.

In considering the usefulness of O-data in measuring masculinity-femininity, it is important to keep the observations of Harkness and his colleagues in mind. It seems possible that some aspects of masculinity-femininity are well suited to observational assessment. Clearly, we sometimes form judgments of masculinity and femininity in others from observing their behavior. Other aspects of masculinity-femininity, such as gender identity and sexual orientation, may be more internal, and their expression in behavior is highly likely to be influenced by their social desirability in particular contexts or by the relationship between subject and observer.

There have been attempts to use O methods in evaluating masculinity-femininity. Green (1987) showed that observers were able to distinguish—with a high degree of reliability—elementary school boys with feminine gender identities from typically developing boys on the basis of the ways they walked and moved. However, most efforts involving O-data have focused on differences in behavior patterns between gay and heterosexual males. Bailey (2003) uses the term "gaydar" to describe the ability to distinguish gay from heterosexual males solely by behavior. He notes that comedians can easily portray a gay male with speech or movements that are recognized by most people as feminine. We discuss efforts to develop specific measures in chapter 2.

Gender Differences in the Structure of Masculinity and Femininity

Gender differences on personality traits may be found on three different levels: mean differences on a trait measure (e.g., males scoring higher than females on a Dominance scale); different elements that compose a trait (e.g., aggressiveness defined as verbal hostility for females but as physical intimidation for males); and differential relationships between traits (e.g., openness and anxiety being closely related in males but not in females). When we refer to structural differences, we are referring to the second of these possibilities:

different components of a trait, which can occur at the item level and/or at the factor level. If there are gender differences in the structure of any psychological phenomena, masculinity-femininity is one area where they might reasonably be expected. This expectation arises from the sense that masculinity in a female may be different from masculinity in a male and, conversely, that femininity in a male may be different from femininity in a female. Such differences could arise from the development of masculinity and femininity under different social and hormonal influences in the two genders. For example, a feminine male might encounter social ridicule that a feminine female would not encounter, and this might have an impact on the development and expression of that femininity.

This issue of sex/gender differences in the structure of masculinity-femininity has been raised since Pedhazur and Tetenbaum (1979) looked at scores for men and women separately on the Bem Sex Role Inventory (Bem, 1974). They identified four factors for women and four similar factors for men, but with different loading patterns. Other studies that have looked at men and women separately have concluded that the factor structure of masculinity-femininity for men and women may be different (Finn, 1986a; Marsh, 1985; Martin, 1991; Martin, 1993). Furthermore, in Finn's (1986a) study, the relationships among comparable factors for males and females were quite different. He found that gender differences in correlations among factors diminished but were still significant even when women were scored on the men's factors and men on the women's factors. Finally, Spence and Sawin (1985) showed that men and women attach significantly different meanings to the words "masculine" and "feminine." Thus, we must consider that there may be gender differences in the structure of masculinity-femininity.

Cultural, Maturational, and Generational Effects on the Measurement of Masculinity and Femininity

Terman and Miles (1936) expressed a special interest in investigating differences in masculinity-femininity between cultures and even at intervals of one or more generations in the same culture. Even though masculinity-femininity may have at least some physiological and biochemical basis, it is reasonable to expect that at least some manifestations of masculinity-femininity are environmentally influenced. These influences could be observed in cultural and generational effects on masculinity-femininity. Japanese ideas of masculinity-femininity may be different from American ideas. The definition of "feminine" during the Civil War in the United States may have been different from what it is today.

Eysenck, Eysenck, and Barrrett (1995) found that British and American adults differed in items on which men and women showed more than 10 percent differential endorsement rate. American males and females differentially endorsed (by 10 percent or more) one-third more items than did British men and women on the Eysenck Personality Questionnaire-Revised. This result suggests that there are cultural differences in male-female differences. Furthermore, such differences occurred in two cultures that are more similar to each other (i.e., British and American) than to many other cultures in the world.

However, Williams and Best (1990) compared twenty-five nations on adjectives that describe personality and found "considerable" similarity across nations in what adjectives differentiated men and women. "Adventurous" and "independent" were associated with males more than with females, whereas "sentimental" and "submissive" were more characteristic of females than males. The degree of differentiation of males and females varied among nations, and the predominant religion of a country had some effect on differentiating characteristics.

Another aspect of the multifaceted study by Loehlin et al. (2005), mentioned earlier, demonstrated similarities in masculinity-femininity across three nations. They applied Lippa's gender diagnosticity approach (see chapter 2) to samples—from the United States (an elderly sample), Sweden, and Australia—that had responded to a common questionnaire. They concluded that "among adults in Western societies, gender diagnosticity scales appear to be highly generalizable" (p. 1312).

Changes in masculinity-femininity also may occur as a result of maturational processes. Such changes could be reflections of biological, psychological, or environmental influences. Men's scores on Scale 5 of the MMPI-2 do not seem to change with age (Butcher et al., 1991); however, if we parcel out the variance in Scale 5, age effects might be observed in some subcomponents. Attitudes, beliefs, values, interests, activity levels, and so on, that characterize one phase of life may be different in subsequent phases of life, even though one's perceived masculinity-femininity may be unchanged. Hence, for example, manifestations of masculinity or femininity in college may be different from what they are in later years. The criteria that one uses to evaluate the masculinity-femininity of an adolescent may be different from those used to judge an octogenarian. Thus, although the adolescent and the octogenarian might be perceived as equally masculine, their relevant attitudes, interests, behavior, etc. could be different in many ways. People who share the same culture may understand and accommodate these different expressions of the underlying trait over the life span in their judgments of masculinity-femininity.

In the same ambitious study previously cited, Loehlin et al. (2005) compared adolescents at ages twelve, fourteen, and sixteen. They found moderate consistency but also discovered that gender discriminability increased between the ages of twelve and fourteen. They also compared adolescents to adults and observed "substantial changes in the content of the items diagnostic of gender . . . over the age span from age 12 to elderly, in terms of correlations with four Eysenck dimensions" (p. 1315).

There are various ways that potential variations in masculinity-femininity might be manifested. Differences between college students and the general U.S. population, which could result from generational, maturational, or even cultural differences, might reflect any of the three levels of differences in traits previously discussed. It is possible that the behaviors and beliefs expressed by two distinct populations on a measure of masculinity-femininity could result in different mean scores, but perhaps with no perceived differences in masculinity-femininity. For example, an adolescent male might score higher on masculinity measures than an octogenarian (i.e., have a higher total score) by endorsing more boisterous, athletic, or thrill-seeking behavior items, but the two may perceive themselves and be perceived by others as equally masculine because age-appropriate behavior is taken into account. Another level of differences in traits could be reflected in similar mean scores between the two populations, but with those traits having different relationships to other traits. For example, adolescents might score similarly to adults on masculinity-femininity measures, but the adolescent score might reflect different levels of the components of the measure than adult scores.

One might argue that masculinity-femininity is simply a composite of various personality characteristics in certain proportions varying from males to females, from time to time, and from population to population. This composite could take many forms. Alternatively, one might argue that there is a stable nucleus of core traits comprising masculinity-femininity, with more variable peripheral characteristics that are important to the full appreciation of the phenomena. Those peripheral characteristics may be closer to the nucleus at some times than at others. Thus, a component of boisterousness in college students (Martin, 1991) may strongly relate to perceptions of masculinity-femininity in this age group but may not be a salient feature of masculinity-femininity for other populations. When boisterousness appears in other populations, such as the elderly, it might be perceived as reflecting some characteristic other than masculinity-femininity (such as immaturity or psychopathology). Such complexities raise the possibility that different measurement instruments for masculinity-femininity may be desirable not only for males and females but also for different cultures, different generations, or different age ranges. This is an empirical question, the answer to which our studies provide insight.

In the face of these enormous complications, the possibility of dropping the terms *masculine* and *feminine* from scientific usage is inviting. However, we must remember that these two words are a common part of most people's vocabulary and that they somehow capture an important aspect of how people appear to others and think of themselves. Thus, they deserve close analytical consideration.

Do Masculinity-Femininity Inventories Capture Something Unique?

The possibility arises that the components of existing measures of masculinity-femininity parallel established personality traits and thus afford little discriminant or incremental validity in personality assessment. If this were true, we could drop the terms *masculinity* and *femininity* with the comfort that their meaning is captured elsewhere.

Lubinski, Tellegen, and Butcher (1981) addressed this issue by evaluating the Bem Sex Role Inventory (BSRI) with respect to scales of the Multidimensional Personality Questionnaire (MPQ). The MPQ carves personality into the broad domains of Negative Emotionality, Positive Emotionality (now subdivided into communal and agentic aspects), and Constraint. Results provided evidence that "masculinity," as measured by the BSRI, is related to the higher-order factor of Positive Emotionality and that "femininity" may be aligned with the higher-order factor of Constraint. Lubinski et al. later confirmed the relationship between the BSRI and Positive Emotionality and found a similar relationship between Spence and Helmreich's Extended Personal Attributes Questionnaire (1986) and Positive Emotionality (Tellegen & Lubinski, 1983).

Antill and Cunningham (1979) showed that the masculine scale of the Personal Attributes Questionnaire shares much variance with Positive Emotionality. O'Heron & Orlofsky (1990) suggested that masculinity-femininity as measured by the Sex Role Behavior Scale (SRBS) is related to psychological adjustment, including depression, anxiety, and social maladjustment. As we discuss later, studies of the MMPI suggested that certain Serkownek subscales of Scale 5 correlate with other dimensions of personality (Schuerger et al., 1987; Ward & Dillon, 1990). Thus, various instruments purportedly measuring masculinity-femininity, including Scale 5 of the MMPI, demonstrate at least some overlap with other psychological dimensions.

However, the overlap is apparently not complete. Factor analyses of the full set of MMPI items have consistently identified unique factors of masculinity and femininity, which have often been described as masculine or feminine "stereotypical interests" (Johnson, Null, Butcher, & Johnson, 1984). Also, when one factor analyzes the basic scales of the MMPI, Scale 5 often defines its own independent factor (Dahlstrom, Welsh, & Dahlstrom, 1975). Furthermore, factor analytic studies of the BSRI often result in one or two factors that retain a label of masculinity or femininity or something closely related (Gruber & Powers, 1982; Pedhazur & Tetenbaum, 1979; Ratliff & Conley, 1981; Ruch, 1984). These results clearly indicate that there is some unique characteristic measured by some masculinity-femininity instruments.

Finn (1986a) proposed that the terms *masculinity* and *femininity* be reserved for those traits that clearly show discriminant validity from existing personality traits. Such a parsimonious approach would limit the possibility that masculinity and femininity become hazy, residual categories reflecting any and all gender differences. Furthermore, it focuses on the concepts in a way that would enhance their incremental validity in describing personality. If there were gender differences in dominance, they might most appropriately be expressed in terms of dominance rather than masculinity-femininity. If there were no incremental validity over existing personality dimensions, there might be little reason to bother with masculinity-femininity. However, even if masculinity and femininity demonstrated no incremental validity, they might still be useful concepts if they defined a pattern of existing personality dimensions that could be reliably discerned and that therefore offered enhanced understanding. As a cake ultimately is the sum of all the ingredients, so masculinity-femininity could be composed of known qualities but ultimately be different than the specific parts.

Summary of the Status of Masculinity-Femininity

In summary, current concepts of masculinity and femininity are not clearly focused, but they have helped people organize their experience of the world for centuries. Masculinity and femininity measures have been confused by over-reliance on differential item endorsement by males and females, by equating gender differences with differences in sexual orientation, by possible unacknowledged gender differences in the structure, and by possible unacknowledged instability across ages, generations, and cultures. Thus, from a scientific standpoint, the concepts of masculinity and femininity have serious defects. Spence and Buckner (1995) concluded that masculinity and femininity are ineffable senses and that they are of no use to science. Goldberg (as cited in Benoist & Butcher, 1977) contends that asking one question, "I am a male:

True or False?", would be as useful as previous masculinity-femininity scales. Efforts to come to a more discriminating, explicit, theoretically based definition of masculinity and femininity may be helpful precursors to their scientific usefulness. Moreover, until this is done, it may make little sense to include masculinity-femininity scales on personality measures.

The Focus of Our Research

The purpose of this book is to explore some of the unanswered questions about masculinity and femininity. First, is there enough consistency in what people mean by masculinity and femininity to make these concepts useful scientifically? If there is sufficient consistency, how can we best operationalize the concepts? Are gender differences viable criteria for establishing masculinity and femininity? Are there gender differences in the structure of masculinity and femininity? Do masculinity and femininity change over the course of the life span? Are there cultural differences in masculinity-femininity? How important are biology and social influences in the development of masculinity and femininity? These and other questions await answers.

Understanding what efforts have gone before us is an important aspect of considering the evidence, and our focus begins there. We present past efforts to measure masculinity-femininity and then consider in depth the history of masculinity-femininity in the MMPI. In our effort to gain a better understanding of the nature of masculinity and femininity and, perhaps, some insight into the potential scientific utility of the constructs, we attempt to stay largely grounded in empirical evidence. The MMPI-2 and the MMPI-A provide excellent data for such explorations.

Value of the MMPI-2 and MMPI-A in the Study of Masculinity-Femininity

The revised version of the Minnesota Multiphasic Personality Inventory-2 (MMPI-2; Butcher, Dahlstrom, Graham, Tellegen, & Kaemmer, 1989) retained the Masculinity-Femininity scale (Scale 5) and added two gender-related scales (GM and GF). The more recent MMPI-A also retained an abbreviated version of Scale 5.

They offer an opportunity to study simultaneously both theoretical and practical aspects of masculinity-femininity. In fact, these situations are not independent, but rather integrally related. Through a better understanding of masculinity-femininity, its measurement can be improved. At the same time, as the measures improve, more penetrating insights can be realized into the nature of masculinity-femininity.

The MMPI-2 and MMPI-A have several advantages for theoretical investigations of masculinity-femininity. First, Scale 5 of the MMPI-2 is by far the most widely administered measure of masculinity-femininity. Its widespread use in clinical practice and research provides a rich source of data and a long history of investigations to consider in our studies and in studies to come. Second, Scale 5 is surrounded by a large item pool (567 total items on the MMPI-2; 478 total items on the MMPI-A) that may be of use in fleshing out components of masculinity-femininity that are inadequately represented on Scale 5. The nearly one hundred items on the GM and GF scales suggest that there are many additional items that are differentially endorsed by the genders and that may potentially improve the measure of masculinity-femininity. Third, the MMPI-2 normative data represent a broad spectrum of the population of the United States. In fact, an effort was made to have the sample representative of the U.S. population in regard to age, educational level, socio-economic background, ethnic and racial groups, and geographic distribution. Although only a rough replication of the country's demographics, the sample is broad and permits investigation with less concern about generalizability than a more limited sample would present. Furthermore, the MMPI-2 normative sample permits some investigation of the potential cultural, educational, and age differences previously discussed.

Fourth, the fact that the MMPI-2 is used with adults (age eighteen and over), whereas the MMPI-A is used with adolescents (age fourteen to eighteen) offers the opportunity to examine developmental aspects of masculinity-femininity. Finally, the fact that the MMPI-2 has already been translated into many languages and is used in other cultures provides future opportunities to investigate cultural differences in masculinity-femininity. Furthermore, the MMPI's ubiquitous use over the years may provide opportunities to study maturational and generational influences as well. Thus, the MMPI-2 and MMPI-A seem well suited to study masculinity-femininity, and the study in turn may improve the utility of Scale 5. Through our bootstrapping efforts, additional answers may begin to come into focus: Are there viable markers of masculinity-femininity in the MMPI? If so, what is the interrelationship of these various components? Is it important to consider education level or ethnicity in interpreting measures of masculinity-femininity on the MMPI? These and other questions are the focus of this book.

Chapter 2

History of the Measurement of Masculinity-Femininity

Folklore has provided some entertaining tests of masculinity-femininity. One such test involves asking respondents to look at their fingernails. If people extend the hand, palm away, they are considered feminine. If they make a loose fist, with the palm turned inward to look at the nails, they are considered masculine. Another test asks respondents to look at the bottom of their shoe. A masculine person purportedly raises her/his foot to the front, with the knee out, whereas a feminine person raises the foot back, with knees together, and looks over their shoulder to see the bottom of the foot. One test includes questions such as, "What is the lightest wood known to man?" This question assumes that males have been exposed to balsa wood in making models whereas females have not. These approaches are entertaining but provide little confidence that an accurate assessment of masculinity-femininity is accomplished.

The history of scientific efforts to measure the constructs of masculinity and femininity is a tortured path that seemingly has only led in a circle. The major approach to measurement has been based on the notion that masculinity and femininity are defined by male-female differences (Gough, 1966; Terman & Miles, 1936). Thus, by compiling a series of written items that are differentially endorsed by males and females, an effective measurement tool is expected. Some researchers have diverged to consider differences between homosexuals and heterosexuals as a barometer of masculinity-femininity (Hathaway & McKinley, 1943). Others have used focal traits, such as instrumentality or expressivity, as at least two aspects of masculinity-femininity (Spence, 1984; Spence & Helmreich, 1986). Yet other efforts to measure the constructs have been founded on judges' intuitive ratings of what traits, activities, or interests comprise masculinity or femininity (Bem, 1974; Orlofsky, 1981; Spence, Helmreich, & Stapp, 1974).

Another recent approach, exemplified by Cleveland, Udry, and Chantala (2001), is to create a measure tailored to a particular sample of males and females by selecting items from a larger set using statistical techniques to predict males and females. This is actually a variation on the technique of choosing items based on gender differences, but, instead of looking for a fixed set of items, one adopts a new set for each sample that is studied. Udry and Chantala (2004) argue that this method provides a measure "not tied to some previous time period, a different age group, or a group of different social composition" (p. 48). This approach assumes that there is a great deal of instability across samples in what constitutes masculinity and femininity. In fact, it is not at all clear that this is true, even from Udry and Chantala's own work.

None of the previously mentioned approaches has provided much clarity to the concepts of masculinity and femininity. Instead, in combination, these methods have left the terms vague, elusive, and potentially contaminated by other factors. Recently, some experts have abandoned masculinity and femininity as constructs altogether and settled for measuring gender-related phenomena (Hoffman, 2001; Spence & Buckner, 1995; Spence, Helmreich, & Sawin, 1980). Instrumentality, expressivity, sex role, sex role identity, sex role orientation, sex role attitude, sex role beliefs, and particularly gender identity are among the related characteristics drawing attention.

Because of confusion about how to measure masculinity-femininity, much research in the past thirty years in this area has been misinformed. A search of PsychInfo reveals that over 1,420 articles have been published citing the Bem Sex Role Inventory (BSRI; Bem, 1974) from 1980 to 2008, with 254 of these studies published since 2000. In addition, 419 studies have cited a version of the Personal Attributes Questionnaire (PAQ; Spence, Helmreich, & Stapp, 1974) from 1980 to 2008, including 68 since 2000. Most of these studies have advanced these instruments as measures of masculinity and femininity, even though Spence and Helmreich (1981, 1986) have explicitly stated that the PAQ is not a measure of masculinity-femininity but rather a measure of instrumental and expressive personality traits. As far as we know, Bem has never published such an admission, although many other researchers have reached a similar conclusion about the BSRI (Hoffman & Borders, 2001; Spence & Buckner, 1995; Lubinski, Tellegen, & Butcher, 1981; Udry & Chantala, 2004).

The fact that studies continue to be published using the PAQ and BSRI as operational definitions of masculinity and femininity is an interesting phenomenon in itself. Clearly, the number of citations reflects the great interest in this domain of personality, as well as the fact that there is no widely accepted alternative measure of masculinity-femininity. We find it unfortunate that energy and resources are seemingly wasted through use of a measure that does not assess the construct that researchers assume it does.

Let us take some time to review in greater detail the history of the measurement of masculinity-femininity, which naturally reflects changing theoretical understandings. This history can be divided into three general periods with different views of masculinity-femininity: as a one-dimensional bipolar construct, as separate dimensions that vary independently, and as a multidimensional construct. Spence and Buckner (1995) judge that the traditional bipolar model and the two-factor model do not pan out: "When the total body of relevant evidence is considered, however, the data support neither perspective. Nor do they support the presumptions on which each theory is predicated" (p. 119). Spence and Buckner support a multifactorial model organized around gender identity. Our research suggests a return to a unidimensional bipolar conceptualization, but only of the more limited core aspects of the constructs, with multiple related constructs correlating to varying degrees with this core.

Traditional Bipolar Measures of Masculinity-Femininity

As might be expected given their relationship to biological sex, traditionally, masculinity and femininity have been viewed as opposite ends of a single bipolar dimension. At one end of the dimension are the characteristics representative of men, and, at the other end, common characteristics of women. Until thirty years ago, the notion that masculinity and femininity represented extremes of a bipolar dimension was largely accepted by lay people and by the scientific community; therefore, it was relatively unexamined empirically. This initial perspective was reflected in early attempts in the seventy-year history of efforts to measure masculinity and femininity. The Attitude-Interest Analysis Test (Terman & Miles, 1936), the Minnesota Multiphasic Personality Inventory (Hathaway & McKinley, 1942), the Guilford-Zimmerman Temperament Survey (Guilford & Zimmerman, 1949), and the California Personality Inventory (Gough, 1966) each provided a single masculinity-femininity score locating an individual somewhere on a continuum from extremely masculine to extremely feminine. The working definition of masculinity and femininity implied by early measures generally covered a broad range of interests and traits based on observed sex differences.

Attitude-Interest Analysis Test (Terman & Miles, 1936)

Terman and Miles were the first researchers to do extensive work in the area of masculinity-femininity. They devoted much time and energy to research on masculinity-femininity, which culminated in their groundbreaking book *Sex and Personality* (1936). They concluded that the domain of masculinity-femininity encompassed two aspects: differences in the direction of interests and differences in the direction of emotions and impulses. They argued that male interests involved exploit and adventure and included the outdoors, machinery and tools, science, inventions, and business. Female interests involved domestic affairs, aesthetic concerns, and more sedentary and nurturing activities. Terman and Miles contended that emotional dispositions supported these interests. The emotional disposition of males included self-assertion, aggressiveness, hardiness, fearlessness, and "more roughness of manners, language, and sentiments" (p. 447). The female disposition included compassion, timidity, sensitivity, emotionality, and the tendency to be "severer moralists, yet admit in themselves more weaknesses in emotional control and in physique" (p. 448).

Terman and Miles pioneered the use of sex differences in item responses as the basis for measuring "mental masculinity and femininity." Although they expressed reservations about relying solely on sex differences as the basis of masculinity-femininity, they did so, and this approach was subsequently used extensively by others in the development of masculinity-femininity measures. Items were selected for their Attitude-Interest Analysis Test (AIAT) if they showed significant male-female endorsement differentials. Bipolarity of the construct was implicit in their design. Two forms of the questionnaire, Form A and Form B, containing 456 and 454 items, respectively, were developed. Each form included seven subtests, ranging from assessment of knowledge to ink blot associations. Interestingly, the seven tests demonstrated low intercorrelations (.30 to .49). Terman and Miles considered the possibility that specific profiles of these tests might reflect different behavior patterns and expressions of masculinity-femininity. They considered weighting the various items according to how central they seemed to masculinity and femininity but abandoned this idea to avoid accentuating "accidental differences in experience" (p. 53).

Exercise 1 of the AIAT asks subjects to select one of four option words that fits "best or most naturally" with a target word. For example, to the word "Knight," an answer of "armor" or "man" is scored as masculine, whereas an answer of "brave" or "Ivanhoe" is scored feminine. "Inkblots" or black ink drawings that are semi-ambiguous are presented in Exercise 2, with a choice of four things that the drawing makes you think of most. Each of the four possible responses is rated as either masculine, feminine, or neutral. (See Figure 2.1 for examples.)

Exercise 3 asks the subject to complete a sentence with the one among four options that makes it true: for example, "Things cooked in grease are boiled (masculine), broiled (masculine), fried (feminine), roasted (masculine)." This section tests for stereotypical knowledge that may be more familiar to one sex than to the other. Exercise 4 rates intensity of emotional response (anger, fear, disgust, pity) for a number of stimuli. Almost all of the seventy items in this section score females as emotionally reactive and males as not having strong feelings. The next part of this exercise section asks subjects to rate the "degrees of wickedness or badness" of certain actions, such as picking flowers in a public

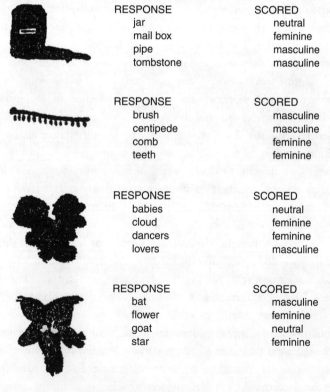

RESPONSE	SCORED
jar	neutral
mail box	feminine
pipe	masculine
tombstone	masculine

RESPONSE	SCORED
brush	masculine
centipede	masculine
comb	feminine
teeth	feminine

RESPONSE	SCORED
babies	neutral
cloud	feminine
dancers	feminine
lovers	masculine

RESPONSE	SCORED
bat	masculine
flower	feminine
goat	neutral
star	feminine

Note. Sample of items selected from Terman & Miles (1936).

Figure 2.1. Examples of Drawings from Exercise 2 of the Attitude-Interest Analysis Test (sample of items selected from Terman & Miles, 1936)

park. Men think only three of the twenty-eight items are more wicked than do women: whispering in school, being a Bolshevik, and being cross to your brother or sister. A final short section to Exercise 4 asks subjects to choose a favorite of two options. For example, making plans is scored masculine, and carrying out plans is scored feminine.

Exercise 5 first asks subjects to rate whether they would like certain types of work, such as architect (masculine), nurse (feminine), florist (feminine), optician (feminine), preacher (feminine), and bookkeeper (feminine). The next section of Exercise 5 asks subjects if they like certain types of people, such as men with beards (masculine), infidels (masculine), very forgiving people (feminine), and very quiet people (masculine). The next section of this exercise asks about liking Charlie Chaplin (masculine), movie love scenes (feminine), adventure stories (masculine), dramatics (feminine), civics (feminine), hunting (masculine), Drop the Handkerchief (feminine), and repairing a door latch (masculine). (You may notice that a number of these items found their way into the MMPI.) The next section of Exercise 5 asks the subject to rate a list of books as liked, disliked, or not read: *Robinson Crusoe* (masculine) and *Peter Pan* (feminine). The final sections of Exercise 5 ask respondents to select which objects they would like to draw if they were an artist, what they would want to write about if they were a newspaper reporter, and what they would like to do and see if they had money and two years to travel.

Exercise 6 presents a list of famous characters and asks if they are liked or disliked by the subject. Christopher Columbus and Herbert Hoover are scored feminine; P. T. Barnum and Jefferson Davis are scored masculine. The second section of Exercise 6 asks true/false questions such as "The weak deserve more love than the strong" ("true" is scored masculine) and "One usually knows when stared at from behind" ("true" is scored feminine). The final Exercise 7 presents yes and no questions covering personal opinions such as "Do you like most people you know?" ("yes" is scored masculine) and "Do people often say you are too noisy?" ("yes" is scored feminine).

As you can see, the AIAT is a lengthy and involved measure. It is also severely culture-bound and time-bound, with such questions as "How bad is it to be a Bolshevik?", "Do you like near-beer?", and "Do you like Judge Ben Lindsey?" Because much of the test is outdated, it seems that it holds little practical value today. However, it was an ambitious test that opened the way to objective measurement of masculinity-femininity. It is interesting to note the similarity of items with those of the MMPI, evidence that the AIAT had a substantial impact on the subsequent measurement of masculinity-femininity. In trying to be exhaustive, the AIAT may have assessed an array of personality dimensions. Regardless of its limitations, the work of Terman and Miles became the foundation for subsequent research in the measurement of masculinity-femininity.

Strong Vocational Interest Blank

The Strong Vocational Interest Blank (SVIB; Strong, 1943) was a survey that compared a respondent's interests with those of people in various occupations. The fact that there were male-female differences in occupational interests made this test well suited to the differential item endorsement procedure used in constructing the AIAT. Strong developed a masculinity-femininity scale (MF) for this test (Campbell, 1971). Slightly over half of the items on the SVIB were included on the MF scale because they demonstrated at least some gender difference in direction of response. Again, the result was one MF total score implying bipolarity of the masculinity-femininity construct.

Test items weighted in the masculine direction included interests in the work of an athletic director, dentist, governor, and criminal lawyer, as well as interest in golf, operating machinery, repairing electrical wiring, acting as cheerleader, discussing ideals with others, making bets, and physics. Vocational interests weighted in the feminine direction included artist, interior decorator, interpreter, landscape gardener, librarian, and private secretary. Other feminine interests on the test were decorating a room with flowers, regular work hours, contributing to charities, foreigners, and literature (Campbell, 1971).

It is clear that the major dimension of the MF scale was stereotypical masculine and feminine interests related to occupation. The MF scale was related to the larger domain of masculinity-femininity, but only on this one dimension. Apparently, for this reason, test users were cautioned against overinterpreting the scale. Campbell (1971) observed: "A Masculinity-Femininity score can be troublesome to use, as men are prone to interpret the score as relevant to their virility—or lack of it. Counselors should be certain to dispel any such ideas. Educated men in particular score toward the feminine end, which usually means they like books and art, to go to concerts, to work inside and keep their hands clean . . . activities that are typically 'feminine' in society as a whole" (p. 236). Perhaps because of such reasons, both the second and third editions of the SVIB, which was revised to become the Strong Campbell Interest Inventory, eliminated the MF scale from the profile (Campbell & Hanson, 1981).

In sum, the MF scale may have been a reasonable measure of stereotypical male and female vocational interests, a subset of stereotypical masculine and feminine interests that we believe is integrally related to masculinity-femininity. As noted in chapter 1, examination of the SVIB interest items over a long period shows that stereotypical masculine and feminine interests have not changed much since the inception of the SVIB in 1943 (Willerman, 1991).

Minnesota Multiphasic Personality Inventory

The Minnesota Multiphasic Personality Inventory (MMPI; Hathaway & McKinley, 1943) was the most widely used personality inventory in the world. The revised version, the Minnesota Multiphasic Personality Inventory-2 (MMPI-2; Butcher, Dahlstrom, Graham, Tellegen, & Kaemmer, 1989), retains this distinction and, at this point, has been translated into many languages. Thus, Scale 5 of this inventory, sometimes called the Mf or the Masculinity-Femininity scale, continues to be the most frequently encountered masculinity-femininity measure. Therefore, it has great importance to the measurement of masculinity-femininity, and the 1989 revision plays a central role in our research. For these reasons, the MMPI, MMPI-2, and MMPI-A are discussed in detail in chapter 3.

Guilford-Zimmerman Temperament Survey

Guilford and Zimmerman (1949) and Guilford, Zimmerman, and Guilford (1976) defined the positive qualities of masculinity as an interest in masculine activities and vocations, not being easily disgusted, being hard-boiled, being resistant to fear, being inhibited in emotional response, and having little interest in clothes and styles. The negative qualities of masculinity (i.e., femininity) were seen largely as being the opposite of masculine: being interested in feminine activities and vocations, being easily disgusted (by poor grooming, manners, etc.), being sympathetic, being fearful, having romantic interests, being emotionally expressive, having much interest in clothes and styles, and having a "dislike of vermin" (Guilford, Zimmerman, & Guilford, 1976).

The M scale on the Guilford-Zimmerman Temperament Survey (GZTS) was the ultimate product of their work and is a measure of masculinity that evolved from Guilford's efforts to find the dimensions of personality using factor analytic techniques (Guilford & Guilford, 1936; Guilford & Zimmerman, 1949; Guilford & Zimmerman, 1956). Consistent with the zeitgeist, masculinity-femininity was considered a single bipolar dimension. Even though differential endorsement by the genders was never a criterion in scale development, mean scores in a normative sample showed that males and females were significantly different; the point-biserial correlation with gender was .75 (Guilford & Zimmerman, 1956). From a modern perspective, the M scale seems multidimensional, with a large portion concerned with stereotypical masculine and feminine values and interests and other portions addressing stereotypical masculine and feminine personality characteristics (i.e., nurturance, sensitivity, emotional expressivity, fearfulness).

California Psychological Inventory

Gough began to measure folk concepts of personality in 1951 and worked to develop a femininity scale that would provide a brief, subtle, and reliable way to differentiate men from women and "deviates" of one gender from "normals" of the same gender (Gough, 1952). He selected many items from the MMPI to include in the California Psychological Inventory (CPI), creating much item overlap between these two measures. (In fact, of the 462 items on the CPI, 194 came from the MMPI.) The fifty-eight-item Femininity scale (Fe) was the result of empirical work using high school and college males and females. The item pool consisted of five hundred items originally developed for a study of political behavior (Gough, 1952). The Fe Scale was incorporated into the CPI (Gough, 1964) and later revised into the thirty-two-item F/M scale.

The single score of both the Fe and the F/M scales implies that masculinity-femininity can be viewed as a single, bipolar dimension. A higher score on the F/M scale suggests that one is "sympathetic, helpful, sensitive to criticism, tends to interpret events from a personal point of view, and often feels vulnerable" (i.e., feminine), whereas a lower score suggests that one is "decisive, action-oriented, takes initiative, is not easily subdued, and is rather unsentimental" (i.e., masculine) (Gough, 1987, p. 7). Gough later suggested dissecting the F/M score into two unipolar scores by dividing it into an F/M-F score, including those fifteen items scored in the true direction (females tend to answer true), and an F/M-M score composed of the seventeen items that are scored in the false direction (females tend to answer false).

Baucom Scales of the CPI

Baucom (1976, 1980) applied to the CPI the concept advanced by Bem that masculinity and femininity were independent dimensions. (We discuss Bem and her measure later.) Baucom developed two unipolar scales by considering the differential item endorsement by the genders. The Baucom masculinity scale (BMS) contains fifty-four items, and the Baucom femininity scale (BFM) forty-two items, from the total CPI pool. One who scores high on both the BMS and the BFM (i.e., androgynous) was considered the most psychologically healthy of the four possible score combinations; one who scores low on both scales was the "most inadequate of the types" (Baucom, 1976, p. 876). Baucom diverged from Bem's ideas by advancing the notion that the absolute scores on BMS and BFM were also important in reflecting absolute amounts of masculinity and femininity (Baucom, 1976, 1980).

The content of both the BMS and BFM scales seems clearly multidimensional. Dominance, emotionality, stereotypical interests, anxiety, aggressiveness, and other traits are represented on both scales. The scales were developed exclusively according to the differential endorsement of test items by the genders, with no further effort to distinguish what components might represent masculinity or femininity. In sum, the CPI F/M scale and the Baucom scales are multidimensional, representing both personality traits and stereotypical interests. Their heterogeneity appears to limit their usefulness in measuring masculinity-femininity.

Observational Measures of Masculinity-Femininity

As mentioned in chapter 1, there are many good reasons to consider observational methods to assess masculinity-femininity. Let us review the work that has been done in the area of observational methods (i.e., O methods) and masculinity-femininity.

Benoist and Butcher (1977) studied nonverbal cues in assigning adjectives to subjects on the basis of a five-minute standardized interview. The high feminine and low feminine females (based on a self-report measure of masculinity-femininity given prior to taping the interview) were discriminated by sixty-two adjectives. High feminine women were judged to be warm, affable, oversocialized, and submissive; low feminine women were seen as dominant. High feminine men were judged to be impulsive, dominant, and socially uneasy; low feminine males were seen as oversocialized and conventional.

Schatzberg, Westfall, Blumetti, and Birk (1975) sought a precise behavioral definition of effeminacy. They developed the Effeminacy Rating Scale (ERS), which systematically rates speech, gait, posture and tonus, mouth movements, upper face and eyes, hand gestures, hand and torso gestures, body type, and body narcissism (e.g., preening hair) in a sixty-seven-item behavior rating scale. They found a .45 correlation between the ERS and sexual orientation (determined by a self-report history of sexual behavior).

Also supportive of the observational assessment of masculinity-femininity is the work of Lippa (1998). He used videotapes of thirty-four college men and thirty-three college women delivering talks to judge extraversion, "gender diagnosticity," masculine instrumentality, and feminine expressiveness. He defines gender diagnosticity as the "Bayesian probability that an individual is predicted to be male or female based on some set of gender-related indicators (such as occupational preference ratings)" (p. 86). Lippa computed gender diagnosticity scores from preference ratings for occupations, hobbies, and activities using discriminant analysis techniques (Lippa, 1991). He concluded that "naïve observers can judge others' M-F [masculinity-femininity] based on brief and limited exposure to their nonverbal cues and physical appearance . . . The validity of M-F judgments is substantial and comparable to that displayed by extraversion judgments" (p. 102). He also found a high correlation between women's physical attractiveness and others' judgments of their masculinity-femininity, with greater physical attractiveness associated with higher feminin-ity ratings.

The most recent work in developing O techniques for the assessment of masculinity-femininity in gay and heterosexual males has been summarized by Bailey (2003). He reviews efforts (including his own) in two behavior areas: body movements and speech patterns.

Ambady, Hallahan, & Conner (1999) conducted a study that concluded that gay men can be distinguished from heterosexuals by brief observations (i.e., "thin slices") of nonverbal behavior. Bailey (2003) found a large differ-ence in how heterosexual and gay males move. He used a scale developed over thirty years ago to measure sex role motor behavior. The criteria used in the rat-ings covered walking, standing, and sitting, with several behavioral differences noted. For example, a masculine walk is characterized by "long strides with free knee action, a minimum hip movement, and arm movement from the shoul-ders," whereas feminine walking is defined by "short strides with controlled knee action, pronounced hip movement, and arm movements from the elbow" (Bailey, 2003, p. 75). Masculine standing is characterized by separated feet, firm wrist action, and hands in pocket; feminine standing has the feet together, limp wrist action, and hands on hips. Differences in sitting include how far the buttocks are from the back of the chair (masculine is further out) and how legs are crossed, as well as hand, arm, and wrist movements. On these criteria, gay males scored between heterosexual women and men (although closer to men).

In studying speech, Bailey (2003) found a large difference (effect size about 2.0) in ratings on a scale gauging speech by listeners to audio recordings of gay and heterosexual males reading a set of sentences that contain all the phonemes (Harvard Sentences). He also found substantial variation among gay males, with approximately 25 percent scoring in the heterosexual range. He notes that, although most people label a gay accent as a feminine accent, this is only a hypothesis. The three things noted by phoneticist consultants in his study were that gay males produce vowels differently, speak more precisely, and pronounce /s/ sounds differently. These linguistic differences are apparently enough to allow some degree of accurate differentiation.

The ultimate utility of observational data in the assessment of masculinity-femininity is unclear; however, we think it represents a promising prospect in enhancing the definition and understanding of masculinity-femininity. There seems to be no other personality trait as often mimicked and mimed as masculinity-femininity.

It is important to note that most of these O-method studies (with the exception of Benoist & Butcher, 1997) are using homosexual-heterosexual differences to define masculinity-femininity. This is a questionable assumption, and one that we argue contributed to confusion about the construct of masculinity-femininity. It is important that these O-methods be studied within gender and within sexual orientation groups, so that the constructs are not confounded with differences unrelated to masculinity-femininity.

Other Measures of Masculinity-Femininity

There have been less well-known attempts to measure masculinity-femininity using techniques other than questionnaire. For example, Franck and Rosen (1949) developed the Drawing Completion Test, which is projective in nature, and Goodenough (1946) developed a word association test. Both of these measures were based on differential responses between the genders and were developed during the 1940s, when masculinity-femininity was considered a bipolar construct. As best we can determine, they are no longer used.

Masculinity and Femininity as Separate Dimensions

C. G. Jung was one of the first to consider alternative conceptualizations to the bipolar structure of masculinity and femininity. However, his conceptualization was on the abstract plane of archetypes. He proposed the concepts of *animus*, the masculine aspect of personality, and *anima*, the feminine side of personality, and advanced the notion that both are present to some degree in any individual (E. Jung, 1972). Jung argued that "just as man is compensated by a feminine element, so woman is compensated by a masculine one" (Jung, 1951, in Campbell, 1971, p. 151). However, the feminine side of a man and the masculine side of a woman might not find outward expression, because this might disturb his or her outer adaptation and self-image (E. Jung, 1972).

Constantinople (1973) was the first modern voice to effectively challenge the notion that masculinity and femininity are opposite ends of a single bipolar dimension. In a seminal article, she leveled three major criticisms of masculinity-femininity research. First, she attacked as untested the assumption that masculinity-femininity was a bipolar construct with masculinity at one end and femininity at the other. Second, she questioned the assumption that masculinity-femininity was unidimensional. Third, she criticized the strategies used to construct masculinity-femininity measures as atheoretical and insufficient. She questioned whether a single score that reflects gender differences in response to test items could adequately measure masculinity-femininity. Introducing a new paradigm to our thinking about these concepts, she broached the possibility that masculinity and femininity might exist as separate, independent dimensions. A flood of research ensued.

Bem Sex Role Inventory

Bem (1974, 1981b) developed the Bem Sex Role Inventory (BSRI) and advanced the notion that masculinity and femininity are independent dimensions. She selected items that reflected instrumental, "getting the job done" traits as the basis of masculinity and items that reflected expressive qualities representing an "affective concern for the welfare of others" as the basis of femininity (Bem, 1974, p. 156).

The BSRI asks the subject to rate how well a characteristic describes himself/ herself on a seven-point Likert scale. From these ratings, masculinity, femininity, and social desirability scores can be computed; from these scores, the subject is classified into one of four categories: masculine (significantly higher score on the masculinity scale than the femininity scale), feminine (significantly higher score on the femininity scale than the masculinity scale), androgynous (high on both scales), or undifferentiated (low on both scales). Bem (1979) later proposed a short form of the BSRI, which has been considered by some to be superior to the original version (Brems & Johnson, 1990).

The BSRI introduced the concept of androgyny and set off a frenzy of research and a period of infatuation with the concept. It represented a major event in social and personality psychology of the late 1970s and early 1980s. The idea of androgyny was appealing to the political climate of the time, when feminism was on the rise. Not until the mid-1980s did the unpopular reality come to the fore that there was little empirical support for the concept of androgyny. Tellegen and Lubinski (1983) and Spence and Buckner (1995) were among the first to arrive at this conclusion.

There have been many efforts to identify the underlying dimensions of the BSRI (Gaudreau, 1977; Waters, Waters, & Pincus, 1977; Whetton & Swindells, 1977; Moreland, Gulanick, Montague, & Harren, 1978; Pedhazur & Tetenbaum, 1979; Ratliff & Conley, 1981; Gruber & Powers, 1982; Ruch, 1984; Brems & Johnson, 1990). The results provide evidence for two to seven factors, with a modal number from these studies being four factors. The common four factors carry various labels but are similar in structure to those identified by Pedhazur and Tetenbaum (1979): Assertiveness, Interpersonal Sensitivity, Self-Sufficiency, and a bipolar factor they labeled Masculinity-Femininity.

Spence (1984) claimed that the BSRI measures socially desirable, self-assertive traits for males (instrumentality) and socially desirable, interpersonally oriented, emotive traits for females (expressivity). As discussed in chapter 1, Lubinski, Tellegen, and Butcher (1981) found that the Masculinity scale correlates substantially with the higher-order personality dimension of Positive Emotionality, whereas the Femininity scale correlates with Constraint. They conclude that the Masculinity scale may be a measure of dominance, whereas the Femininity scale may reflect nurturance-warmth.

Spence (1984) argued that instrumentality and expressivity may be two of many traits that show gender differences, but that they do not reflect a masculinity-femininity bipolar dimension. The results of her study trace the effects noted by Frable (1989) and others, which support the notion of the bipolar nature of masculinity-femininity and the BSRI's ability to measure it, to two items on the BSRI: rating oneself on how "feminine" and how "masculine" one perceives oneself. Spence contends that these two items assess gender identity (i.e., one's sense of being male or female) and that these two items are responsible for occasional results suggesting that the BSRI measures sex role identity.

Furthermore, Leaper (1995) found that scores on the BSRI do not match people's ideas of masculinity-femininity. Subjects did not equate the terms masculine and feminine with instrumental and "socioemotional" adjectives. Wiggins and Holzmuller (1978) correlated the BSRI scales with eight general personality dimensions and concluded that the Masculinity scale lies close to the dominant-ambitious marker of the resulting "interpersonal circumplex," whereas the Femininity scale lies close to the warm-agreeable marker. In both cases, the BSRI scales align with higher-order personality dimensions and thus provide little incremental validity beyond existing personality measures.

Choi and Fuqua (2003) summarized twenty-three separate exploratory factor analyses of the BSRI. They conclude that "masculinity/femininity has not been adequately operationalized in the BSRI. It is clear that the lack of theoretical dimensions of masculinity and femininity adversely affects the construct validity of the BSRI" (p. 884).

Finally, Hoffman and Borders (2001) argue that the assumption underlying the development of the BSRI, that masculine and feminine traits are mutually exclusive, is not accurate. They contend that "instrumentality and expressivity do not equal masculinity and femininity" (p. 52). In this article, they conclude that the enormous amount of research done using the BSRI is misguided, because masculinity and femininity are inaccurately defined by the measure. Furthermore, they state that "neither a sex role theory nor an androgyny theory approach to understanding human behavior is any longer efficacious" (p. 52).

Unfortunately, this growing consensus does not appear to keep some researchers from using the BSRI as a measure of masculinity-femininity.

Personal Attributes Questionnaire

About the time that Bem was developing the BSRI, Spence, Helmreich, and Stapp (1974) developed the Personal Attributes Questionnaire (PAQ) to measure two dimensions that they related to masculinity-femininity. They aligned self-assertive, goal-directed qualities with masculinity and interpersonally oriented, nurturant characteristics with femininity. Factor analysis of the PAQ has suggested that it measures two orthogonal factors (Helmreich, Spence, & Wilhelm, 1981). They initially suspected that the two dimensions were independent and that they possibly reflected the dimensions of androgyny. However, the authors eventually argued that the PAQ is not a measure of masculinity-femininity, but rather of dimensions (expressivity and instrumentality) that represent only components of the multidimensional, global concepts of "masculinity" and "femininity," which, by themselves, lack validity (Spence, 1984; Spence & Helmreich, 1986). Spence (1985) later contended that the PAQ measures only "two specific constellations of gender-differentiating personality traits" (i.e., goal-directed assertiveness and interpersonal nurturance) and concluded that "gender related phenomena are multidimensional" (p. 3).

The M scale included those items that were deemed socially desirable in both genders but that were judged more typical of males. This generally encompassed self-assertive, instrumental traits. The F scale included items that were socially desirable in both genders but that were more typical of females. These described more interpersonally oriented, expressive traits. The content of each scale is unidimensional. The third scale, M-F scale, was composed of those traits that were deemed stereotypical of males or females but that were also considered socially desirable for one gender, but not for the other. The M-F scale is bipolar; scores on the M-F scale correlated positively with the M scale and negatively with the F scale (Spence & Helmreich, 1986).

This original questionnaire was reduced to twenty-four items (three eight-item scales) by retaining only the items that most enhanced the psychometric properties of the scales and, in the case of the M and F scales, that best assessed instrumental or expressive traits (Helmreich, Spence, & Wilhelm, 1981). Later, an effort was made to expand the PAQ to include socially undesirable traits on the measure. The resulting longer version of the PAQ (forty items) is referred to as the Extended Personal Attributes Questionnaire (EPAQ).

Masculinity and Femininity as Multidimensional Constructs of Gender-Related Traits

The idea that masculinity-femininity might be a multidimensional construct was recognized in scientific literature in the early 1970s (Lunneborg, 1972; Lunneborg & Lunneborg, 1970; Wakefield, Sasek, Friedman, & Bowden, 1976). The idea has gained credence with many experts agreeing that masculinity-femininity is a collection of related traits (Coan, 1989; Marsh, 1985; Spence, 1984; Tellegen & Lubinski, 1983). The bulk of the evidence has resulted from factor analyses to establish the underlying components of masculinity-femininity measures.

Helmreich, Spence, and Wilhelm (1981) recognized the multidimensional nature of masculinity-femininity "whose components are not strongly related to each other and not necessarily related to criterion variables in the same way or to the same degree" (p. 1107). As mentioned previously, the BSRI has been the focus of many such factor analyses, finding dimensions such as Assertiveness, Interpersonal Sensitivity, Self-Sufficiency, and a bipolar factor they labeled Masculinity-Femininity (Pedhazur & Tetenbaum, 1979).

The masculinity-femininity scale of the MMPI (Scale 5) has also been explored for dimensionality. Factor analysis of Scale 5 by Graham, Schroeder, and Lilly (1971) resulted in the identification of seven "significant and psychologically interpretable" (p. 370) factors, including Sensitivity-Narcissism, Feminine Interests, Masculine Interests, Demographics, Homosexual Concern-Passivity, Social Extraversion, and Exhibitionism. Furthermore, low intercorrelations among these resulting factors prompted Schuerger, Foerstner, Serkownek, and Ritz (1987) to conclude that masculinity-femininity, as measured by the MMPI, is multidimensional. Thus, whether or not masculinity-femininity is multidimensional, at least several important purported measures of masculinity-femininity are clearly multidimensional.

Measures of Gender-Related Characteristics

Male-Female Relations Questionnaire

In an effort to further elucidate different areas of gender-related phenomena, Spence, Helmreich, and Sawin (1980) developed the Male-Female Relations Questionnaire (MFRQ). The MFRQ measures the extent to which one's behavior and one's expectations for behavior of the other gender are aligned with conventional sex role expectations in the United States. Spence and her colleagues use the term "sex role" to refer to "normative expectations about the duties, responsibilities, and rules for behavior in specific situations that men and women in a given society should assume" (Spence et al., 1980, pp. 3–4).

Factor analyses resulted in three scales for each gender. For males, these included Social Interaction (sixteen items), Expressivity (four items), and Marital Roles (ten items). For females, the scales were Social Interaction (sixteen items), Male Preference (four items), and Marital Roles (ten items) (Spence, Helmreich, & Sawin, 1980). The Social Interaction scales measure one's tendency to modify one's behavior to meet sex role demands, and the Marital Roles scales reflect one's preferred relationship with one's spouse. The Expressivity scale for males measures one's willingness to express emotions and be considered sensitive; the Male Preference scale measures a female's preference for masculine, dominant men. The MFRQ may be related to stereotypical masculine and feminine characteristics.

In a sample of college students, Storms (1979) found that masculine items correlated highly negatively with feminine items (−.64 for males and −.74 for females, both $p < .001$). He took this to suggest that masculinity and femininity, at least in terms of sex role identity, are not separate dimensions, but rather represent a single dimension. The MFRQ is relevant to the measurement of masculinity-femininity in that it does seem to address a core aspect, perhaps gender identity.

Sex Role Behavior Scale

Orlofsky (1981) also argued that sex role is not a unitary phenomenon but rather is composed of sex-typed traits, sex-typed attitudes, and sex-typed social roles and behaviors. (To clarify terminology, sex role traits are supposedly gender-related personality traits such as those reflected in the BSRI and PAQ. Sex role attitudes are gender-related beliefs such as those measured in the MFRQ. Sex role interests are represented as components of other masculinity-femininity measures such as the MMPI and are largely stereotypical masculine and feminine interests.) Orlofsky set about to develop a sex role interests test to measure social roles and behavior, because he believed that these three components of sex roles needed to be assessed independently and that existing measures focused on only sex role traits and sex role attitudes. He developed the Sex Role Behavior Scale (SRBS).

A male-valued score, a female-valued score, and a sex-specific score are computed from the SRBS. The sex-specific scale is bipolar, with higher scores reflecting more masculine interests and behaviors and lower scores reflecting more feminine interests and behaviors. Orlofsky (1981) found a moderate positive correlation between the male-valued scale and the female-valued scale for both men ($r = .50$) and women ($r = .38$), from which he deduced that male and female interests are not mutually exclusive or bipolar but, in fact, overlap. However, the masculine and feminine items on the sex-specific scale did appear to be more mutually exclusive, correlating with each other −.69. Thus, these items reflect more extreme male and female interests, which do not overlap.

Orlofsky, Ramsden, and Cohen (1982) developed a longer version in an effort to make fine-grained distinctions between the four categories represented on the test (recreational activities, vocational interests, social and dating behavior, and marital behavior). For practical purposes, Orlofsky and O'Heron (1987) shortened the SRBS by selecting ninety-six items from the long form that covered the domain of behavior areas. The resulting scale is a combination of stereotypical masculine and feminine interests and conventional social sex role behavior (i.e., socially prescribed behaviors determined by one's sex). The difference from the MFRQ is that rather than asking a respondent how others should act, the SRBS assesses how the respondent himself/herself believes and behaves.

Other Measures

The Behavioral Self-Report of Masculinity (Keisling, Gynther, Greene, & Owens, 1993) and the Behavioral Self-Report of Femininity (Greene & Gynther, 1994) both identify behaviors that distinguish males and females. Greene and her colleagues asked undergraduate college students to rate the frequency of engaging in a list of what they believed were potentially feminine behaviors. Of the fifty-seven items included in the Behavioral Self-Report of Femininity that differentiated between males and females, six factors emerged: Social Connectedness, Romantic, Domestic/Dutiful, Concern for Age/Sexual Attractiveness, Concern with Appearance, and Traditional/Conservative. The test developers concluded that femininity is a multidimensional construct.

Sex role transcendence, a concept conceived by Hefner, Rebecca, and Oleshansky (1975) in the wake of Constantinople (1973) and Bem (1974), refers to the "achievement of a dynamic and flexible orientation to life in which assigned gender is irrelevant" (Hefner, Rebecca, & Oleshansky, 1975, p. 143). Gender role transitions (i.e., changes in how one views his/her gender role) were hypothesized to "occur when there are demonstrations, reevaluations, and integrations of masculinity and femininity over the lifespan" (O'Neil & Fishman, 1986, p. 142). Hefner, Rebecca & Oleshansky (1975) originally proposed three stages, including Undifferentiated, Polarized, and Sex Role Transcendence. In the first two stages, a child gradually learns sex role distinctions. Transition to the third stage represents a paradigm shift to the point where "behaviors and life-styles are chosen that are appropriate and adaptive for the particular individual in the specific situation" (p. 143), which is free of sex role limitations. These ideas subsequently expanded to include five stages (O'Neil & Egan, 1992). However, they remain abstract, and there is no empirical evidence to support them.

Nonetheless, the Gender Role Journey Measure (O'Neil, Egan, Owen, & Murry, 1993) was developed to assess gender role developmental changes and explore phases of the gender role journey. It tested the idea that sex role orientation develops through five phases of life: Acceptance of Traditional Gender Roles, Ambivalence, Anger, Activism, Celebration and Integration of Gender Roles. Factor analysis supported only three phases: Acceptance of Traditional Gender Roles; Gender Role Ambivalence, Confusion, Anger, and Fear; and Personal-Professional Activism. Test-retest reliabilities were low (.53 to .77). Also, the first and third phase scores correlated −.46, indicating they were not separate constructs, but rather perhaps a bipolar construct. Although this area of theorizing has been popular, there is little evidence to support its line of development.

As described earlier, Lippa (1991) developed the concept of "gender diagnosticity" and used preference ratings of occupations, school subjects, activities, hobbies, and entertainment to predict probability of maleness or femaleness using discriminant analysis. The gender diagnosticity approach does not advocate central markers of masculinity-femininity that apply to all samples but rather advises that markers be identified in any sample by using items that discriminate males form females in that specific sample. Thus, masculinity-femininity is left to vary with the uniqueness of the specific population considered. Although Lippa generally has used avocational and vocational interests as the basis of gender diagnosticity measures, he has also used personality questionnaires (Lippa & Hershberger, 1999). Lippa's approach implies that masculinity-femininity may manifest differently in various cultures, age ranges, and eras. He claims success in using the gender diagnosticity measure to identify masculinity-femininity both between the genders and within genders. He also found that resulting masculinity-femininity scores did not correlate highly with the BSRI, PAQ, or the five personality dimensions identified by McCrae and Costa (1987), including neuroticism, extraversion, openness, agreeableness, and conscientiousness (Lippa, 1991). To this point, Lippa's prolific work has not seemed to have much impact on the field, perhaps because, as mentioned earlier, it has not resulted in a standardized measure that can be used in different samples. From our reading, we also question whether there is more similarity between samples in what constitutes masculinity-femininity than Lippa assumed at the outset of his research.

Loehlin et al. (2005) used the gender diagnosticity approach with some success in their study of masculinity-femininity across the United States, Sweden, and Australia, as well as across age ranges mentioned in the previous chapter. Their findings suggest that the gender diagnosticity approach offers a flexible tool in exploring masculinity-femininity across cultures and ages. Again, however, there were substantial similarities between different samples in what effectively differentiated the genders.

Hoffman and colleagues have developed the Hoffman Gender Scale to assess the "intensity of one's belief that she or he meets her or his personal standards of femininity and masculinity" (Hoffman, 2001, p. 480). She contends that this new scale measures two factors: gender self-definition (i.e., how important masculinity-femininity is to one's self-concept) and gender self-acceptance (i.e., how comfortable one is with one's gender). Hoffman echoes Lewin's (1984) contention that personal interpretations of being male or female are important. Furthermore, she questions whether culture has developed to the extent that masculinity and femininity are no longer viable or important concepts.

Measures of Gender Identity

The measurement of gender identity as a distinct psychological phenomenon has a relatively brief history. Initially conceived of as a categorical trait, gender identity is more likely a dimensional trait that can be measured in terms of degree. Spence (1993) defends a multifactorial gender identity theory from which other aspects of masculinity-femininity spring. She suggests that when people rate their masculinity and femininity, they "tend to blend together their self-images of gender identity . . . and the qualities they use to verify this identity, along with a weighted summary of the ways that they perceive themselves resembling their own sex" (p. 22).

Ruble and Martin (1998, cited in Martin, 1999) cautioned researchers "not to assume that there is not unity in gender constructs, especially for young children" (p. 46). They point out that gender effects are "pervasive and powerful in children," and that gender identity plays an important role in organizing gender development. Furthermore, they discuss some "areas of unity" in gender, including observations that people typically "develop gender identities congruent with their biological sex, develop gender-typed interests, prefer same-sex playmates, develop gender stereotypes and apply these when making judgments of others, and later develop a sexual interest in the other sex" (p. 46). Several researchers have developed scales to measure gender identity, some of which we describe.

Feminine Gender Identity Scale

Freund, Nagler, Langevin, Zajac, & Steiner (1974) developed the Feminine Gender Identity Scale (FGIS) in an effort to measure that aspect of femininity that is relevant to transsexual males and possibly homosexual males. To avoid errors in assuming that femininity in homosexual males is the same as that which differentiates males and females, Freund and colleagues used homosexual transsexual males as the extreme of femininity. Scale development suggested that gender identity was related to, but different from, sexual orientation. The FGIS has been used as a measure of masculine gender identity since that time, but not until 1983 was a similar scale published for females, when Blanchard and Freund (1983) developed the Masculine Gender Identity Scale (MGIS) to be used with females.

Sex Role Identity Scale

In his work to investigate the relationship between sex role stereotypes and sex role attributes, Storms (1979) developed a measure of what he called "sex role identity," which he defined as a "global self-concept of one's masculinity and femininity." The SRIS is short; it is composed of six face-valid items, which ask respondents to rate themselves on three masculine and three feminine items: "How masculine/feminine is your personality?"; "How masculine/feminine do you act, appear, and come across to others?"; and "In general, how masculine/feminine do you think you are?" Storms (1979) showed satisfactory internal consistency for the scale by computing, for a sample of 104 male and 110 female college students, the average correlation of the three masculine items (.66 for males and .68 for females) and the three feminine items (.80 for males and .70 for females). We believe that the SRIS is best conceived of as a measure of gender identity, and that this label better fits with Storms's original definition of "sex role identity."

Gender Identity Scale

Although it is unpublished, the Gender Identity Scale (GIS) was developed by Finn (1986a) from items written by psychologists familiar with masculinity-femininity research. Using factor analysis of a large item pool, he constructed a form for males and a form for females, each containing twenty items to be answered true or false. The internal reliability of the scales was demonstrated to be high (alpha coefficient of .89 for the male form and of .88 for the female form). For males, the measure seems to represent three distinct but closely related areas: female identification, incongruence with masculinity, and childhood gender atypical behavior. For females, the components are male identification, male sex-typed childhood behavior, and dis-identification with feminine behavior.

Both the male form and the female form measure an aspect of masculinity-femininity that has often been overlooked in the past. Freund's Feminine Gender Identity Scale (FGIS) is better established, but Finn's measure is promising. Freund's measure for males contains some questions that might be off-putting to conventional males and thus may limit its utility. For example, there are three questions about wearing women's underwear or clothing. Also, nine of twelve questions in the first part of the Freund's measure for females (MGIS) and eighteen of twenty in the first part of their measure for males (FGIS) are about specific behavior and thoughts during the childhood of the respondent's life. This may be satisfactory when college students are the respondents, because those memories are close and accessible, but may be a limitation with older respondents. Finn's measure has a few questions about childhood, but they are more general questions that might be easily answered by older respondents. Finally, Finn's measure has more subtle items and showed more variance in a normal population than did that of Freund and colleagues.

Using a sample of seventy-five men and ninety-four women who rated themselves as exclusively heterosexual, Spence and Buckner (1995) correlated shortened versions of Finn's scale with a variety of other gender-related measures. They concluded that Finn's measure did seem to be saturated with gender identity, but that it also was contaminated with other variance, such as one's acceptance of socially dictated gender expectations. Instead of Finn's measure, Spence and Buckner recommended that researchers use a single-item measure of gender identity, in which respondents use a Likert scale to rate the strength of their feelings of maleness or femaleness.

Continuous Gender Identity (CGI) and Childhood Gender Nonconformity (CGN)

Bailey and colleagues (Bailey, Dunne, & Martin, 2000; Bailey, Finkel, Blackwelder, & Bailey, 1996; Gangestad, Bailey, & Martin, 2000) separated out several aspects of Finn's (1986a) Gender Identity Scale to construct two separate scales. One, the Continuous Gender Identity (CGI) scale, uses seven of Finn's items that have to do with male/female identification (e.g., "In many ways I feel more similar to women/men than to men/women."). The items are rated on a seven-point Likert rating scale, and, although the shortened scale has reduced internal consistency, it has proved useful in several studies. For example, in a study of lesbian and gay couples, CGI scores were moderately related to partners' ratings of respondents' masculinity-femininity (Bailey et al., 1996).

The other measure, Childhood Gender Nonconformity (CGN), retrospectively assesses childhood sex-typed behavior (i.e., participation in sex-stereotypic games and activities) and gender identity (i.e., internal feelings of maleness and femaleness). Items were selected from Freund's MGIS and Finn's FGIS and from several existing scales measuring recalled childhood play activities. Different forms of the measure were developed for men and women, and coefficient alpha was .79 for both men and women (Gangestad et al., 2000). In a large study of Australian twins, Bailey et al. (2000) found some evidence that the CGN scale measures a heritable trait.

Gender Identity Questionnaire

Acknowledging that recent views of gender identity advance a multidimensional construct, Willemsen and Fisher (1999), developed the Gender Identity Questionnaire. This questionnaire includes "personality traits as well as behaviors, preferences, and intentions in the areas of social relations, leisure time, the expression of emotion, and gender roles" (p. 361). It contains four subscales, two that form the Femininity scale (Feminine Traits and Feminine Behaviors) and two that form the Masculinity scale (Masculine Traits and Masculine Behaviors). It was developed in the Netherlands with a random mailing to one thousand males and one thousand females. The response rate was 314 males and 451 females. Although Willemsen and Fischer present data supporting the measure, there are problems with it. Methodologically, it is possible that the sample that responded is not random. Most important, although the scale is labeled "gender identity," the authors do not seem to have conceived of this construct in the specific sense that most people now do (i.e., as one's sense of oneself as male or female, masculine or feminine). Instead, the instrument assesses a mishmash of gender-related traits and behaviors. At best, the questionnaire reflects the persistence and allure of the masculinity and femininity constructs, as well as the confusion that reigns in the general area.

Return to the Bipolar Concept of Masculinity-Femininity

The result of years of attempting to delineate the multitude of gender-related differences has led to an appreciation of just how complex this area is. Twenge's (1999) work exemplifies how unwieldy the multifactorial understanding of gender-related characteristics can be. She concluded that "the various aspects of gender appear to be even more diffuse than theorized: several variables that should have been in the same proposed area were not highly or even moderately correlated. Thus, we still have a long way to go in formulating a theory of gender-related attributes and in predicting which characteristics are related" (p. 498).

However, emerging from research over the past twenty years is the possibility that a more limited dimension of gender-related attributes may serve as a core construct. Research by Marsh (1985) using the Comrey Personality Scales' (Comrey, 1970) masculinity-femininity scale and by Pedhazur and Tetenbaum (1979) using the BSRI suggests evidence of a higher-order bipolar factor of masculinity-femininity. Although there are many dimensions in traditional measures of masculinity-femininity, they found one aspect that retained a bipolar nature. Thus, the traditional single factor concept of masculinity-femininity may still be valid in some limited way. Furthermore, this higher-order factor shows discriminant validity from recognized personality dimensions, suggesting that some unique attribute is being captured by it. These findings suggest a core masculinity-femininity that has been confounded with other dimensions of personality as the result of previous methods employed in the development of masculinity-femininity measures.

The Search for Masculinity-Femininity

What might the core masculinity-femininity be? There are a number of possibilities. Stereotypical sex-typed interests, gender identity, sexual orientation, some aspects of personality, and even cognitive styles and aptitudes all show some gender differences, and at least some of these have been advanced as integral to conceptualizations of masculinity-femininity.

In support of stereotypical interests being central to masculinity-femininity is the fact that whether masculine and feminine interests are considered a single bipolar dimension or two separate dimensions, they appear frequently in some form in factor analytic studies of various measures of masculinity-femininity (Gaudreau, 1977; Graham, Schroeder, & Lilly, 1971; Pedhazur & Tetenbaum, 1979; Ratliff & Conley, 1981; Ruch, 1984). Furthermore, masculine and feminine values seem central to the "stereotypical interests" factor, consistently appearing in factor analyses of the entire MMPI item pool, capturing some unique variance (Archer & Klinefelter, 1991; Johnson, Null, Butcher, & Johnson, 1984).

Willerman (1991) considered interest patterns to be one of the largest and most stable gender differences. Spence (1984) argued that people begin in early childhood and continue through life to seek out those activities and behaviors (i.e., masculine and feminine) that confirm their gender identity. Even as U.S. society evolves, rough-and-tumble play, hunting, and tinkering with cars are still largely male behaviors and are strongly considered masculine, whereas arranging flowers and sewing are still largely female behaviors and are considered feminine. It is likely that one's interest pattern, or gender role orientation, is central to one's sense of masculinity-femininity. The obverse of this may be true as well: that people's sense of masculinity-femininity is central to their interest patterns. Finally, intuition suggests that one of the most common bases of judging masculinity-femininity in others is their interest patterns. A man's interest in sewing or a woman's interest in boxing is likely to influence how others rate their masculinity-femininity.

Research suggests that sexual orientation may be related to masculinity-femininity. Willerman (1991) noted that the sex of one's preferred mate is one of the largest psychological gender differences. Lippa (2002) notes that scores on his gender diagnosticity measure "are strongly related to sexual orientation in both men and women" (2001, p. 189). In data obtained from an Internet survey (301 males and 738 females), Lippa found that gay men and lesbians showed significant differences from same-gender heterosexuals on his measure of gender diagnosticity (effect size for males, 1.14; for females, 0.53). In their studies of the effects of prenatal testosterone on sexual orientation and masculinity-femininity, Udry and Chantala (2006) used a loose adaptation of the Terman and Miles method of masculinity-femininity assessment (1936) to assess masculinity-femininity in adolescent males and females. Six years later, the males who scored as feminine at the first testing had "several times the probability of being attracted to same-sex partners, several times the probability of having same-sex partners, and several times the probability of self-identifying as homosexuals, compared with more masculine males" (p. 797). Females did not show any significant relationship in masculinity-femininity scores and later sexual orientation. Thus, sexual orientation is another construct to consider in elucidating masculinity-femininity, at least for males.

Spence (1993) contends that gender identity is a primary sex difference. Again, Willerman (1991) identified gender identity as another psychological characteristic with large sex differences. Perhaps gender identity is part of a core masculinity-femininity.

Masculinity-femininity measures consistently put forth personality differences as central to masculinity-femininity. From Terman and Miles's (1936) assertion that men and women differ in the "direction of emotions and impulses" to Spence's (1984) original contention that instrumentality and expressivity are elements of masculinity-femininity, personality factors are implicated.

Willerman (1991) and Feingold (1994) list personality traits on which males and females differ. A past best seller (Tannen, 1990) advances the long-popular notion that men are more dominant and controlling than women. The popular book *Mars and Venus on a Date* (Gray, 1997) asserts without hesitation that "feminine radiance" is self-assured, receptive, and responsive, whereas masculine presence is confident, purposeful, and responsible.

However, those personality variables showing gender differences are most likely not distinct from existing personality dimensions, unless they represent some as yet unmeasured dimension of personality. It is possible that personality factors or a combination of personality factors may be part of the constellation of masculinity-femininity. But in order to be a useful concept that is not merely a recapitulation of existing traits, masculinity-femininity must capture something beyond common personality dimensions.

Finally, why not consider cognitive styles or aptitudes as characteristics central to masculinity-femininity? Neither of these phenomena has been included in the more widely studied tests of masculinity-femininity, so less is known about their relationship to masculinity-femininity. Evidence suggests that there are gender differences in a number of cognitive skills and even perceptual abilities (although the differences are typically not large). As mentioned in chapter 1, Swaab et al. (2001) contend that there are numerous known functional sex differences. Recent proof of this statement includes the work of McFadden (2002), who found that females have greater hearing sensitivity than males, whereas males are better at locating sounds than women. He suggests that these differences may result from the effects of androgen exposure. Another gender difference has been documented in visual and spatial memory (Lowe, Mayfield, & Reynolds, 2003). On average, young females have better verbal memory, as assessed by the Test of Memory and Learning (Reynolds & Bigler, 1994), whereas young males have better spatial memory. This finding supports widely established gender differences in verbal and spatial skills.

However, cognitive styles and aptitudes display only weak correlations with masculinity-femininity scores. Thus, it is unlikely that they would be integral to a higher-order bipolar construct. Moreover, cognitive styles and aptitudes would likely not be central to the layperson's conception of masculinity-femininity.

Summary of the Measurement of Masculinity-Femininity

In summary, there have been many tools developed since the work of Terman and Miles in the 1930s in an attempt to measure masculinity and femininity accurately. None have proved satisfactory. One lesson that stands out is that the label of a scale does not necessarily reflect what is actually measured. This is a basic lesson in the concept of construct validity (Cronbach & Meehl, 1955). For example, Storms's measure is labeled the Sex Role Identity Scale, but it appears to be a measure of gender identity. Willemsen and Fischer's (1999) purported measure of "gender identity" is a measure of a variety of gender-related characteristics. Most significant, innumerable studies have been done using the BSRI scale as a measure of masculinity and femininity, and yet many people do not realize that these scales are measures of expressivity and instrumentality—or of nurturance/warmth and dominance/poise, if one prefers the terms used by Tellegen and Lubinski (1983).

We have moved from a bipolar notion of masculinity-femininity to consideration of masculinity and femininity as separate dimensions, to a multidimensional perspective, and perhaps back to a bipolar view of a more circumscribed dimension. Through all this wandering, the concepts of masculinity and femininity have remained central aspects in how everyday people describe individuals in everyday life. Any viable measure of masculinity-femininity must capture that common understanding shared by a population that uses the terms widely in everyday discourse.

The nature of a bipolar construct of masculinity-femininity would be an important and useful clarification. It may only have been obscured by the imprecise measures that have been developed over the past seventy years, with inaccuracies being adopted into mainstream scientific thinking. From our vantage point, clearly much of the research on the Bem Sex Role Inventory has only further muddied understanding of masculinity-femininity. The same might be said of the development of Scale 5 of the MMPI, which attempted to identify masculine and feminine characteristics by contrasting homosexual males with heterosexual males. (The development of Scale 5 is discussed in detail in chapter 3.) Although this approach is now widely regarded as faulty, it is interesting to note that a recent effort to develop a masculinity-femininity scale in Mexico followed the same ill-conceived path (Corona & Izquierdo, 2003).

Clearly, a prominent reason for the mismeasure of masculinity and femininity is the lack of a well-conceived, well-developed instrument to accomplish the task. Furthermore, the lack of such an instrument stems in part from the murky conceptual understanding of masculinity and femininity. Given this situation, it is understandable that many researchers have suggested that it may never be possible to measure masculinity-femininity adequately; have concentrated on developing sample-specific, local measures of the construct rather than nomothetic measures that can be used in many settings; or have turned their attention from the construct of masculinity-femininity to more circumscribed characteristics that show gender differences.

Our hope is that a clearer understanding of masculinity and femininity can be reached and operationally defined that allows these seemingly meaningful dimensions of personality to be scientifically useful.

Chapter 3

The Measurement of Masculinity-Femininity on the MMPI

We now focus our attention on the central topic of this book: how masculinity-femininity has and can be measured on the MMPI, MMPI-2, and MMPI-A. In this chapter, we review the development of Scale 5 and other MMPI scales related to aspects of masculinity-femininity. Duckworth (1984) commented that Scale 5 is the most misunderstood of all the MMPI clinical scales; we agree and believe that this is partly the result of confusion about its original purpose, the complexities of its construction, and the resulting psychometric heterogeneity of the scale. Thus, we begin with a detailed recounting of how Scale 5 was developed. We then present a critical review of the many research studies that have been done concerning masculinity-femininity and the MMPI instruments—including efforts to refine the interpretation of Scale 5—from the publication of the original MMPI until this book went to press.

The Development of Scale 5 of the MMPI

In comparison with the other MMPI scales, information about the methods used to construct Scale 5 is somewhat sketchy and inconsistent. Colligan, Osborne, Swenson, and Offord (1983) have compiled the most complete information, based on a variety of sources. Nichols (2001) also presents a useful summary of what is known. Our version relies heavily on these two accounts.

A preliminary version of Scale 5 was presented in the original 1942 MMPI manual and then again in the revised manual published in 1943 by Hathaway and McKinley. Although Hathaway was interested in studying various forms of sexual deviance, apparently this was not the sole or even major motivation behind developing the scale (in contrast to what many contemporary books report). The 1942 manual labels the sixty-item scale "The Interest Scale" and states that it was constructed to assess "the tendency toward masculinity or femininity of interest pattern . . . a high score indicates a deviation of the basic interest pattern in the direction of the opposite sex" (p. 8). The 1942 manual then elaborates: "The Mf score is often important in reference to vocational choice. Generally speaking, it is well to match a subject vocationally with work that is appropriate to his Mf level" (p. 8).

Item Selection

Thirty-seven of the items on Scale 5 were drawn from the original 504 MMPI items; another twenty-three were added sometime during 1940–42, and were part of a set of fifty-five items adapted from "sections 5, 6, and 7 of the Terman and Miles Attitude-Interest Test" (Dahlstrom, Welsh, & Dahlstrom, 1972, p. 5). The twenty-three items did not survive Hathaway's multiple comparisons and make it onto Scale 5. However, they were retained in the MMPI. The AIAT (Terman & Miles, 1938) is described in detail in chapter 2. As Greene (1980) noted, adding fifty-five items to the original item set would have produced 559 items, yet the MMPI contained only 550 items. No one has been able to explain what happened to the other nine items.

The rationale and procedures through which the sixty MMPI items were selected are not entirely clear, but there is general agreement that multiple steps were used and that an attempt was made to cross-validate the items. (This point is glossed over in many contemporary critiques of Scale 5.) At least some of the items were apparently selected on the basis of gender differences in endorsement frequencies, although no one seems sure to what extent or exactly at what point such contrasts were performed. Hathaway and McKinley (1942) wrote, "The items were originally selected by a comparison of the two sexes" (p. 8). But Hathaway (1956) later contradicted this, stating that: "A final less important criterion [for selecting items] was the comparison of male and female frequencies" (p. 110). Dahlstrom et al. (1972) said the twenty-three added items were selected because of their "promise in identifying sexual inversion as shown in the studies of Terman and Miles" (p. 201), and this seems to agree with Hathaway's (1956) general emphasis on the goal of identifying homosexuals. Constantinople (1973) posited that original MMPI items discriminating men and women among the Minnesota Normals (the original normative sample) were added to those derived from the AIAT and then subjected to further analyses. Although this hypothesis makes sense, there is no way to confirm it.

In another step, item responses were compared between a criterion group of "thirteen homosexual invert males"—for whom no demographic information was reported—and "average males" (Hathaway, 1956, p. 110). The thirteen homosexual men appear to have been selected on the basis of their overt effeminacy, which Hathaway and McKinley believed indicated a constitutional factor underlying their homosexuality (Hathaway, 1956). This was in contrast to "pseudo-homosexuals," who were believed, in the prevailing clinical wisdom of the time, to be heterosexual men who engaged in homosexual behavior because of some form of psychopathology. Thus, the thirteen men in the criterion group were also selected because of their lack of pronounced neurotic, psychotic, or psychopathic features (Dahlstrom & Welsh, 1960), although one wonders how well this goal was achieved. If one imagines the life of highly effeminate gay men in Minnesota in the 1940s, it is difficult to believe that they could have been completely free of psychological distress.

And who were the "average males" to whom Hathaway (1956) referred? Dahlstrom and Welsh (1960) later clarified that, because some of the Scale 5 items were added to the test after the original MMPI normative sample was collected, "special groups of normals had to be gathered for this scale construction work" (p. 64). The initial contrast group is reported to have been fifty-four male soldiers (Dahlstrom & Welsh, 1960). Besides being used in analyses with the thirteen homosexual men, the item responses of this same group were compared in a later step to a group (of unknown size) of men with high scores on the Inversion scale of the Terman and Miles (1936) Attitude-Interest Analysis Test. (Items on this AIAT scale were themselves selected because of their ability to differentiate normal males from a group of "passive homosexual men.") We do not possess other information about the men selected for this criterion group or about how highly they scored on the AIAT Inversion scale. However, Colligan et al. (1983) ingeniously deduced that they might have resembled the description that Terman and Miles provided for the typical "invert" personality in their book on AIAT. Such men were to be distinguished by the following characteristics:

[F]astidiousness with respect to dress, cleanliness, and care of person; in their preoccupation with domestic affairs; in their preference for feminine types of occupations and for working with women rather than with men; in their fondness for sentimental movies and romantic literature; in their feminine timidity when faced by physical danger; in their religious interest; and in their liking for literature, art, music, and dramatics . . . by their repudiation of everything that is characteristically masculine: aggressive leadership, energetic activity, physical courage, masculine pursuits, and interest in warfare, adventure, outdoor sports, science and things of a mechanical nature . . . an excessive amount of sex consciousness, especially consciousness of the forbidden nature of their sex lives . . . and a great variety of responses which indicate social maladjustment, nervousness, lack of self-confidence, a low degree of self-control, and a marked tendency to worry and anxiety. (p. 282)

Terman and Miles also reported that inverts had "lax ethical standards" (p. 283). Note that if Colligan and his colleagues are correct in their conclusion, a broad range of psychopathological features might have characterized this second criterion group, possibly contaminating Scale 5 with such characteristics and working against Hathaway's and McKinley's original intention not to confound the scale with neuroticism or psychopathy.

Nichols (2001) asserts that the final comparison performed was between the male soldiers and a group of sixty-seven female airline employees. Items surviving all these contrasts comprise the sixty items on the original MMPI Scale 5. These are listed in Appendix A. One can easily see that those items from the original MMPI item pool are saturated with psychological distress and disturbance, whereas those derived from the AIAT primarily reflect gender-stereotypical vocational and avocational interests.

Norms

The 1942 manual presented T score derivations based on the responses of forty-nine male and seventy-three female students in psychology classes at the University of Minnesota, explaining that "no general normative group was available, since these items were added late" (p. 18). The tables of standard scores listed in the 1943 manual are based on yet two other samples. The first was a group of 117 men, of whom "54 per cent were engineers of various ages and 46 per cent were unselected army noncommisioned men" (Hathaway & McKinley, 1943, p. 11). The norms for women were based on the responses of "108 females of various ages. Of these 62 per cent were employed clerical workers, 21 per cent were night-school students, and the rest were hospital patients" (Hathaway & McKinley, 1943, p. 11). We know from the article by Hathaway and Briggs (1957) that the means and standard deviations for Scale 5 in these two samples were, respectively, 20.44 and 5.13 (for males) and 36.51 and 4.83 (for females). Unfortunately, we have been unable to locate the actual frequency distributions of Mf raw scores in this sample.

Separate Scale for Women

Finally, it is worth noting that Hathaway and McKinley apparently had some discomfort with the assumption that masculinity and femininity were essentially the same for both men and women. Hathaway (1956) described an attempt to derive a separate scale for women:

> A scale designated Fm was derived by a process similar to that used for Mf. The new scale correlated .78 to .95 with Mf on a number of samples. This correlation and the fact that cross-validation did not particularly favor the new scale, even for the identification of homosexual females, indicated its abandonment. (p. 110)

To our knowledge, the item composition of this potential scale has been lost.

Research on Homosexuality and Scale 5

As mentioned earlier, the first two MMPI manuals suggest that Scale 5 was originally intended in part as a measure of vocational interests. To be sure, the 1942 manual states that "males with very high Mf scores have frequently been found to be either overt or repressed sexual inverts" (p. 8). However, in both of the first two manuals, Hathaway and McKinley were adamant that homo-sexual "abnormality *must not be assumed* on the basis of a high score without confirmatory evidence" (1942, p. 8; 1943, p. 5). Similarly, in 1951, Hathaway and Meehl cautioned: "T scores of 60 to 75 are not uncommon among males in literary and artistic lines of work. One would never be justified in assuming an identity between high scores on this scale and the existence of homosexual practices" (p. 81).

In spite of these caveats, much of the early research on Scale 5 concerned its ability to distinguish male homosexuality, with results confirming Hathaway and Meehl's (1951) assertion. For example, Burton (1947) compared Mf scores of "20 rapists, 34 sexual inverts, and 84 other delinquents," finding that the thirty-four homosexual men scored significantly higher than the other two groups but that the scale could not be used for individual classifi-cation without producing high error rates. Gough (1947) also demonstrated that Scale 5 was susceptible to conscious impression management. When instructed to do so, a majority of homosexual males in his sample were able to lower their Scale 5 scores into the normal range. Interestingly, in spite of these early results and Hathaway and Meehl's (1951) admonition, over the years, a number of studies have tried to discriminate male homosexuals using Scale 5 (e.g., Aaronson & Grumpelt, 1961; Fraas, 1970; Friberg, 1967; Horstman, 1975; Krippner, 1964a; Manosevitz, 1970, 1971; Singer, 1970). Many found substantial mean differences between heterosexual and homo-sexual men. For example, Hiatt and Hargrave (1994) found a fourteen-point mean difference on MMPI Scale 5 between sixty homosexual and sixty-five

heterosexual male law-enforcement applicants. Our impression is that interpretation of the high scores in many clinical settings continues to be tied to
homosexuality, at least for men.

Other Early Research

Other early studies investigated the construct validity of Scale 5 through its
correlations with other measures of masculinity-femininity, such as those drawn
from the Strong Vocational Interest Blank and the Kuder Preference Record
(Heston, 1948), Terman and Miles's AIAT (de Cillis & Orbison, 1950), Guilford
Zimmerman Temperament Survey (Murray, 1963a), Franck Completion (a
projective test that has since disappeared; Shepler, 1951), and the Thematic
Apperception Test (Caligor, 1951). Given the lack of theoretical clarity regarding masculinity-femininity, it is not surprising that evidence for convergent
validity was generally lacking. Researchers were similarly disappointed to find
that Scale 5 scores did not predict such criteria as the gender of the figure drawn
on the Draw-a-Person Test (Granick & Smith, 1953). Aaronson (1959) noted
that a huge error rate resulted if one attempted to use Mf scores to differentiate
males from females. Importantly, evidence also began to accumulate that Scale
5 scores were related to social class, education, and IQ (e.g., Clark, 1953; Fry,
1949; Goodstein, 1954; Murray, 1963b; Sopchak, 1952; Winfield, 1953). This
finding led major clinical texts (e.g., Graham, 1977; Greene, 1980) to recommend a modified interpretation of high Scale 5 scores for highly educated men
and women, with a "correction factor" of up to ten T score points for those with
graduate degrees. For example, Graham (1987) recommended that, for men,
"homoerotic trends" should only be strongly considered if a respondent's Scale
5 score deviated "markedly from what is expected based on the subject's intelligence, education, and social class" (p. 51). Still, the correlation of Scale 5 scores
with socioeconomic status apparently did not lead most people to question the
construct validity of the scale for measuring masculinity-femininity.

Other early studies appeared to ignore all these problems, accept the validity
of Scale 5 as a measure of masculinity-femininity, and correlate the scale with
various other measures to investigate the relationship of masculinity-femininity
with other constructs, such as personal values (Didato & Kennedy, 1957), intel-
lectual abilities (Krippner, 1964b), and creativity (Littlejohn, 1967).

Studies of Individuals with High 5 Scores

One approach to fleshing out the meaning of Scale 5 scores was to follow
the traditional MMPI code type approach and to investigate the characteristics

of individuals who scored high or low on the scale. Hathaway and Meehl (1957, cited in Dahlstrom et al., 1972) studied peer ratings of normal men and women. They found that high-scoring males were characterized as "sensitive and prone to worry, idealistic and peaceable, sociable and curious, and having aesthetic interests" (Dahlstrom et al., 1972, p. 205). Women with high Mf scores were described as adventurous. Low-scoring men were judged to be "practical, balanced, cheerful, self-confident, and independent," whereas low-scoring women were seen as "sensitive and responsive, as well as modest, grateful, and wise" (Dahlstrom et al., 1972, p. 206).

Gough, McKee, and Yandell (1955) used expert judges to assess the characteristics of normal men with high and low Scale 5 scores. As summarized by Friedman, Lewak, Nichols, and Webb (2001), "the high Scale 5 man [was described as] inner-directed and intellectually curious. Work and achievements provided these men significant gratification, and they were seen as mature, self-aware individuals. They had good judgment and common sense. They could communicate effectively and were quite verbal. Some of the adjectives typical of . . . high Scale 5 men included ambitious, clear-thinking, effeminate, imaginative, nervous, organized, sensitive, and submissive" (p. 118). Low-scoring men were seen as "lacking insight into their own motives, preferring action to thought, and having narrow interests. They did not appear to have the psychological complexity or inner-directedness that the high Scale 5 men had" (Friedman et al., 2001, p. 118). More recently, King and Kelley (1977) and Tanner (1990) investigated MMPI two-point codes involving Scale 5 among psychiatric outpatients. Both found that elevations on Scale 5 were quite rare in psychiatric samples (perhaps because of the correlation of Mf and social class). Also, as King and Kelley summarized, Scale 5 had "significant, but normal correlates" (p. 185) and "homosexuality was not a significant descriptor associated with any Scale 5 elevation, either alone or in combination with other scales" (p. 184).

Hathaway and Monachesi (1963) added to interest in Scale 5 with their classic study of adolescent MMPI responses. Between 1948 and 1954, they assessed 15,300 boys and girls in Grade 9 in the Minnesota school system. Also, 3,856 of these students were retested when they reached Grade 12 in 1956–57. The authors reported that boys who had their highest scores on Scale 5 came from families with highly educated parents and had a lower incidence of delinquent or antisocial behaviors, even when they came from populations where these behaviors were frequent. Boys with low scores on Scale 5 tended to be delinquent and do poorly in school, and they had lower intelligence test scores than boys scoring high on Scale 5. Hathaway and Monachesi concluded that Scale 5 worked as an "inhibitor" of aggressive and delinquent tendencies among adolescent boys. The results for girls were less clear: those with low scores on Scale 5 did better on intelligence testing and showed higher academic achievement. However, girls scoring high on Scale 5 did not show delinquency, although they did less well in school and tended to come from rural environments.

Williams and Butcher (1989) compared boys and girls scoring high (in the top 25 percent) on MMPI Scale 5 with those in the lower three quartiles in a clinical sample of 844 adolescents that was later used in validating the MMPI-A. Using a variety of external rating measures, the authors expected to replicate Hathaway and Monachesi's finding that Scale 5 was negatively predictive of acting-out problems. However, this proved not to be true; there were virtually no significant differences on any measure between high scorers on Scale 5 and the rest of the sample for either boys or girls. Unfortunately, correlations between Scale 5 and the other measures were not reported; we suspect that such a procedure might have illuminated significant external relationships of Scale 5. (As we report, Butcher, Williams, Graham, Archer, Tellegen, Ben-Porath, and Kaemmer, 1992, reanalyzed this data in examining correlates of MMPI-A Scale 5.)

Other MMPI M-F Measures

As many studies accumulated showing that Scale 5 did not demonstrate expected empirical relationships, some researchers seem to have gone back to the MMPI item pool to see if they could derive other MMPI indices that would work better for their purposes. For example, Panton (1960) and Marsh, Hilliard, and Liechti (1955) developed MMPI scales to identify homosexuality and sexual deviancy, respectively, using empirical keying to select items that differentiated normal from criterion groups. Neither of these scales showed much validity or utility, however, and we found no evidence that they were ever widely used.

Nichols (1980) reported on the Acceptance of Passivity (Ap; Harris) scale, a rationally developed index which, although it was never published, developed quite an underground following and was apparently used in a configural manner with Mf to clarify the interpretation of scores. For example, among men, high scores on both Mf and Ap were supposed to indicate "acceptance of passivity" and either overt or covert homosexual tendencies, whereas low scores on both were taken to imply "accentuated masculinity" (Nichols, 1980). As far as we know, there are no published studies using the Ap scale, and it seems to have faded into obscurity. (Out of curiosity, we examined Ap's performance in our data; see chapter 6.)

An interesting variation on the strategy of creating new item scales was the "Mf Index" developed by Aaronson (1959) based on a person's scores on Scales 1, 3, 6, and 7. Aaronson showed that his linear combination of these scales more successfully differentiated the genders than did Scale 5 but was relatively unrelated to Scale 5 scores. He concluded from this that "male and female personality differences comprise more than a single dimension" (p. 50).

A more recent MMPI-based measure related to masculinity-femininity is the Gender Dysphoria (Gd) scale, developed by Althof, Lothstein, Jones, and Shen (1983) to identify males with gender dysphoria or transsexualism. Althof and his colleagues identified thirty-one MMPI items that significantly differentiated between men applying at a university sex reassignment program for surgery and a matched group of male psychiatric outpatients. Admirably, Althof et al. cross-validated the Gd scale—before publishing it—with independent groups of gender dysphorics and controls. Also, shortly after its publication, a separate group of researchers in Australia (Ross, Burnard, & Campbell, 1988) showed that the Gd scale had excellent sensitivity and specificity for differentiating male gender dysphorics from mixed psychiatric outpatients. The scale did not perform as well, however, in differentiating "primary gender dysphorics" (those men diagnosed as transsexuals) from "secondary gender dysphorics" (those men seeking sex reassignment for other reasons).

Inspection of the Gd scale shows that eleven of its thirty-one items overlap with Scale 5; others are non–Scale 5 items that appear to reflect stereotypic masculine and feminine interests (e.g., Like fishing, #423; Liked to play hopscotch, #463; Would like to be a dressmaker, #538; and Would like to be a secretary, #557). Many of these are items derived from the Terman and Miles (1938) AIAT that were added to the MMPI item pool in 1940–42 but which did not make it onto Scale 5. Remaining Gd items seem related to emotional/physical distress and are expressed in language that might be more typical of women than men (e.g., Muscles don't twitch, #103; Not more nervous than most, #242).

Although apparently never used in clinical practice, two other relevant MMPI scales resulted from the first published item-level factor analysis of the full MMPI (Johnson, Null, Butcher, & Johnson, 1984). Twenty-one replicated factors were derived from an orthogonal varimax solution, using ratings from 5,506 inpatients and outpatients at the Missouri Department of Mental

Health, and a cross-validation, using 5,632 respondents from the same setting. Two of the resulting factors were Stereotypic Femininity, comprised of twenty items, and Stereotypic Masculinity, using thirteen items. Inspection of these items on these two scales shows that all but eleven are scored on Scale 5. Again, most of the remaining items are gender stereotypic interest items from the AIAT that did not survive the multiple comparisons to make it onto Scale 5. Finn (1986b) examined the retest stability over thirty years of the Stereotypic Femininity and Stereotypic Masculinity scales—along with other of the Johnson et al. (1984) factor scales—in two groups of men followed at the University of Minnesota for a study of cardiovascular disease. In the first cohort (seventy-eight business professionals who were middle-aged at the inception of the study in 1947), the thirty-year retest coefficients were .62 for Stereotypic Femininity and .58 for Stereotypic Masculinity. For the second cohort (ninety-six college students who were in their twenties when the study began), Finn found retest correlations of .45 for Stereotypic Femininity and .55 for Stereotypic Masculinity. These findings are unique in suggesting that the masculine and feminine interests may be fairly stable in men across the entire adult life span.

Archer and Klinefelter (1991) conducted an MMPI item factor analysis very similar to that of Johnson et al. (1984), but they used a sample of 1,762 adolescents receiving psychiatric services at the time they took the MMPI. Among the factors they identified were one that they labeled Masculinity, consisting of twenty items, and one labeled Femininity, containing twenty items. These factor scales were extremely similar to those identified by Johnson et al. (1984). In fact, twelve of the twenty items on Archer and Klinefelter's Masculinity factor are also on the Stereotypic Masculinity scale of Johnson et al.; thirteen items from Archer and Klinefelter's Femininity scale are scored in the same direction on the Stereotypic Femininity scale of Johnson et al. As with the factors in Johnson et al. (1984), we are not aware that the Archer and Klinefelter scales were ever used clinically.

Scale 5 Subscales

Another attempt to improve on Scale 5 concerned the development of subscales. Shortly after Harris and Lingoes (1955/1968) developed their well-known rational subscales for the clinical scales, Pepper and Strong (1958) developed a similar set of subscales for Scale 5 using fifty-seven of the sixty items. The subscales were labeled (1) Personal and emotional sensitivity, (2) Sexual identification, (3) Altruism, (4) Feminine occupational identification, and (5) Denial of masculine occupations (Dahlstrom, Welsh, & Dahlstrom, 1972). According to Graham (1987), these subscales were never widely used. However, there was increasing recognition that a number of dimensions underlay Scale 5 of the MMPI, as well as other existing inventories purporting to measure masculinity-femininity (Engel, 1966; Lunneborg, 1972; Lunneborg & Lunneborg, 1970; Reece, 1964).

Eventually, another set of Scale 5 subscales gained more recognition and use: the Serkownek subscales (Schuerger, Foerstner, Serkownek, & Ritz, 1987; Serkownek, 1975). Serkownek based his subscales on a factor analysis of Scale 5 items done by Graham, Schroeder, and Lilly (1971) on responses from 422 individuals, including both men and women and psychiatric inpatients, outpatients, and normals. Items were assigned to separate subscales based on their having factor loadings of .30 and higher. Subsequently, the subscales were named on the basis of item content and correlations with other MMPI scales in an independent sample of outpatients (Schuerger et al., 1987). The resulting subscales were: Mf1, Narcissism-Hypersensitivity; Mf2, Stereotypic Feminine Interests; Mf3, Denial of Stereotypic Masculine Interests; Mf4, Heterosexual Discomfort-Passivity; Mf5, Introspective-Critical; and Mf6, Socially Retiring. Whereas most of the items in the subscales were scored in the same direction as they were on Scale 5, fourteen items were scored in the opposite direction, to be consistent with the factor loadings in the Graham et al. (1971) study. Graham (1987) reported six-week retest reliability coefficients for the Serkownek subscales, based on work done by Moreland (1985). For males, the reliability coefficients ranged from a high of .83, for Mf1, Narcissism-Hypersensitivity, to .67 for Mf4, Heterosexual Discomfort-Passivity. For females, the retest reliabilities went from .83, for Mf3, Denial of Stereotypic Masculine Interests, to .69, for Mf4, Heterosexual Discomfort-Passivity.

Although we have located little empirical research using the Serkownek subscales, they were included in a number of clinical texts on the MMPI and in many MMPI scoring programs, and hence they were used by a number of clinicians up until the publication of the MMPI-2. One interesting fact highlighted by Wong (1984) is that in the original study by Graham et al. (1971), the seven factors extracted (mirroring the Serkownek subscales and another factor concerning education and social class) accounted for only 25 percent of the common variance. This raises questions about how adequately the Serkownek subscales ever captured the variability in personality measured by Scale 5. Also Foerstner (1986; cited in Friedman et al., 2001) showed that at least some of the Serkownek subscales appeared to be more related to constructs such as depression and social introversion than to what is generally conceived of as masculinity or femininity.

Scale 5 and Androgyny Theory

As discussed in chapter 2, in 1973, Anne Constantinople published her now-famous critique of existing measures of masculinity-femininity, including the Mf scale of the MMPI. Constantinople's complaints about Scale 5 were well taken and included (1) the limited criterion groups used to develop the scale; (2) the confounding of many constructs (e.g., sexual orientation, gender differences, gender-related interest patterns) in its implicit definition of masculinity-femininity; and (3) the assumption of a single, bipolar dimension of masculinity-femininity. Shortly after this article was published, Bem (1974) and Spence, Helmreich, and Stapp (1975) published their own measures purporting to measure "masculinity" and "femininity" and related them to the politically attractive concept of "androgyny."

Not surprisingly, in the flood of research that followed, various studies correlated Scale 5 with Bem's BSRI and Spence et al.'s EPAQ or contrasted groups of individuals formed using these measures (e.g., "Masculine," "Feminine," "Androgynous," and "Undifferentiated") on Scale 5 and sometimes on other MMPI scales (Adams & Sherer, 1982; Alumbaugh, 1987; Evans & Dinning, 1982; Todd & Gynther, 1988; Volentine, 1981; Wakefield, Sasek, Friedman, & Bowden, 1976). Almost all of these studies found little or no relationship between Scale 5 and the popular contemporary measures of "sex role orientation"; in retrospect, this result seems expected, given the vastly different conceptualizations of masculinity-femininity reflected in Scale 5 and these other instruments.

Other researchers used various approaches to assess whether Scale 5 measured an underlying bipolar dimension or better fit the idea of independent unipolar dimensions (e.g., Goen & Lansky, 1968; Lunneborg, 1972; Sines, 1977). Despite little consensus on the question of bipolarity, there was general agreement that Scale 5 was psychometrically multidimensional (as were other widely used measures of masculinity-femininity).

Given these findings and given psychology's love affair with androgyny theory during this period, perhaps it is not surprising that, in 1984, Wong published an influential article, "MMPI Scale Five: Its Meaning or Lack Thereof," reiterating many of Constantinople's criticisms and seeming to call for a moratorium on the use of Scale 5. In his concluding sentence, Wong asserted: "Rigid, synthetic, dichotomies such as those suggested in interpretations of . . . MMPI Scale Five serve to perpetuate status quo myths that apparently were never more than 13 moving shadows on a laboratory cave wall" (p. 283).

The Development of Scale 5 for the MMPI-2

Item Content

When the MMPI was revised, four items were deleted from Scale 5, leaving it with fifty-six items (Butcher et al., 1989). The items cut from the original scale were the following: #69, Attracted to people of my own sex; #70, Liked Drop-the-Handkerchief; #249, Believe in Hell, and #295, Liked "Alice in Wonderland." Items #70 and #295 were considered outdated, whereas items #69 and #249 were considered too intrusive for many settings in which the MMPI-2 is now used (e.g., for employment screening). All of these deleted items were keyed True for males, and all but item #69 were keyed True for females. It is noteworthy that, with the elimination of item #69, there is no longer any explicit question about sexual orientation on the MMPI-2. Six other Scale 5 items were also rewritten to improve their clarity (Butcher et al., 1989, Table 8, p. 8).

Response Shifts

One interesting question is to what extent the endorsement of Scale 5 items changed in the years since the measure was first developed. Unfortunately, this is not so easy to determine. Hathaway and Briggs (1957) listed the original means and standard deviations on the sixty-item scale as 20.44 and 5.13, respectively, for men (N = 117) and as 36.51 and 4.83 for women (N = 108). The means and standard deviations in the modern restandardization sample for the revised fifty-six-item scale are 26.01 and 5.08 for men (N = 1,138) and 35.94 and 4.08 for women (N = 1,462). Hence, although it seems that men in the new normative sample answered more items in the "feminine" direction compared to those in the original sample, it is impossible to say whether this is a result of cultural shifts between the 1940s and the 1980s or to other differences between the two samples. There was much less change in the endorsement of Scale 5 items by women in the two samples. Also, it is difficult to determine the exact effect of having dropped the four Scale 5 items. Butcher et al. (1989) were able to calculate means and standard deviations for the other shortened basic scales on the original Minnesota normative group; however, data on the original Scale 5 normative groups could not be located. When the MMPI-2 was first published, some critics suggested that the increased Scale 5 raw scores for men were an artifact of a predominantly "yuppie" normative sample that was unrepresentative of the U.S. population. However, Schinka and LaLone (1997) constructed a census-matched subsample of the MMPI-2 normative group. The Scale 5 mean T score and standard deviation for men in the stratified subsample (N = 482) were 47.51 and 9.33, respectively. These were not significantly different statistically from those for the full male normative sample.

Psychometric Properties

As might be expected, Scale 5 was one of the basic scales with the lowest internal consistency for men in the MMPI-2 normative sample, with an alpha coefficient of .5809. For women, Scale 5 had the lowest internal consistency of all the basic scales, .3689 (Butcher et al., 1989). Retest reliability over a one-week interval was adequate, however: .83 for men and .74 for women (cf. Appendix E in Butcher, Graham, Ben-Porath, Tellegen, Dahlstrom, & Kaemmer, 2001). Scale 5 correlated with the other basic scales very much as it had on the original MMPI—quite low (cf. Table F-1 in Butcher et al, 1989). This was true even with Scale 0, with which it shares nine items. Also, Butcher et al. (1989) factor analyzed the basic validity and clinical scales for the normative males and females separately, and Scale 5 behaved much as it had in numerous previous factor analyses of the MMPI. (See Dahlstrom, Welsh, and Dahlstrom (1975) for a summary of these early studies.) For both males and females, Scale 5 largely defined a separate factor, on which the L scale also had a moderate loading. For males, this factor accounted for 8.5 percent of the common variance; for females, it encompassed 8.7 percent of the variance (cf. Tables F-2 and F-3 in Butcher et al., 1989).

As with Scale 0, Scale 5 on the MMPI-2 is plotted using linear T scores, not the uniform T scores derived for the other clinical scales. The standard error of measurement for Scale 5 is 4.15 and 5.09 for males and females, respectively, indicating that retest differences for one respondent falling within these ranges are not meaningful.

Association with Socioeconomic Status and Education

As discussed earlier, Scale 5 scores from the original MMPI showed a substantial relationship to social class and education. Thus, when the MMPI-2 was published, there was considerable interest in whether this correlation would continue to be true. Unfortunately, there has been some confusion on this issue. Butcher (1990) performed the first relevant analyses on the MMPI-2 normative sample and showed that, among males, Scale 5 was the basic scale that had the highest correlation with education (.348). For the normal females, the Scale 5 correlation with education was much less than for males (−.152), and several other basic scales had nearly as high correlations with education (e.g., L = −.143,

Scale 0 = −.149). After examining the mean Scale 5 scores of different educational groups in the normative sample, Butcher concluded that the MMPI-2 Scale 5 scores showed minimal effects from education. He did suggest, however, that small adjustments in interpretation might be required for respondents with less than a high school education or those with postgraduate training.

Dahlstrom and Tellegen (1993) analyzed essentially the same data sets and reported an eleven-point T score difference between the least and most educated men, but negligible differences (i.e., 5–6 T score points) between comparable groups of women. They also showed an influence of education on profile shape: for normative men, the majority of profiles with peak scores on Scale 5 came from those respondents with the highest education level. As might be expected, for women, the opposite was true: those with less education were more likely to have Scale 5 as their profile high point.

Greene (2000) reached a conclusion similar to that of Butcher (1990) after analyzing two data sets: the MMPI-2 normative sample and Caldwell's (1997) clinical dataset of 52,543 MMPI-2s of inpatients and outpatients collected from his scoring service. Greene reported correlations between Scale 5 and years of education to be .100 for the normal respondents and .091 for the clinical respondents and concluded that "Scale 5 . . . on the MMPI-2 [is] not affected by years of education, unlike on the MMPI" (p. 452). However, Greene combined men and women in the MMPI-2 normative sample in his calculations, which obscures the differences that appear to exist when males and females are considered separately.

As regards occupational level, Dahlstrom and Tellegen (1993) found very small, clinically insignificant differences on Scale 5 scores between the highest and lowest occupational groups in the MMPI-2 normative sample, for either men or women. This fact was also noted by Greene (2000).

The Masculine Gender Role (GM) and Feminine Gender Role (GF) Scales

With the publication of the MMPI-2, two new scales became available that were expected to be related to masculinity-femininity: the Masculine Gender Role (GM) and Feminine Gender Role (GF) scales. As detailed by Peterson and Dahlstrom (1992), these scales essentially represent an effort to apply androgyny theory—with its assertion that masculinity and femininity are independent, unipolar dimensions—to the MMPI-2. Following a procedure pioneered by Baucom (1976) with the California Personality Inventory (CPI), Peterson (1991) examined MMPI-2 item endorsement frequencies by gender in the restandardization sample. She selected forty-seven items that were endorsed in one direction by at least 70 percent of men and for which the endorsement frequency for women was at least 10 percent less than that for men; these became the GM scale. Nine of the GM items are scored in the same direction as on Scale 5. Similarly, forty-six items were identified that were endorsed by at least 70 percent of women and for which the endorsement frequency in men was at least 10 percent less; these comprised the GF scale. Sixteen of the GM items overlap with Scale 5 and are scored in the same direction. There are no overlapping items between GM and GF.

Peterson and Dahlstrom (1992) reported that, as hoped, GM and GF were highly independent of each other, correlating −.10 within each gender in the MMPI-2 normative sample. They also had low to moderate correlations with Scale 5, and, as expected from their method of construction, each scale showed a bimodal distribution of scores by gender. Also not surprisingly, the two scales were only moderately internally consistent, with GM having Kuder-Richardson coefficients of .72 and .78 for males and females, respectively, and GF yielding coefficients of .57 and .58, respectively. One-week retest reliabilities were adequate, however. For GM, the retest correlations were .73 for males (N = 82) and .89 for females (N = 111); for GF, the coefficients were .86 and .78, for males and females, respectively. Peterson and Dahlstrom used median splits on the scales within each gender to classify the normative subjects into "androgynous" (i.e., high GM-high GF), "masculine stereotyped" (high GM-low GF), "feminine stereotyped" (low GM-high GF), and "undifferentiated" (low GM-low GF) groups. They then compared the groups on their mean Scale 5 scores. For each gender, the "masculine-stereotyped" individuals had the lowest raw scores on Scale 5, and the "feminine-stereotyped" individuals had the highest raw score means. The "androgynous" and "undifferentiated" groups did not significantly differ on Scale 5 raw scores, which was taken as evidence that Scale 5 "confounds" these two subtypes.

As part of the MMPI-2 restandardization project, GM and GF were correlated with spouse ratings for a subset of 832 women and 823 men from the normative sample. Statistically significant correlates bore little or no resemblance to lay conceptions of masculinity and femininity. For example, for both males and females, GF was related to "misuse of prescription drugs and alcohol," and GM was correlated with "self-confidence" and "persistence towards one goal." As Peterson (1991) detailed, she also administered the MMPI-2, BSRI, PAQ, and Baucom's (1976) masculinity and femininity scales for the CPI to an undergraduate sample of 198 men and 198 women. GM showed fairly good convergent validity with the masculinity scales of these other inventories and fairly good discriminant validity from their femininity scales. For example, correlations of GM with BSRI Masculinity were .38 and .35 for males and females, respectively, and correlations with BSRI Femininity were .00 and −.11, respectively. GF had moderate correlations with Baucom's Femininity scale (.57 for men and .53 for women), which is to be expected given their item overlap. However, GF showed very poor convergent and discriminant validity with the Femininity and Masculinity scales of the BSRI and PAQ. This suggested that the GF operational definition of femininity bore little resemblance to feminin- ity as conceptualized by the developers of the BSRI and PAQ.

As far as we know, since the MMPI-2 was introduced, there have been only four published investigations of GM and GF that are independent of the work of Peterson and Dahlstrom. Johnson, Jones, and Brems (1996) gave a rather damning assessment, based on their examination of the scales in 173 female and 90 male undergraduate students. They felt that the internal consistencies of the two scales in their sample were too low for individual comparisons (although they were similar to those found in the MMPI-2 normative sample). They also judged that relevant correlations with the BSRI and with Orlofsky and O'Heron's (1987) Sex Role Behavior Scale (SRBS-Short) were too low to demonstrate con- vergent validity. (The significance of this point rests on whether one believes that the BSRI and SRBS measure important aspects of masculinity and feminin- ity.) More important, in our eyes, was the conclusion that Johnson and his col- leagues reached from correlating GM and GF with the 16-PF (Cattell, Eber, & Tatsuoka, 1970) and from noticing its very poor discriminant validity with well- understood personality traits: "It is possible that these two scales [GM and GF], like other sex-role measures, are not measures of femininity and masculinity at all, but of personality traits that are predominantly gender-typed" (p. 166).

Castlebury and Durham (1997) seem to have provided further evidence of this point. They set out to examine the relationship between masculinity, femininity, and "androgyny" (as measured by median splits on GM and GF) with psychological well-being in a sample of three hundred male and female college students. GM and, to some extent, GF had substantial correlations with scales of SCL-90-R (Derogatis, 1977) and the Tennessee Self-Concept Scales (Roid & Fitts, 1991), with both indices correlating positively with scales of psychological well-being and negatively with scales related to psychopa- thology. Castlebury and Durham interpreted their results as supporting the idea that "psychological well-being is actualized when an individual adopts a masculine-role orientation" (p. 890); however, they also admitted the possibil- ity that "'masculinity' and 'femininity' may be misnomers for what [GM and GF] are measuring" (p. 891).

Cellucci, Wilkerson, and Mandra (1998) first classified 117 undergraduate students (64 women and 53 men) into "sex-typed, androgynous, undifferentiated, and cross sex-typed" groups based on their scores on Spence, Helmreich, and Stapp's (1974) Personal Attributes Questionnaire (PAQ; see chapter 2). The authors then examined respondents' scores on GM and GF and Ego Strength (Es). The PAQ classified groups showed few differences in their GM and GF scores. GM was correlated with the M scale of the PAQ for both men and women (.40 and .41, respectively), and GF was correlated with the F scale for women (.37), but not for men (.01). For both men and women, GM was positively correlated with Es (.66 and .57, respectively), leading the authors to conclude that "these scales (and particularly . . . GM) may reflect general psychological well-being" (p. 754).

Woo and Tian (2006, 2008) examined relationships between GM and GF and two MMPI-2 markers of "psychological well-being," Es and Low Self-Esteem (LSE), in mixed clinical samples of Australian (N = 107) and Singaporean (N = 70) patients. Using both median-split and multiple regression approaches, the authors determined that GM was significantly related to Es and LSE, whereas GF was not. Correlations of GM in the combined sample were .72 for Es and −.61 for LSE. The authors concluded that "individuals with more masculine traits have better psychological adjustment" (2006, p. 418), but again, this statement rests on the assumption that GM is a measure of masculinity.

Our opinion is that GM and GF do almost nothing to clarify the interpretation of MMPI-2 Scale 5 or the measurement of masculinity-femininity. In effect, these scales are best thought of as "gender typicality" scales, with high and low scores showing whether an individual endorsed MMPI-2 items that are more typical of one of the genders. Beyond this, the scales do not appear to be highly meaningful or to be related to important aspects of personality that are not found elsewhere in the MMPI-2. There is some evidence that GM scores correlate with other self-report measures of psychological adjustment, but, in our mind, this does not lead to the conclusion that "masculinity is associated with psychological well-being." An alternative explanation is that GM is in part of a measure of positive and negative emotionality, as are the BSRI and PAQ Masculinity Scales (see chapter 2).

Recent Research on Masculinity-Femininity with the MMPI-2

Since the introduction of the MMPI-2, four published studies have directly focused on Scale 5 and/or the measurement of masculinity-femininity on the MMPI-2. Long and Graham (1991) used the same spousal ratings as did

Peterson (1991) from the subset of 819 heterosexual couples included in the MMPI-2 normative sample (Butcher et al., 1989). In their study, Long and Graham examined correlations between spousal ratings and Scale 5 scores for men. Of the 110 items in the spousal rating form, ten positive and ten negative ones were rationally selected because they seemed to capture descriptors that are traditionally associated with men who score high on Scale 5. These items were correlated with obtained Scale 5 scores and with education. Only one of the selected descriptors was found to be significantly correlated with Scale 5 ($r = -.21$): "Is passive and obedient to superiors." When the effects of education were partialed out, this correlation dropped to $-.14$ but was still statistically significant. In contrast, educational level significantly correlated with eight of the spousal rating descriptors. Long and Graham concluded that their study did not offer "much support for the use of Scale 5 of MMPI-2 for describing the behaviors and personality characteristics of normal men." Although this is certainly true of their investigation, we remind the reader that certain aspects of masculinity-femininity, such as gender identity or the nature of one's erotic fantasies, may not be very amenable to observer ratings. Thus, further study is warranted before concluding that Scale 5 is no longer useful with men in nonclinical populations.

Blais (1995) examined associations between Scale 5 and the personality disorder scales of the Millon Clinical Multiaxial Inventory-II (MCMI-II; Millon, 1987) in a sample of seventy-six female psychiatric inpatients. Pearson correlation coefficients showed that Scale 5 scores were significantly positively associated with the following MCMI-II PD scales: Narcissistic (.23), Antisocial (.26), Aggressive/Sadistic (.38), Passive-Aggressive (.23), and Paranoid (.41). Blais then separated his sample into two groups: (1) high-Mf (Scale 5 T score > 50, with a mean of 59T) and (2) low-Mf (Scale 5 T score ≤ 50, with a mean of 42T). He then performed contrasts on the MCMI-II PD scales. The women scoring above the mean on Scale 5 had significantly higher scores on the Narcissistic, Antisocial, Aggressive/Sadistic, and Paranoid MCMI-II scales than did those women scoring below the mean. Although these results are intriguing in suggesting that Scale 5 scores may be associated with certain types of personality pathology, it is difficult to know how far one can generalize Blais's findings. As we demonstrate later in this book, it is possible for clients to achieve elevations on Scale 5 in substantially different ways, and the meanings of these elevations vary widely depending on which content areas of Scale 5 are endorsed. It is quite possible that the high-scoring female inpatients in Blais's sample were alike in certain ways and also were quite different than female outpatients or nonpatients who score high on Scale 5.

A relatively recent, statistically sophisticated study by Haslam (1997) subjected the Scale 5 scores of the 1,138 men in the MMPI-2 restandardization sample (Butcher et al., 1989) to taxometric analyses, in an attempt to gain information on whether male sexual orientation is continuous or categorical. Two premises of the study were that Scale 5 is a valid measure of male sexual orientation and that it reflects a unitary underlying variable. Haslam concluded that Scale 5 measures a continuous rather than categorical underlying trait. Because we reject the ideas that Scale 5 measures sexual orientation in men or reflects a unitary underlying dimension, to us, this study speaks to the dimensionality of those traits comprising the majority of the variance in Scale 5. (We will be able to say more about what these traits are after we report on our own investigation.)

McGrath, Sapareto, and Pogge (1998) set out to develop a new scale, which they called the Masculine-Feminine Pathology Scale (Mfp), in which the items would show gender differences but would also be related to psychopathology. Using a sample of 988 psychiatric patients, they constructed a bipolar, fifty-four-item scale, by selecting MMPI-2 items that first met the criteria used by Baucom (1976) and Peterson (1991) in developing their scales (i.e., at least 70 percent of the items were endorsed in one direction by one gender, with the endorsement frequency for the other gender being at least 10 percent less). (As expected, thirty-one of the fifty-four Mfp items are found on either GM or GF, and nine of the items overlap with Scale 5.) A second criterion was that an item's keyed response had to represent a symptomatic feature that was typical of one of the genders. For example, item #23 ("Uncontrollable laughing and crying Retaliate when wronged") is more frequently endorsed by women and judged to be symptomatic in that direction. Item #27 ("Retaliate when wronged") is more likely to be endorsed by men and is associated with character pathology when keyed in that direction. Items selected for each gender were combined into a bipolar scale, with the "male" items being keyed oppositely to those for women. High scores were set so as to be more typical of women.

Not surprisingly, McGrath and his colleagues found that the Mfp items were structurally complex and represented multiple dimensions, such as "interpersonal hypersensitivity" and "amorality." Although they do not report it for their sample, clearly this scale has very low internal consistency. Correlations with ratings done by the patients' primary therapists showed that high scores were associated with anxious distress. The researchers expected low scores to be associated with acting-out characteristics, but such behaviors were not adequately represented on the therapist rating instrument that was used. Our best sense is that Mfp represents a scale of internalizing versus externalizing symptomatology, and, although future research may reveal its utility, we question both its conceptualization and its almost certain lack of discriminant validity from other established scales, such as A and R. We also fail to see how it might be clinically useful to know that a certain patient's symptomatology is more typical of men than of women or vice versa.

In summary, recent research on Scale 5 and/or masculinity-femininity on the MMPI-2 seems to suffer from the same kind of theoretical and methodological confusion that typified earlier research.

A Recent Controversy: Gendered vs. Nongendered Norms

Although tangential to our discussion of masculinity-femininity and Scale 5, a relatively recent issue concerning gender differences on the MMPI-2 seems worthy of note. As most users of the MMPI-2 know, since the inception of the original MMPI, norms for each of the scales have been developed separately for men and women. That is, women have always been compared to other women, and men have been compared to men. However, the Federal Civil Rights Act of 1991 explicitly forbids consideration of race, color, religion, gender, or national origin in hiring practices. Thus, there was concern that using gendered MMPI-2 norms in employment screening would go against this prohibition. Tellegen, Butcher, and Hoeglund (1993) and Ben-Porath and Forbey (2003) explored the effects of using nongendered norms on a variety of scales for the MMPI-2 (excluding Scale 5, GM, and GF). Ben-Porath and Forbey concluded that nongendered norms had virtually no effect on any MMPI-2 scale examined, with the exceptions of the Content Scale Fears and the Content Component Scale FRS2 (Multiple Fears) for men and the PSY-5 Scale Disconstraint and the Content Component Scale ASP-2 (Antisocial Behavior) for women. If one uses the nongendered norms, men produce slightly lower scores on FRS and FRS2 than if one uses gendered norms; women score slightly lower on nongendered versions of Disconstraint and ASP-2 than with the usual gendered norms. Thus, in almost all settings, it seems advisable for most test users to continue to refer to the traditional gendered norms.

Scale 5 of the MMPI-A

Development

Of the basic MMPI scales, Scale 5 was changed the most in the development of the MMPI-A. In fact, sixteen of the sixty original Scale 5 items were eliminated completely for the MMPI-A, including the four items dropped from the MMPI-2. These eliminated items (with their MMPI-2 item numbers) are listed in Table 3.1. Butcher et al. (1992) explained that they thought it would be beneficial to shorten this scale because it was quite long and because the item content was somewhat redundant. Items were deleted "if they were objectionable or irrelevant to adolescents, if their endorsement frequencies failed to differentiate between the two genders, and if they were scored on the Mf scale and were not highly correlated with the total score of the scale" (p. 47). As one can see in Table 3.1, more than half of the deleted items had to do with stereotypic feminine interests. Six other items were revised: two because they referred to adolescent experiences in the past tense and four because of grammatical errors or other problems with their language.

Although it is not the shortest of the basic clinical scales, MMPI-A Scale 5 had the lowest internal consistency coefficients of all the scales: .43 for boys and .40 for girls in the normative sample, and .44 and .35 for boys and girls, respectively, in the clinical sample (Butcher et al., 1992). These are lower than the internal consistencies found for Scale 5 in the adult normative sample, but this is to be expected given the shorter scale length. The test-retest correlation over one week was .82, yielding a standard error of measurement of 2.12 T score points. The raw score means and standard deviations were 21.28 and

Table 3.1. Items on Scale 5 of the MMPI Not Included on Scale 5 of the MMPI-A

4.	Like library work.
19.	On a new job, find out who is important.
25.	Would like to be a singer.
74.	Would like to be a florist.
112.	Like theater.
121.	Don't engage in unusual sex.
184.	Seldom daydream.
187.	Would like to report theater news.
191.	Would like to be a journalist.
194.	Never had worrisome skin rashes.
207.	Would like to be a member of several clubs.
236.	Would like to be an artist who draws flowers.

3.98, respectively, for boys (N = 805), and 28.24 and 3.73 for girls (N = 815). As on the MMPI-2, linear T scores rather than uniform T scores were used with Scale 5.

Butcher et al. (1992) reanalyzed the data from the previously discussed study by Williams and Butcher (1989), which looked for external correlates of various MMPI scales in a clinical sample of 844 adolescents. Using correlational procedures, instead of the contrasting groups approach that had been previously used, Butcher et al. identified the following significant correlates of MMPI-A Scale 5 raw scores: for boys, "increase in disagreements with parent(s)" (r = .19); "placed on probation" (r = −.20); and "court appearance" (r = −.19); for girls, "suspended from school" (r = −.20); "change in schools" (r = −.21); "acting-out behaviors" (r = −.23); "eating problems" (r = .22); and "history of learning disabilities" (r = −.24). Similar correlates were found for girls in the normative sample: "number of school problems" (r = −.22), and "suspended from school" (r = −.21). These findings provide new evidence for Hathaway and Monachesi's (1963) conclusion that Scale 5 is an "inhibitory" scale for predicting acting-out behaviors for boys; they also suggest that this principle may be extended to contemporary adolescent girls. This relationship persisted even with the shortening of Scale 5 on the MMPI-A.

Recent Research

Several other studies have followed up on the relationship between Scale 5 and externalizing tendencies in adolescents by examining MMPI-A Scale 5 scores (and others) in samples of known delinquents. Peña, Megargee, and Brody (1996) found that Scale 5 scores were significantly lower in their sample of 162 delinquent boys in a residential training school than in boys in the MMPI-A normative sample. Cashel, Rogers, Sewell, and Holliman (1998), using a sample of ninety-nine juveniles who had been committed to a correctional facility for delinquent youth, found that the MMPI-A Scale 5 mean score was the third most deviant from the normative mean. Morton, Farris, and Brenowitz (2002) improved on these studies using their sample of 655 incarcerated male juvenile delinquents. They found low scores on Scale 5 to be the most frequent deviation; the average score in their sample was 41.9, with a standard deviation of 7.93. When the delinquent and normative samples on the MMPI-A basic validity and clinical scales are compared, Scale 5 had of the largest effect sizes, and many of the delinquents' profiles were best defined by their low scores on Scale 5. Thus, at this time, it seems quite clear that low MMPI-A Scale 5 scores may be quite useful in assessing delinquency in adolescent boys. The same may be true for girls, but more research is needed.

Finlay and Kapes (2000) expressed great concern as a result of their study of the comparability of Scale 5 on the MMPI and MMPI-A among sixty emotionally disturbed adolescents. Half of the respondents took the MMPI first, then the MMPI-A approximately thirteen days later; for the other half, the order of administration was reversed. Finlay and Kapes found a mean difference of 11.52 T score points between the two administrations, with MMPI Scale 5 scores being higher, but this finding is confounded by three variables: retesting, the different scales, and the different norms used. For the MMPI-A, Finlay and Kapes used the established norm set; for the MMPI, they used the adolescent norms developed by Marks and Briggs (1972). More puzzling still was the reported correlation between respondents' two Scale 5 scores: r = .13, which was much lower than correlations for any of the other standard scales. This result is so unexpected, given the forty-four-item overlap between the two scales, and so deviant from known retest correlations for Scale 5 on either the MMPI or MMPI-A that we find it hard to interpret. Given the preponderance of evidence, we don't agree with Finlay and Kapes's conclusion that "until further research brings clarity . . . Scale 5 scores from the MMPI-A should not be used in any interpretation . . . based on . . . research or clinical experience with the MMPI." However, this study does seem to indicate that further research is needed on the correlates of MMPI-A Scale 5.

The MMPI-2-RF and the Elimination of Scale 5

In 2008, the Minnesota Multiphasic Personality Inventory-2 Restructured Form (MMPI-2-RF) was published (Ben-Porath & Tellegen, 2008; Tellegen & Ben-Porath, 2008). The MMPI-2-RF is a reworking of the MMPI-2 item pool into a number of psychometrically sound homogeneous subscales, correcting many of the problems with the MMPI and MMPI-2 scales. The MMPI-2 clinical scales were "restructured" (i.e., factor analyzed with the intent of removing the common Demoralization factor from each) into the MMPI-2 RC Scales (Tellegen, Ben-Porath, McNulty, Arbisi, Graham, & Kaemmer, 2003), and these then were incorporated into the MMPI-2-RF (Ben-Porath & Tellegen, 2008). Scales 5 and 0 were not included in the published RC Scales, but the RC Scales monograph (Tellegen et al., 2003) describes the factor analyses used to restructure them. A four-factor solution in four archival samples produced (1) a Demoralization factor, (2) a factor of items associated with a traditional "feminine gender role," (3) a factor of "mixed extraverted-aggressive-cynical content," and (4) a factor with loadings on several traditionally masculine items

(Tellegen et al., 2003, p. 16). Factors 2 and 4 were retained, and Factor 2 was augmented with other items outside of Scale 5, resulting in the two "interest" scales of the MMPI-2-RF, labeled Aesthetic-Literary Interests (AES) and Mechanical-Physical Interests (MEC), respectively. Of the nine items on MEC, three are not originally from Scale 5 but are instead Terman-Miles items that were adapted for the original MMPI but that did not make it onto Scale 5. All seven of the AES items are original Scale 5 items. Also of note, three of the AES items are false-keyed items on the GM scale of the MMPI-2, whereas seven of the nine MEC items are false-keyed items on GF. The "neutral" names for the two scales were chosen to be descriptive of their content and also to avoid any direct connotations of masculinity-femininity (Ben-Porath, 2008).

Table 3.5 of the *MMPI-2-RF Technical Manual* (Tellegen & Ben-Porath, 2008) reports the test-retest reliability coefficients for AES and MEC in a subset of men and women (N = 193) from the MMPI-2 normative sample: .86 and .92, respectively. Alpha consistency coefficients for the two scales were also calculated in the full normative sample, and in three large archival clinical samples (one outpatient and two inpatient). These analyses showed that the two interest scales have adequate internal consistency for most purposes, with the alphas for women ranging from .49 to .66 in the different samples (with a median of .60) for AES, and from .55 to .60 (with a median of .55) for MEC. The alpha coefficients for men were slightly higher, ranging from .61 to .67 (with a median of .66) for AES, and from .60 to .64 (with a median of .62) for MEC. Tables 3.17 to 3.22 of the *Technical Manual* show the intercorrelations of AES and MEC in these same samples. They range from −.03 to .16 for men, with a median of .06, and from .07 to .24 for women, with a median of .22. Hence, the two scales are largely orthogonal.

Tellegen and Ben-Porath (2008) also reported correlations in the archival samples between AES and MEC and the complete set of MMPI-2 and MMPI-2-RF scales. Not surprisingly, given the number of items that they share with Scale 5, AES and MEC were the two MMPI-2-RF scales that were most correlated with Scale 5 in almost every sample. For men, the correlations with Scale 5 ranged from .46 to .54 for AES, with a median of .49, and from −.41 to −.45 for MEC, with a median of −.43. For women, the correlations with Scale 5 ranged from .41 to .45 for AES, with a median of .43, and from −.26 to −.30 for MEC, with a median of −.28. AES and MEC were not substantially correlated with any of the other MMPI-2 or MMPI-2-RF scales, supporting the interpretation that they are not measures of psychopathology. Inspection of the linear T score conversion table (A-4) of the MMPI-2-RF interpretive manual (Ben-Porath & Tellegen, 2008) shows that both interest scales have adequate ranges but relatively low ceilings. For AES, the maximum T score that a respondent (male or female) can achieve (by endorsing all seven items) is 73T. For MEC, the maximum possible T score is 78T.

In keeping with their formulation as interest scales, Ben-Porath and Tellegen interpret AES and MEC in a straightforward manner. The MMPI-2-RF manual states that high scores ($\geq 65T$) suggest that a respondent has indicated an "above average interest in activities or occupations" of either "an aesthetic or literary nature" (for AES) or "a mechanical or physical nature" (for MEC). Low scores ($T < 39$) are also interpreted and are said to indicate "no interest in activities or occupations" in the specified area. As with other MMPI-2-RF scales, interpretation is not based entirely on item content. Each scale is noted to have "empirical correlates" that go beyond its content interpretation. High scores on AES are associated with being "empathic" and "sentient" (i.e., "appreciative and responsive to sensory experiences"), whereas high scores on MEC are correlated with "adventure-seeking" and "sensation-seeking" (Ben-Porath & Tellegen, 2008, p. 58).

Readers who wish to know the details of these empirical correlates can refer to a remarkable resource provided for the MMPI-2-RF: Appendix A of the *Technical Manual*. The tables in this appendix provide correlations between the scales of the MMPI-2-RF and a variety of criterion variables in the various archival samples referred to earlier. A close inspection of these tables yields the following conclusions regarding AES and MEC. First, with few exceptions, AES and MEC scores were not highly correlated with most external clinical criteria, such as intake diagnoses, presenting problems, historical variables, such as history of sexual abuse, mental status variables, or discharge medications. As expected, many other scales of the MMPI-2-RF had much higher correlations with such variables than did AES and MEC. This result further adds to the construct validity of these scales as measures of interests rather than of psychopathology.

Second, AES and MEC scores were correlated with gender-related characteristics in a number of domains. Ben-Porath and Tellegen (2007) summarized some of these correlates of AES and MEC, and we replicate some of their analyses here. In Table 3.2, we have assembled all the correlations of AES and MEC from Appendix A of the *Technical Manual* that equaled or exceeded |.20|. As you can see, there are more correlations that equal or exceed |.20| for men than for women. For men in the outpatient community health center sample, AES and MEC were correlated with overt markers of masculinity-femininity on the Patient Description Form (PDF) (filled out by

Table 3.2. Correlations of Aesthetic-Literary Interests Scale (AES) and Mechanical-Physical Interests Scale (MEC) in Appendix A of the *MMPI-2-RF Technical Manual* That Equal or Exceed |.20|

Men	Correlations	
Variable	AES	MEC
Insecure[a]	—	−.24
Anxious[a]	—	−.21
Depressed[a]	—	−.22
Introverted[a]	—	−.21
Stereotypic masculine interests[a]	−.31	.22
Stereotypic masculine behavior[b]	−.30	.20
Worrier[b]	—	−.21
Rejects traditional gender role[b]	.22	−.26
Acute psychological turmoil[b]	—	−.23
Communicates effectively[b]	.20	—
Stereotypic masculine interests[b]	−.30	—
Low frustration tolerance[b]	−.21	—
Depressed[b]	—	−.25
Sad[b]	—	−.19
Self-doubting[b]	—	−.21
Physically abusive[b]	−.24	—
Concerns about homosexuality[b]	—	−.25
Difficulty making decisions[b]	—	−.21
Eccentric[b]	—	−.22
Stereotypic feminine behavior[b]	.20	—
Mental Status: Tangential[c]	.21	—
Internal States Scale: Activation[d]	—	.28
Machiavellian IV Scale: Distrust of People[d]	—	−.26

(Continued)

Table 3.2. (*Continued*)

Men	Correlations	
Variable	AES	MEC
BIS/BAS: Drive[d]	—	.24
BIS/BAS: Fun-Seeking[d]	—	.31
NEO PI-R Extraversion[e]	.31	.26
NEO PI-R Openness to Aesthetics[e]	.55	—
NEO PI-R Openness to Ideas[e]	.40	.22
Beck Hopeless Scale Total[e]	−.22	—
Barratt Impulsivity Scale: Cognitive[e]	−.21	—
MPQ Social Closeness: Gregarious[f]	−.20	—
MPQ Aggression[f]	—	.25
MPQ Aggression: Physically Aggressive[f]	−.21	.22
MPQ Aggression: Enjoys Aggression[f]	—	.30
MPQ Harm Avoidance[f]	—	−.24
MPQ Harm Av.1: Dislikes Dangerous Activities[f]	—	−.24
MPQ Harm Av.2: Dislikes Dangerous Predicaments[f]	—	−.33
MPQ Absorption Total[f]	.42	—
MPQ Absorption1: Sentient[f]	.39	—
MPQ Absorption2: Prone to Imaginative and Altered States[f]	.32	—

Women	Correlations	
Variable	AES	MEC
Substance Abuse[g]	—	.21
Mood Instability[h]	.22	—
Number of Previous Arrests[i]	—	.21
Frequency of Cocaine Use[i]	—	.23
MPQ Well-Being1: Cheerful, Optimistic[f]	—	.20

(*Continued*)

Table 3.2. (*Continued*)

Women	Correlations	
Variable	AES	MEC
MPQ Social Closeness1: Gregarious[f]	−.21	—
MPQ Constraint Superfactor[f]	—	−.25
MPQ Harm Avoidance[f]	—	−.35
MPQ Harm Av.1: Dislikes Dangerous Adventures[f]	—	−.35
MPQ Traditionalism4: Endorses Strict Rearing[f]	−.21	—
MPQ Absorption[f]	.49	—
MPQ Absorption1: Sentient[f]	.50	—
MPQ Absorption2: Prone to Imaginative and Altered States[f]	.39	—

Notes. [a] Outpatients, Community Mental Health Center, Patient Description Form Scales

[b] Outpatients, Community Mental Health Center, Patient Description Form Items

[c] Inpatients, Community Hospital/VA Hospital, Intake Mental Status Variables

[d] Outpatients, VA Hospital, Selected Self-Report Measures

[e] Substance Abuse Treatment, VA Hospital, Selected Self-Report Measures

[f] College Students

[g] Disability Claimants, Detailed Assessment of Post-Traumatic States Scales

[h] Pre-Trial Criminal, Record Review Form Scales

[i] Pre-Trial Criminal, Record Review Form Items

therapists). Importantly, this is the first example we know of in which MMPI self-ratings (S data) are related to observer ratings (O data) in the area of masculinity-femininity. AES was negatively correlated with "stereotypic masculine interests" (−.31) and "stereotypic masculine behavior" (−.30) and positively correlated with the PDF items "rejects traditional gender role" (.22) and "stereotypic feminine behavior" (.20). MEC was positively correlated with "stereotypic masculine interests" (.22) and "stereotypic masculine behavior" (.20) and negatively correlated with "concerns about homosexuality" (−.25). These same items did not show significant correlations with AES and MEC for women.

Also, for men, AES seemed to function a bit as a constraint marker: it was negatively correlated with items such as "low frustration tolerance" (−.21) and "physically abusive" (−.24) in the community mental health sample, and with MPQ scales "Gregarious" (−.20) and "Physically Aggressive" (−.21) in the college sample. In contrast, MEC seems related to activation, confidence, and disconstraint in men, in that it correlated negatively with such items as "insecure" (−.24), "self-doubting" (−.21), and "difficulty making decisions" (−.21), and positively with BIS/BAS Drive (.24), BIS/BAS Fun Seeking (.31), and MPQ Aggression (.25). For women, AES was negatively correlated with MPQ Gregarious (−.21) in the college sample. MEC was positively correlated with certain acting-out variables in several clinical samples: substance abuse (.21), number of previous arrests (.21), and frequency of cocaine use (.23), and it was negatively correlated with MPQ Constraint (−.25) and MPQ Harm Avoidance (−.35) in the college sample.

The highest correlation reported for AES (.55) was with the NEO PI-R facet scale, "Openness to Aesthetics," in the VA substance abuse treatment sample. This supports the construct validity of the scale as a measure of aesthetic interests. The next highest correlation (.50) was with the MPQ Absorption facet scale, "Sentient," in the college women. The two highest correlations with MEC were the MPQ Harm Avoidance (−.35) scale previously mentioned and the Harm Avoidance facet scale, "Dislikes Dangerous Adventures" (−.35). These correlations support the interpretation that high MEC scores are associated with excitement-seeking and adventure-seeking.

In summary, although Scale 5 was dropped in the MMPI-2-RF, two aspects of its content were retained in the two interest scales, AES and MEC. The research to date (and reported in the *Technical Manual*) supports the interpretation of these scales as measures of aesthetic-literary interests and mechanical-physical interest, respectively. Although not presented as measures of masculinity-femininity, AES and MEC are correlated with gender-differentiating characteristics, such as sentience (for AES) and constraint vs. excitement-seeking (for MEC). Also, the correlation of the two scales with external ratings of gender role behavior, at least in men, raises the question of whether they continue to capture some variance related to masculinity-femininity. Further research is needed to address this question, but it seems possible that AES and MEC are, to some extent, markers of masculinity-femininity. This would not surprise us. As mentioned in chapter 1, Willerman (1991) concluded that male-female differences in interests are among the largest and most stable gender differences known to exist. Also, as described in chapter 2, gender-related interests have played a major role in many previous measures of masculinity-femininity and appear to be correlated with other possible components of masculinity-femininity, such as gender identity. For these reasons, although Scale 5 was eliminated from the MMPI-2-RF, this does not mean that the instrument is devoid of information on masculinity-femininity.

Summary and Conclusion

The measurement of masculinity-femininity on the MMPI began with the Mf scale (now referred to as Scale 5) of the original MMPI, published in 1942. Since that date, numerous attempts have been made to establish what Scale 5 is actually measuring and to develop Scale 5 subscales or other auxiliary MMPI scales to clarify the assessment of masculinity-femininity using the MMPI, MMPI-2, and MMPI-A. Perhaps more than any other basic scale of the MMPI, Scale 5 has been subject to intense criticism over the years, and there have been periodic assertions that it is so outdated or flawed that it should be permanently retired. Some of these critiques have reflected changing political attitudes toward the very concepts of masculinity and femininity; others have been based on actual psychometric complexities of the scale. As a result, responsible researchers and practicing clinicians are left wondering about the meaning of Scale 5 scores or, even more disheartening, must wince periodically at the bold interpretations certain of their colleagues make concerning the significance of high or low scores on Scale 5. Although Scale 5 does not appear on the MMPI-2-RF, many clinicians continue to use the MMPI-2 and would benefit from more clarity about Scale 5. Also, it is intriguing to consider the new interest scales of the MMPI-2-RF. Do AES and MEC have implications for masculinity-femininity? Preliminary data suggest that they may. Moreover, even if these scales are not robustly related to masculinity-femininity, will some clinicians assume that they are?

From our review of the literature concerning Scale 5 and masculinity-femininity, we conclude that it captures unique and potentially useful variance in individual differences that is not captured by other frequently used scales on the MMPI-2 and MMPI-A. We also believe that Scale 5—and masculinity and femininity in general—are comprised of multiple, complex, related dimensions. Much of the confusion about Scale 5 could be resolved if we better understood its underlying structure and the relationship of its components to other dimensions of personality. Also, such an investigation could potentially teach us much about the constructs of masculinity and femininity in general. Thus, we now turn to an exploration of the dimensions underlying Scale 5.

Chapter 4

Dimensions of Scale 5 of the MMPI-2

The MMPI-2 was developed to improve upon and replace the original MMPI. As we have mentioned, Scale 5 was retained; however, evidence suggests that interpreting a single Scale 5 score is fraught with dangers (Long & Graham, 1991; Wong, 1984). It is likely a mixture of constructs related in part to the psyche of a homosexual male of the 1940s. In order to clarify the concepts of masculinity and femininity, we believe that it is helpful to distinguish the variance in Scale 5 that is best described as masculinity-femininity from that variance reflecting other personality characteristics. Our effort is similar to the work of Tellegen, Ben-Porath, McNulty, Arbisi, Graham, and Kaemmer (2003) and Ben-Porath and Tellegen (2008) in their restructuring of Scale 5 and their development of the two interest scales (AES and MEC) for inclusion in the MMPI-2-RF. However, Tellegen et al. were not focused on exploring masculinity-femininity per se, and we believe they may have overlooked variance in Scale 5 that may be related to this domain of personality. Our other major hope was that by carefully exploring the dimensions underlying Scale 5, we could build a foundation for enhanced insight into the nature of masculinity and femininity.

We explored the dimensions of Scale 5 using a multistage approach. First, we factor analyzed the normative data for the MMPI-2 to arrive at empirical factors. Initially, we conducted the factor analyses separately on males and females to investigate any potential gender differences in factor patterns. We found no substantial differences between males and females. Accordingly, we then combined the male and female data and factor analyzed the combined data, to give one set of factors for both genders. Final factors were based on this empirical work and considered in light of rational analysis. The steps used to develop Scale 5 factors were the following:

Step 1. Principal components analysis by gender

Step 2. Factor analysis by gender

Step 3. Compare factors by gender

Step 4. Factor analysis of combined male and female data

Step 5. Add items that correlate with factors

Step 6. Eliminate insufficient factors

Step 7. Principal components and factor analysis of unassigned items

Step 8. Addition of factors and items

Step 9. Optimize internal consistency

Step 10. Name the final factors

Developing Empirical Factors of Scale 5

The multistage approach we used is similar to that used in development of subscales for Scale 0 of the MMPI-2 (Ben-Porath, Hostetler, Butcher, & Graham, 1989). Further details about the procedures used in this exploration may be found in Martin (1993). We performed the factor analytic procedures on data from the MMPI-2 normative sample. This sample is composed of 1,462 females and 1,138 males; it is roughly representative of the U.S. population in regard to geographic, racial, and ethnic parameters. Subjects ranged from eighteen to ninety years of age. Further information about this sample is contained in the MMPI-2 manual (Butcher, Dahlstrom, Graham, Tellegen, & Kaemmer, 1989).

Step 1. Principal Components Analysis by Gender

In the first step of clarifying the dimensions of Scale 5, we subjected the fifty-six items of Scale 5 to principal components analysis, using the male data and the female data separately. We plotted eigenvalues for the possible solutions and examined these solutions using Cattell's scree test (1966). We then selected a range of the most likely factor solutions. For males, this range included from four to eight factors; for females, it included from four to seven factors.

Step 2. Factor Analysis by Gender

Each of these possible solutions, five solutions for males and four solutions for females, was then factor analyzed, using squared multiple correlations as communality estimates, and rotated to promax criteria, a method that allows nonorthogonal factors. We used an oblique rotation because it is likely that components of masculinity-femininity are correlated. We then assigned items to each factor of each solution by considering item loadings. An item was included in a factor if its loading on that factor was greater than or equal to .35 but not loading higher than .25 on any other factor. We also included an item if its factor loading was below .35, but greater than or equal to .30, and if the item loaded at least .10 higher on that factor than on any other factor of that solution.

We then selected the best solutions for males and females, respectively, from the resulting possible factor solutions. We did this by examining which rotated solution made the most sense psychologically, by forming distinct, cohesive psychological constructs. Accordingly, we selected the six-factor solution for males, which provided only five factors under the item selection criteria used (one factor dropped out because it did not meet criteria), and the five-factor solution for females as the best of the available possibilities (see Appendix B for the male solution and Appendix C for the female solution).

Step 3. Compare Factors by Gender

We then compared the numerous possible solutions and the preferred solutions for males and females and found they demonstrated substantial similarity in factor patterns and item content. This similarity between the male and female factor structures suggested that the structure among items was sufficiently the same for males and females to allow one set of factors for both genders. Thus, we combined the male and female data, and the analyses in Steps 1 and 2 were repeated.

Step 4. Factor Analysis of Combined Male and Female Data

The scree plots and eigenvalues from the principal components analysis of the combined data suggested that five to nine factors should be extracted. These solutions were performed and then rotated to promax criteria. We selected the six-factor solution as the most psychologically comprehensible. These six factors served as the initial provisional factors. They closely paralleled the factors previously identified for males and females separately (see Appendix D).

Step 5. Add Items that Correlate with Factors

In an effort to capture any items not then included on a provisional factor that might enhance the measurement of that dimension of Scale 5, we considered item correlations with composite scores. Accordingly, we computed composite scores for each of the initial provisional factors by counting the number of items on that factor endorsed in the scoring direction. We then correlated the provisional factors' composite scores with all the Scale 5 items that were not then included on any of those six provisional factors. Any such item that correlated with a provisional factor greater than .20 and correlated at least .10 less with any other provisional factor was added to that provisional factor. This resulted in the addition of one item to provisional factor 1, two items to provisional factor 2, and one item to provisional factor 6.

Step 6. Eliminate Insufficient Provisional Empirical Factors

We next computed alpha coefficients of internal consistency (Cronbach, 1970) for each of the resulting six provisional factors. Provisional factor 5 had the lowest alpha consistency coefficient (.40) and also contained only three items. Thus, we dropped this provisional factor 5 at this point. The internal consistency of the remaining five provisional factors (alphas of .63, .66, .60, .48, and .55, on the factors, respectively) suggested reasonably cohesive factors. Thus, five provisional factors were retained at this stage.

Step 7. Principal Components and Factor Analysis of Unassigned Items

In the next step, we determined whether any substantial as yet unrecovered factors remained in the unassigned items. Thus, we subjected the twenty-three remaining Scale 5 items that were not included on one of the five provisional factors to principle components analysis. Using Cattell's scree test (1966), this analysis suggested that between two and six additional factors might exist. We then factor analyzed each of these possible solutions using the promax criteria used previously. The two-factor solution was chosen as the preferred solution. These additional factors, the first containing four items and the second containing six items, reflected reasonably comprehensible psychological constructs (i.e., gender-related phenomena and boisterousness) and were retained as provisional factors 6 and 7, respectively.

Step 8. Addition of Factors and Items

We then correlated the composite scores for each of the now seven provisional factors with all items in Scale 5 not then included on one of these factors. At this point, we considered items that correlated with more than one provisional factor for inclusion on the provisional factor with which they had the highest correlation. The allowance for multiple correlations was in recognition that factors of a masculinity-femininity measure may well be somewhat intercorrelated. We also considered compatibility of an item's content with the provisional factor in these additions. In every instance, the content of the items suggested for inclusion seemed appropriate to the highest correlating provisional factor. Thus, one item was added to each of the first four provisional factors. We did not allow item overlap.

Step 9. Optimize Internal Consistency

Next, we calculated alpha internal consistency coefficients in a stepwise fashion, and items were deleted that detracted from a provisional factor's internal consistency. Only one item was deleted (from provisional factor 1) for this reason. All other items included on the provisional factors enhanced to some degree the internal consistency of their factor. At this point, the alpha internal consistency coefficient for each provisional factor suggested reasonably cohesive factors when computed from the data of the combined (male and female) normative sample. These coefficients are shown in Table 4.1.

Table 4.1. Provisional Factors for Scale 5 of the MMPI-2

DENIAL OF STEREOTYPICAL MASCULINE INTERESTS: (alpha for combined data = .63, for males = .54, for females = .42)

> (–) 001. Like mechanics magazines.
> (–) 069. Would like being a forest ranger.
> (–) 197. Would like to be a building contractor.
> (–) 199. Like science.
> (–) 201. Like hunting.
> (–) 133. Would like to be in military.

HYPERSENSITIVITY/ANXIETY: (alpha for combined data = .66, for males = .65, for females = .66)

> (–) 063. Feelings not hurt easily.
> 166. Worry about sex.
> (–) 184. Seldom daydream.
> (–) 194. Never had worrisome skin rashes.
> 196. Frequently worry.
> 205. Habits of some family members very irritating.
> (–) 237. Don't mind not being better looking.
> (–) 239. Wholly self-confident.
> 251. Often strangers look at me critically.
> 256. Occasionally hate family members I love.
> 219. Disappointed in love.
> 271. Feel more intensely than most.
> 268. Bothered by sexual thoughts.

(*Continued*)

Table 4.1. (*Continued*)

STEREOTYPICAL FEMININE INTERESTS: (alpha for combined data = .61, for males = .46, for females = .43)

> 064. Like romances.
> 074. Would like to be a florist.
> 080. Would like being a nurse.
> 119. Like collecting plants.
> 236. Would like to be an artist who draws flowers.
> 004. Like library work.

LOW CYNICISM: (alpha for combined data = .52, for males = .51, for females = .51)

> (−) 026. Keep quiet when in trouble.
> (−) 027. Retaliate when wronged.
> (−) 076. Hard to convince people of truth.
> (−) 104. People honest because they don't want to be caught.
> (−) 193. I avoid stepping on sidewalk cracks.
> (−) 254. People have friends because they're useful.

AESTHETIC INTERESTS: (alpha for combined data = .55, for males = .59, for females = .49)

> 187. Would like to report theater news.
> 112. Like theater.
> 191. Would like to be a journalist.
> 067. Like poetry.
> 025. Would like to be a singer.

FEMININE GENDER IDENTITY: (alpha for combined data = .59, for males = .21, for females = .05)

> 062. Wish was a girl or happy that am.
> 137. Kept a diary.
> (−) 257. Would like to be a sports reporter.
> (−) 272. Never liked to play with dolls.

RESTRAINT: (alpha for combined data = .46, for males = .46, for females = .43)

> (−) 086. Like loud parties.
> (−) 207. Would like to be a member of clubs.
> (−) 209. Like to talk about sex.
> (−) 231. Like being with people who play jokes on one another.
> (−) 019. On a new job, find out who is important.
> (−) 068. Tease animals.

Note: Test item numbers are included for each item along with the direction in which the item is scored (a minus sign in parentheses preceding the item number indicates the item is scored when the response is "false"; the absence of a minus marker indicates the item is scored when the response is "true").

As a way to correct for factor length in determining the cohesiveness of a factor, we used the Spearman-Brown formula to determine average item correlations. The average item correlations for the combined data were .22, .13, .21, .15, .20, .26, and .12 for provisional factors 1 through 7, respectively. Thus, the provisional factors displayed acceptable cohesiveness in the normative sample. At this point, we considered that we had a group of workable factors that identified the dimensions of Scale 5.

Step 10. Naming the Factors

Our next task was to identify the construct reflected in each factor and to develop descriptive names that would appropriately capture their nature. After much consultation, we decided to score all the factors in what seemed to be a "feminine" direction, so that elevations on any factor would suggest an elevation in femininity or qualities related to it. We decided that scoring all factors in the same "trait" direction would aid interpretation. We chose the "feminine" direction to reflect high scores because this led to the clearest factor labels, not because of any inherent judgments about which trait direction is normal or preferred. Our choice in this matter also parallels that of Serkownek (1975) for his Scale 5 subscales for the original MMPI.

The items on factor 1 clearly reflect traditional masculine activities and interests. Thus, we reversed the scoring of items in factor 1 and assigned the name "Denial of Stereotypical Masculine Interests." This is the Serkownek (1975) label for his similar factor on the original MMPI. This factor is highly similar to that identified by Tellegen et al. (2003) and eventually included in the MMPI-2-RF as "Mechanical-Physical Interests" (MEC). Items in factor 2 reflected a heightened emotional sensitivity, insecurity, and excessive worry, so we adopted the name "Hypersensitivity/Anxiety" for this factor. Again, this name is similar to the similar subscale identified by Serkownek on the original MMPI. Factor 3 clearly included items related to traditional feminine activities and interests, so we assigned the name "Stereotypical Feminine Interests." This factor is highly similar to that identified by Tellegen et al. (2003) and eventually included in the MMPI-2-RF as "Aesthetic-Literary Interests" (AES). The items on factor 4 suggested a skepticism and lack of trust in the intentions of others. In keeping with the pattern of item correlations, we reversed the items on this factor and assigned the name "Low Cynicism."

The items in factor 5 reflected expressive, aesthetic interests. We decided the name "Aesthetic Interests" was an appropriate moniker. Items in factor 6 represented wishes, activities, and interests closely associated with being female.

The highest loading item was #62 ("Wish was a girl or happy that am"). Also, one item #272 ("Never liked to play with dolls") reflected gender stereotypic interests in childhood that are known to be highly correlated with adult gender identity (Finn, 1986a; Bailey & Zucker, 1995). Thus, we selected the name "Feminine Gender Identity." Finally, the items in factor 7 reflected boisterous, exhibitionistic, and impulsive activities. To score it in the feminine direction, we reversed all the items and assigned the name "Restraint." The provisional factors with their respective names are shown in Table 4.1.

Preliminary Conclusions

Thus far, the analyses confirm that the items on MMPI-2 Scale 5 are not unidimensional but, in fact, highly multifactorial. Using a variety of accepted procedures, we were able to identify seven clusters of items in Scale 5 that were relatively homogeneous in terms of their item correlations and content. Recognition of these item clusters should aid our understanding of Scale 5.

Several of the current Scale 5 factors resemble those subscales previously identified by Serkownek (1975) based on factor analyses of Scale 5 performed by Graham, Schroeder, and Lilly (1971). At this point, it is unclear how to interpret differences between our factors and Serkownek's subscales. Such differences may reflect differences in items in the pool, in the samples used for the factor analyses, in item correlations between 1971 and the late 1980s (when the MMPI-2 normative data were collected), or scale development procedures.

As might be expected given the diverse procedures and ideas guiding the selection of items for MMPI Scale 5, only three of the clusters that we identified (Denial of Stereotypical Masculine Interests, Stereotypical Feminine Interests, and Feminine Gender Identity) appear to reflect core aspects of masculinity-femininity (Finn, 1986a; Spence, 1985). The other factors (Hypersensitivity/Anxiety, Low Cynicism, Aesthetic Interests, and Restraint) appear to reflect gender-related personality traits. Further analyses that are necessary to clarify the differences between the clusters of factors suggested at this point are described in chapter 5.

Characteristics of the Factors

In our next analyses, we began to investigate the parameters and construct validity of the factors by examining their characteristics in the normative sample and two independent samples. Gender differences in factor scale scores, gender differences in internal consistency, factor intercorrelations, and the amount of variance in Scale 5 explained by the factors were examined before we considered the stability of the factors across samples.

Gender Differences in Factor Scores

Because we are dealing at least in part with factors associated with masculinity-femininity, means that combine both males and females may not tell us much other than general factor parameters. Thus, we computed the means and standard deviations on each factor for males and females separately, and gender differences were considered. Table 4.2 shows the mean scores for males and females in the normative sample. A multivariate analysis of variance resulted in a highly significant difference between males and females ($F = 715.64$, $p < .0001$). Post hoc t-tests showed significant differences between the genders on every factor (see Table 4.2). However, not surprisingly given their apparent relationship to core aspects of masculinity-femininity, the differences between the genders on Denial of Stereotypical Masculine Interests, Stereotypical Feminine Interests, and Feminine Gender Identity were greater than one standard deviation, whereas the differences on the other scales were no more than half a standard deviation. The huge effect size (2.12) for Feminine Gender Identity supports its construct validity, because gender identity is believed to be the aspect of masculinity-femininity most correlated with gender (Finn, 1986a; Spence, 1985).

Table 4.2. Comparison of Male and Female Factor Means in the Normative Sample

	Males mean (std dev) n = 1,138	Females mean (std dev) n = 1,462	t	Effect Size[a]
Denial of Stereotypical Masculine Interests	3.03 (1.45)	4.63 (1.09)	31.09 [b]	1.26
Hypersensitivity/Anxiety	5.04 (2.66)	6.12 (2.65)	10.23 [b]	.41
Stereotypical Feminine Interests	1.35 (1.25)	3.15 (1.40)	34.59 [b]	1.36
Low Cynicism	4.14 (1.43)	4.46 (1.35)	5.81 [b]	.23
Aesthetic Interests	2.12 (1.48)	2.67 (1.37)	9.82 [b]	.39
Feminine Gender Identity	1.10 (.91)	3.03 (.84)	55.41 [b]	2.21
Restraint	3.70 (1.48)	4.29 (1.35)	10.35 [b]	.42

Note. Normative sample contains 1,462 females and 1,138 males.

Note. [a] Cohen's (1988) *d*.

[b] denotes $p < .0001$.

Gender Differences in Internal Consistency

We next computed internal consistency coefficients for males and females separately to determine whether the factors provided cohesive factors for each gender independently. These coefficients are shown in Table 4.1. For Hypersensitivity/Anxiety, Low Cynicism, Aesthetic Interests, and Restraint, the internal consistency coefficients were substantially similar for males and females. However, the internal consistency in the other three factors declined when calculated in the genders separately. These three factors are those that demonstrated the largest gender differences in means.

Denial of Stereotypical Masculine Interests and Stereotypical Feminine Interests showed lower internal consistency when scored on the male data alone (.54 and .46, respectively) compared to the combined data (.63 and .61) and even lower internal consistency when scored on the female data alone (.42 and .43, respectively). The internal consistency of Feminine Gender Identity computed with the genders combined (.59) dropped to very low levels when computed separately by gender (males = .21, female = .05).

This decline in factor cohesiveness is not surprising when we consider the large-scale reduction in the variance of gender-related constructs when the genders are considered separately. The reduction in variance in Denial of Stereotypical Masculine Interests and Stereotypical Feminine Interests suggests a moderate narrowing of variance in these factors when calculated separately by gender. The variance in Feminine Gender Identity dropped precipitously when the genders were considered separately. The fact that the distribution of males on this factor was positively skewed (.47), whereas the distribution of females was negatively skewed (−.73), supports the notion of a bimodal distribution. The skew of the distributions also supports Finn's (1986a) observation that gender identity shows highly skewed distributions in "normal" samples. Thus, the low internal consistency within gender and the pattern of skew both support the construct validity of this factor.

Factor Intercorrelations

We then computed the intercorrelations between the factors in the combined normative sample and on males and females in the normative sample separately. We also included Scale 5 scores in the intercorrelations. These results are displayed in Table 4.3. In the combined data, the highest correlations were between Feminine Gender Identity and Stereotypical Feminine Interests (.47) and between Feminine Gender Identity and Denial of Stereotypical Masculine Interests (.45). These high correlations reduced to .17/.07 and .10/.11 when

Table 4.3. Intercorrelations of the Factors of Scale 5 of the MMPI-2 in the Normative Sample for Male, Female, and Combined Data

	S1	S2	S3	S4	S5	S6	S7	Scale 5
S1	—	.08	−.14	.16	.01	.10	.18	.41
		.01	**−.16**	**−.05**	**−.12**	**.11**	**.08**	**.22**
S2	.14	—	.07	−.19	.16	.15	−.19	.57
			−.01	**−.16**	**.14**	**−.04**	**−.19**	**.41**
S3	.19	.13	—	−.03	.35	.17	−.09	.36
				−.03	**.19**	**.07**	**−.04**	**.39**
S4	.11	−.15	.04	—	.00	.11	.16	.32
					.05	**.08**	**.13**	**.35**
S5	.06	.18	.32	.05	—	.17	−.16	.49
						.05	**−.13**	**.43**
S6	.45	.18	.47	.15	.21	—	.06	.45
							.00	**.27**
S7	.22	−.14	.06	.16	−.10	.17	—	.14
								.28
Scale 5	.55	.56	.58	.30	.48	.66	.21	—

Note. S1 = Denial of Stereotypical Masculine Interests, S2 = Hypersensitivity/Anxiety, S3 = Stereotypical Feminine Interests, S4 = Low Cynicism, S5 = Aesthetic Interests, S6 = Feminine Gender Identity, S7 = Restraint.

Note. Intercorrelations from the combined male and female normative data are in the lower triangle of the matrix. Male (on top) and Female (in bold) intercorrelations are in the upper triangle of the matrix.

males/females, respectively, were considered separately. This reduction appears to be the result of the diminished variance in Feminine Gender Identity when the genders are considered separately, as previously mentioned.

The next highest correlation in Table 4.3 is .32, between Stereotypical Feminine Interests and Aesthetic Interests, suggesting that these two factors are related. When the genders were considered separately, the correlation in males ($r = .35$) was higher than that in females ($r = .19$). A Bonferroni-adjusted comparison of these correlations suggested this difference is statistically significant ($z = 4.33$, $p < .05$ or .0018 adjusted).

The only other factor intercorrelations above .20 were between Denial of Stereotypical Masculine Interests and Restraint ($r = .22$) and Aesthetic Interests and Feminine Gender Identity ($r = .21$). When the genders were considered separately, males showed higher correlations ($r = .18$ and .17, respectively) than females ($r = .08$ and .05) in each instance. Again, a Bonferroni-adjusted comparison suggested that both gender differences were statistically significant ($z = 3.00, p < .05$ and $z = 2.50, p < .05$, respectively).

Finally, we were intrigued by the relationship between Denial of Stereotypical Masculine Interests and Stereotypical Feminine Interests. These factors were negatively related in both males ($r = -.14$) and females ($r = -.16$) when considered separately by gender, but positively related when the genders were combined ($r = .19$). Furthermore, their correlation in the combined data is lower than expected, given the relatively high correlations both Denial of Stereotypical Masculine Interests and Stereotypical Feminine Interests have with Feminine Gender Identity (.45 and .47, respectively).

Reduced variance might explain reduced correlations but not the reversal of sign. One possible explanation for this result is that there may be two underlying components to each factor: masculinity-femininity and something like "breadth of interests." Within gender, the latter slightly predominates, but, across genders, it is washed out by the gender-related differences. With these few exceptions (the most notable being the appearance of the higher-order masculinity-femininity factor), the intercorrelations among the factors were generally low and suggested that the factors are fairly independent.

Relationship of the Factors to Scale 5

In the next step, we explored how much of the variance in Scale 5 scores is explained by the factors. We performed a stepwise multiple regression analysis, using the factors to predict the MMPI-2 Scale 5 score. The variance accounted for by the factors (adjusted R^2), when scored on the male normative data, was .90, and, when scored on the female normative data, was .85. This predictability was based on the forty-six items that are included in the factors out of the fifty-six total items on Scale 5 and thus is affected by part-whole correlations. These results are shown in Table 4.4.

Each factor explained a significant amount of variance for both genders ($p > .10$). There were gender differences in the importance of the factors in explaining variance of Scale 5. For example, the Hypersensitivity/Anxiety factor by itself explained the most variance for males ($R^2 = .32$) whereas it explained less variance than Aesthetic Interests for females. This suggests that the meaning of Scale 5 scores may generally be somewhat different for males and females.

Table 4.4. Incremental Percent of the Variance of Scale 5 Explained by the Factors (Normative Sample)

Males

Subscale	R^2
Hypersensitivity/Anxiety	.32
Low Cynicism	.52
Aesthetic Interests	.67
Denial of Stereotypical Masculine Interests	.75
Feminine Interests	.82
Stereotypical Feminine Gender Identity	.86
Restraint	.90

Females

Subscale	R^2
Aesthetic Interests	.18
Hypersensitivity/Anxiety	.31
Restraint	.48
Low Cynicism	.60
Stereotypical Feminine Interests	.72
Denial of Stereotypical Masculine Interests	.81
Feminine Gender Identity	.85

Discussion of Factor Characteristics

The factors for Scale 5 exhibit characteristics consistent with what is expected, given the constructs that they appear to measure. Four of the factors show negligible gender differences. However, three of the factors show different patterns of relationship for males and females. Denial of Stereotypical Masculine Interests, Stereotypical Feminine Interests, and Feminine Gender Identity demonstrate significantly different means when considered separately by gender. The variance in these three factors diminishes when considered separately by gender, which affects the internal consistency of the factors when computed on males and females separately. Furthermore, these three factors show the highest intercorrelations among all the factors. These results lend credibility to the emerging notion that they represent something similar that is distinct from the other dimensions of Scale 5. Before we explore this possibility by examining their validity, we use a separate sample to explore the reliability of the factors.

As we discussed in chapter 1, when we talk about differences in the structure of masculinity and femininity between males and females (or between adults and adolescents in chapter 7), we refer to the item level and the factor level. An example of the item level arises here. The item "Like cooking" (#128) does not load on the Stereotypical Feminine Interests factor for women, but it does for men. Thus, this item may be viewed by females as a human activity, something they and others do that has little to do with masculinity and femininity. Males, on the other hand, may generally view cooking as a feminine characteristic. Thus, males and females (or different generations) may differ in their perceptions of an item's reflection of masculinity or femininity. Similarly, perceptions of a factor may differ. For example, adolescents may view boisterousness as a primary characteristic of masculinity; whereas older adults may not give boisterousness much weight in their calculations of masculinity. We examine this possibility in chapter 7 when we explore the dimensions of Scale 5 in adolescents.

These potential differences in structure present an interesting debate. Spence (1985, 1993) and others, specifically Deaux (1999), argue that

> all people do not share the same meanings of masculinity and femininity. Furthermore, people can selectively pick from their own experiential history, taking on those aspects of masculinity and femininity that they find compatible with other values and dismissing those attributes that may be viewed as central by others. In other words, the package label may say masculine or feminine, but a careful look at the contents may hold some surprises. (Deaux, 1999, p. 21)

Hence they reason that the terms should be abandoned as imprecise and confusing. We maintain the possibility that when the terms are carefully defined, they may offer a relatively coherent construct that is useful to science. If the differences between groups are greater than the differences within groups, the terms may be useful in expressing important information. If there were not substantial similarities (as well as differences) between individuals, no coherent factors would have emerged from our analyses. Idiographic differences may still exist, but a nomothetic consensus remains. Finally, the effect sizes and the loss of variance that we observe in the factors previously discussed support the possibility that we may arrive at a useful, albeit more circumscribed, definition of masculinity and femininity.

Stability of the Scale 5 Factors across Samples

In order to investigate the stability of the Scale 5 factors, we scored the factors using data gathered from a college sample. Gender differences in factor scores, internal consistency coefficients, and intercorrelations among the factors were computed and compared to those generated from the normative sample.

The college sample (UT90 data) included 817 students (434 females and 383 males) in Introductory Psychology classes at the University of Texas at Austin. These students participated in this research as part of the course requirements. They completed a three hundred-item questionnaire that included all items on Scale 5 of the MMPI-2 intermixed with items from other measures of masculinity-femininity, gender identity, sexual orientation, and personality. The data were collected during the summer and fall semesters of 1990. The average age of the males was 20.8 years (standard deviation = 2.7; range = 19 to 55 years). The female average age was 20.5 years (standard deviation = 2.8; range = 19 to 50 years). (See Martin, 1991, for further information.)

Gender Differences in Factor Scores in a College Sample

Similar to the normative data, a multivariate analysis of variance of male and female scores resulted in a highly significant difference between males and females in factor scores ($F = 249.38$, $p < .0001$) (see Tables 4.4 and 4.5). Similar to the normative data, post hoc t-tests showed significant differences between the genders on every factor. The effect sizes were similar for each factor in the normative data and the UT90 college sample.

Table 4.5. Comparison of Male and Female Subscale Means in the UT90 College Sample

	Males mean (std dev)	Females mean (std dev)	t	Effect Size[a]
Denial of Masculine Interests	3.56 (1.48)	5.02 (1.00)	14.23 [b]	1.18
Hypersensitivity/Anxiety	7.22 (2.64)	8.14 (2.55)	5.53 [b]	.35
Feminine Interests	.53 (.83)	2.38 (1.36)	23.83 [b]	1.69
Low Cynicism	3.62 (1.37)	4.15 (1.41)	5.18 [b]	.38
Aesthetic Interests	1.86 (1.47)	2.64 (1.46)	7.59 [b]	.53
Feminine Gender Identity	.99 (.94)	3.20 (.87)	34.61 [b]	2.44
Restraint	2.31 (1.44)	2.74 (1.43)	3.85 [b]	.30

Note. UT90 sample contains 434 females and 383 males.

Note. [a] Cohen's (1988) *d*.

[b] denotes $p < .0001$.

Similar to the normative data, there was a much larger difference between males and females on Denial of Stereotypical Masculine Interests, Stereotypical Feminine Interests, and Feminine Gender Identity than on the other factors. Once again, we see the substantial reduction in variance observed in the normative sample in Denial of Stereotypical Masculine Interests, Stereotypical Feminine Interests, and Feminine Gender Identity. This supports the previously advanced notion that, on measures related to gender, there is more variance when the genders are combined than when considered separately. Thus, the same general patterns exist in the UT90 college sample as in the normative sample.

Internal Consistency of the Factors in a College Sample

The UT90 College sample was not large enough to replicate the factor analyses that we performed with the Scale 5 items in the normative sample; thus, the structural stability of the factors was examined by computing internal consistency in the student sample and comparing that to the factors already developed. The internal consistencies of the factors computed in the combined (i.e., both male and female) student sample were acceptably high for all but Restraint, which was .39. However, it increased to .43 with the deletion of one item. In all the factors, only two other items detracted from the alpha coefficient. These internal consistency coefficients are shown in Table 4.6 (See Table 4.1 for alphas in the normative data) and suggest that the factor items are generally appropriate for the two different populations.

When internal consistency coefficients were calculated by gender separately (also shown in Table 4.6), the results were again similar to the results from the

Table 4.6. Internal Consistency of the Scale 5 Factors from the UT90 Sample

	Combined data[a]	Male data[a]	Female data[a]
Denial of Stereotypical Masculine Interests	.62	.55	.43
Hypersensitivity/Anxiety	.63	.61	.63
Stereotypical Feminine Interests	.62	.29	.49
Low Cynicism	.45	.39	.48
Aesthetic Interests	.63	.61	.60
Feminine Gender Identity	.70	.33	.25
Restraint	.39	.40	.39

Note. [a] Alpha internal consistency coefficients from the UT90 sample.

normative data. Hypersensitivity/Anxiety, Low Cynicism, Aesthetic Interests, and Restraint held up well, whereas Denial of Stereotypical Masculine Interests and Stereotypical Feminine Interests deteriorated somewhat, and Feminine Gender Identity deteriorated substantially. The deterioration is, again, most likely a result of diminished variance in these factors when the genders are considered separately. The low internal consistency for males on Stereotypical Feminine Interests is likely a result of the low variance observed in that group for that factor. Other college samples have not produced such low variance in this factor for males (i.e., UT92, discussed in subsequent chapters).

Intercorrelations of Factors in a College Sample

Factor intercorrelations computed on the UT90 sample with males and females calculated separately as well as combined showed a very similar pattern to the normative data. These intercorrelations are shown in Table 4.7.

Some of the gender differences observed in the intercorrelation of the factors in the normative sample were not observed in the UT90 sample, but at least one gender difference remained. The difference between males and females in the correlation of Stereotypical Feminine Interests and Aesthetic Interests in the normative sample (male $r = .35$ and female $r = .19$) disappeared in the college sample (male $r = .28$ and female $r = .29$) ($z = .25, p > .05$). The gender difference between Denial of Stereotypical Masculine Interests and Restraint in the normative sample (male $r = .18$ and female $r = .08$) was not observed in the college sample (male $r = .00$ and female $r = -.04$) ($z = 1.00, p > .05$). However, the gender difference in the correlation of Feminine Gender Identity and Aesthetic Interests in the normative sample (male $r = .17$ and female $r = .05$) was again significant in the college sample (male $r = .30$ and female $r = .12$) ($z = 4.5, p < .05$). These findings suggest some small sample differences in the relationship among traits, which could be generational; however, the basic similarity of the intercorrelations supports the reliability and construct validity of the factors by demonstrating fair consistency across populations.

Finally, multiple regression analysis was performed using the factors in the UT90 college data to predict Scale 5 scores. The amount of the variance of Scale 5 explained by the seven factors was 83 percent for females and 91 percent for males. These figures are nearly identical to those for the normative data and suggest that the factors perform similarly in both populations.

Thus, the factors appear to have very similar qualities in both the sample of college students and the normative sample. The differences that do exist are small and are consistent with what we would expect in a college population. This stability across samples supports the reliability of the factors.

Table 4.7. Intercorrelations of the Factors of Scale 5 of the MMPI-2 in the UT90 Sample

	S1	S2	S3	S4	S5	S6	S7	Scale 5
S1	—	.10	−.08	.01	−.02	.03	.00	.32
		.11	**−.23**	**−.11**	**−.11**	**.06**	**−.04**	**.12**
S2	.18	—	.09	−.18	.33	.27	−.14	.65
			.04	**−.27**	**.04**	**.01**	**−.15**	**.32**
S3	.22	.15	—	.05	.28	.33	.05	.40
				.05	**.29**	**.18**	**−.01**	**.44**
S4	.06	−.19	.15	—	.14	.08	.19	.28
					.14	**.06**	**.16**	**.40**
S5	.08	.21	.37	.18	—	.30	−.04	.59
						.12	**−.08**	**.48**
S6	.41	.22	.60	.19	.33	—	.11	.54
							.02	**.41**
S7	.06	−.11	.11	.20	−.02	.16	—	.20
								.32
Scale 5	.50	.46	.67	.37	.55	.76	.29	—

Note. Intercorrelations from the combined male and female normative data are in the lower triangle of matrix. Male (on top) and Female (in bold) intercorrelations are in the upper triangle of the matrix.

Note. S1 = Denial of Stereotypical Masculine Interests, S2 = Hypersensitivity/Anxiety, S3 = Stereotypical Feminine Interests, S4 = Low Cynicism, S5 = Aesthetic Interests, S6 = Feminine Gender Identity, S7 = Restraint.

Conclusion

Seven factors that are applicable to both males and females emerged from the multistep approach used in this study. This result reconfirms the multifactorial nature of Scale 5. The factors include Denial of Stereotypical Masculine Interests, Hypersensitivity/Anxiety, Stereotypical Feminine Interests, Low Cynicism, Aesthetic Interests, Feminine Gender Identity, and Restraint, and they demonstrated sufficient internal consistency to be considered viable measures. Intercorrelations among the factors generally suggested that they measured separate constructs. However, the correlations among Denial of Stereotypical Masculine Interests, Stereotypical Feminine Interests, and Feminine Gender Identity (components of a proposed higher-order factor of masculinity-femininity) were sufficiently large to suggest that these constructs are closely related. The two interest factors are similar to those identified by Tellegen et al. (2003) in their restructuring of Scale 5. Feminine Gender Identity is unique and appears to be closely related to the core of masculinity-femininity.

Furthermore, the evidence gathered suggests that the factors are stable across two diverse populations. The internal consistencies of the factors in both samples suggest that the factor items cohere similarly in both populations. The similar pattern of gender differences in scores with generally predictable differences among factors between the two samples supports the reliability of the factors. Also, the similar factor intercorrelations in the two samples and the fact that the factors explain similar amounts of variance in both samples suggest that the factors are stable at least across these two populations. There is evidence of subtle differences in how different ages and genders conceptualize traits related to masculinity-femininity. However, there are also substantial similarities, as demonstrated by our ability to find a consensus set of factors that work well in both males and females both in a sample of the general population and in a college sample.

Three major questions remain: First, is there a way to enhance the factors by using items that fall outside Scale 5? Second, can an effective composite measure of masculinity-femininity be developed? Third, what are the factors measuring? In the next two chapters, these questions are addressed.

Chapter 5

Further Exploration of Masculinity and Femininity in the MMPI-2

In chapter 4, we investigated the factor structure of Scale 5. As we suspected from our review of the original development of Scale 5, from Serkownek's work (1975), and from the work of Tellegen, Ben-Porath, McNulty, Arbisi, Graham, and Kaemmer (2003; see chapter 3), we found a variety of psychological dimensions represented in Scale 5: Hypersensitivity/Anxiety, Low Cynicism, Aesthetic Interests, and Restraint. Additionally, three factors emerged that showed higher intercorrelations than the other factors and that seemed to reflect central aspects of masculinity-femininity. These three factors may capture in part a higher-order factor of masculinity-femininity that permeates Scale 5. We labeled these core factors Denial of Stereotypical Masculine Interests, Stereotypical Feminine Interests, and Feminine Gender Identity.

In the analyses described in this chapter, we examined MMPI-2 items outside of Scale 5 to determine whether any contributed to the core dimensions of masculinity-femininity represented in the Scale 5 factors. Then, we explored the higher-order structure of these core dimensions and constructed a composite factor of masculinity-femininity on the MMPI-2 that is related to the first and dominant higher-order factor. We then examined the parameters of the augmented factors and the composite marker, before considering in detail what these factors measure (described in chapter 6).

Augmenting the MF Factors

Non-Scale 5 MMPI-2 Items and Masculinity-Femininity

We wanted to ascertain whether MMPI-2 items that were not contained on Scale 5 might enhance the three core masculinity-femininity factors that emerged in our work. We were aware that new items were added to the MMPI-2 during its restandardization, at least one of which seemed to be related to the core aspects of masculinity-femininity (i.e., #371, "Wished were member of opposite sex").

As a first step, we correlated the Denial of Stereotypical Masculine Interests, Stereotypical Feminine Interests, and Feminine Gender Identity factors with all items on the MMPI-2 that were most likely to be related to masculinity-femininity, including items from GM and GF and additional items selected from the larger MMPI-2 item pool. Items from the GM and GF scales were selected because these two scales comprise items from the MMPI-2 that show at least a 10 percent differential endorsement rate (in the same scoring direction) by the males and females in the normative data (Peterson & Dahlstrom, 1992). Our reasoning was as follows. Differential endorsement by males and females partly underlay the selection of items for the original MMPI Scale 5 (see chapter 3) and may be a marker, in many cases, that an item measures masculinity-femininity (see chapter 2). Nine of forty-seven items in GM also appear on Scale 5; sixteen of the forty-six GF items are also scored in Scale 5. Thus, sixty-eight items were left for consideration.

However, because the GM and GF items might not contain some potentially useful masculinity-femininity items, we also used judges to rationally pick additional items for consideration. An item such as the one previously mentioned (#371, "Wished were member of opposite sex") might not show differential male-female endorsement rates but might be a useful item—for example, on the Feminine Gender Identity factor.

Three judges who were familiar with masculinity-femininity research, MMPI-2 research, and clinical use of the MMPI-2 inspected the remaining MMPI-2 item pool. They were asked to identify items that might be related to masculinity-femininity. Items independently selected by at least two of the three judges were included, resulting in ten additional items (see Appendix E).

The seventy-eight items thus selected from either GM or GF or by our judges were then correlated with the item totals for the three masculinity-femininity factors, to determine whether any item correlated at least .20 with one of the factor scales. These computations were performed using the normative data for each gender separately and for both genders combined. We gave more weight to the single-gender correlations than to those from the combined sample, in order to downplay items that merely distinguished between the genders and to focus on items that captured within-gender variance as well. Some items correlated above .20 with more than one of the factors. When this occurred, we examined the content of the item to determine which factor seemed most appropriate and assigned that item accordingly.

As a result of these correlations, five items were added to Denial of Stereotypical Masculine Interests, none to Stereotypical Feminine Interests, and three to Feminine Gender Identity. These non–Scale 5 items selected to be included on the factors are the following:

Denial of Stereotypical Masculine Interests additions:

(–) 467. Like science

(–) 465. Like to fix things

(–) 417. Would like to race cars

(–) 474. Prefer adventure stories to romances

(–) 477. Like to play football

Feminine Gender Identity additions:

384. Liked playing "house"

426. Liked to play hopscotch and jump rope

371. Wished were member of opposite sex.

Item #371 is scored in opposite directions for males and females.

Parameters of the Factors

Our next step was to examine the augmented factors to determine their characteristics in the combined normative data, as well as for males and females separately.

Internal Consistency

First, we calculated the internal consistency coefficients for the augmented factors in a stepwise fashion using the normative data. The resulting alphas are shown in Table 5.4. The internal consistency of the augmented Denial of Stereotypical Masculine Interests factor increased to .77 in the combined sample (up from .63 in its previous version) and to .66 in the male sample and .63 in the female sample. The expansion of the factor increased the average item correlations to .23, .15, and .13 for the combined, male, and female data, respectively. Because of these increases in internal consistency, we believed that the augmented factor was potentially a better representation of the construct than the unaugmented version.

The internal consistency of Feminine Gender Identity increased with the deletion of two original factor items ("Kept a diary" and "Would like to be a sports reporter"). The addition of the three non–Scale 5 items ("Wished were member of opposite sex," "Liked playing 'house,'" and "Liked to play hopscotch and jump rope") and the deletion of the two original items substantially increased the internal consistency of the measure. The coefficients of internal consistency increased to .81 in the combined sample (up from .59 in its previous version) and to .43 in both the male and female data separately. The average item correlations for this augmented factor were .46 in the combined sample and .13 in both the male and female data. This increase substantially enhanced the reliability of the factor scale, making it a better measure of the underlying dimension than the unaugmented version.

The internal consistencies of the augmented core factor scales are sufficient for use in nomothetic comparisons (Helmstadter, 1964) and would be expected to increase further in populations with more variance on the characteristics they capture (e.g., among homosexual men).

Means and Standard Deviations

We then calculated the means and standard deviations of the two new augmented factors in the normative data. The results are shown in Table 5.1.

The scales clearly demonstrated the same patterns between genders that they exhibited in the unaugmented versions, with females scoring much higher than males in the "feminine" direction on each scale. The effect size (Cohen's *d*) of these male-female differences for the augmented Denial of Stereotypical Masculine Interests factor was 1.52 (compared to 1.26 in the unaugmented version); for the augmented Feminine Gender Identity factor, it was 3.00 (compared to 2.21 in the unaugmented version). Thus, the pattern of male-female differences

Table 5.1. Means and Standard Deviations for the Factors in the Normative Sample

	Combined Mean (s. d.)[a] (n = 2,600)	Males Mean (s. d.)[a] (n = 1,138)	Females Mean (s. d.)[a] (n = 1,462)
Augmented	6.81	5.00	8.22
Denial of Masculine Interests	(2.64)	(2.30)	(1.94)
Augmented	3.02	1.32	4.34
Feminine Gender Identity	(1.80)	(1.10)	(.91)

Note. [a] indicates standard deviation.

discussed in chapter 4 was maintained in the augmented factor scales, with further increases in the differences between males and females on measures that we believe are directly related to the higher-order construct of masculinity-femininity. These increases further suggest that the augmented versions of the factors are superior markers of the underlying constructs.

Multiple Regression

We recomputed a stepwise multiple regression to determine how much of the variance was explained by the augmented factors. These calculations were performed on males and females separately. These results are shown in Table 5.2.

As we would expect, these percentages decreased slightly over those computed on the unaugmented factors because these augmented factors contain some items that are not included on Scale 5. For example, by comparing Table 4.4 with Table 5.2, we see that, in females, the amount of variance explained is, of course, the same for the first five factors (unaugmented fac-

Table 5.2. Incremental Percent of the Variance of Scale 5 Explained by the Augmented Factors (Normative Sample)

Males

Subscale	R^2
Hypersensitivity/Anxiety	.32
Low Cynicism	.52
Aesthetic Interests	.67
Denial of Stereotypical Masculine Interests	.75
Stereotypical Feminine Interests	.81
Restraint	.85
Feminine Gender Identity	.86

Females

Subscale	R^2
Aesthetic Interests	.18
Hypersensitivity/Anxiety	.31
Restraint	.48
Low Cynicism	.60
Stereotypical Feminine Interests	.72
Denial of Stereotypical Masculine Interests	.79
Feminine Gender Identity	.80

tors). However, the incremental variance explained by the last two factors, Denial of Stereotypical Masculine Interests and Feminine Gender Identity, declines from 0.81 and 0.85 in the unaugmented factors to .79 and .80 in the augmented factors. The decline was minimal. The augmented factors clearly capture an adequate amount of the variance in Scale 5.

Intercorrelations

Next, we computed in the normative sample the intercorrelations among the factors, substituting the two augmented factors for their unaugmented counterparts. We also included Scale 5 scores. These correlations are shown in Table 5.3.

Table 5.3. Intercorrelations of the Augmented Factors in the Normative Sample

	Aug-S1	S2	S3	S4	S5	Aug-S6	S7	Scale 5
Aug-S1	—	.07	−.11	.11	.00	−.07	.21	.37
		.03	**−.09**	**−.05**	**−.14**	**.08**	**.08**	**.21**
S2	.16	—	.07	−.19	.16	.08	−.19	.57
			−.01	**−.17**	**.14**	**−.05**	**−.19**	**.41**
S3	.28	.13	—	−.03	.35	.25	−.09	.37
				−.03	**.19**	**.15**	**−.04**	**.39**
S4	.09	−.15	.04	—	.01	.03	.17	.32
					.05	**.02**	**.13**	**.35**
S5	.06	.18	.32	.05	—	.20	−.16	.50
						.04	**−.14**	**.43**
Aug-S6	.47	.16	.53	.10	.23	—	−.07	.26
							−.05	**.15**
S7	.23	−.14	.06	.17	−.10	.12	—	.14
								.28
Scale 5	.57	.56	.59	.30	.49	.60	.22	—

Note. Intercorrelations from the combined male and female normative data are in the lower triangle of the matrix. Male (on top) and Female (in bold) intercorrelations are in the upper triangle of the matrix.

Note. Aug S1 = augmented Denial of Stereotypical Masculine Interests, S2 = Hypersensitivity/Anxiety, S3 = Stereotypical Feminine Interests, S4 = Low Cynicism, S5 = Aesthetic Interests, Aug S6 = augmented Feminine Gender Identity, S7 = Restraint.

The relationships were similar to those observed among the original factors. This suggests that the augmented factors and the factors from which they were developed have similar relationships to the other factors.

These intercorrelations were similar to those of Greene (2000, p. 153). He used Caldwell's (1997) clinical sample of over 50,000 MMPI-2s and computed correlations between Scale 5 and other MMPI-2 scales, including the factors that we developed here. He only looked at males and females combined, but he found a similar pattern of correlations between our factors and Scale 5. In that very large sample, Scale 5 correlated −.582 with Stereotypical Masculine Interests (augmented but not reversed); .430 with Hypersensitivity/Anxiety; .646 with Stereotypical Feminine Interests; −.233 with Low Cynicism (not reversed); .388 with Aesthetic Interests; .708 with Feminine Gender Identity (augmented); and −.251 with Restraint (not reversed).

Distribution of Scale 5 Factor Scores in the Normative Sample

We then examined the distribution of scores on the factors in the normative data. These results are displayed in the following graphs, Figure 5.1 through Figure 5.7. Notice the differences in distributions when the male and female data are considered separately. The distribution of scores on the Denial of Stereotypical Interests factor showed a substantial gender difference, with females scoring higher than males. The graph of the combined data smoothed out the differences between males and females and produced a flatter curve.

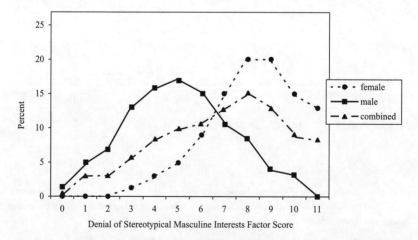

Figure 5.1. Distribution of Scores on the Denial of Stereotypical Masculine Interests Factor

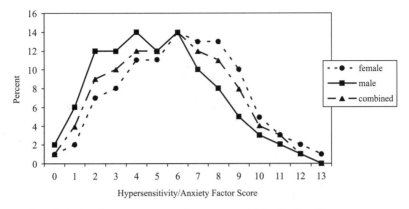

Figure 5.2. Distribution of Scores on the Hypersensitivity/Anxiety Factor

On the Hypersensitivity/Anxiety factor, the genders scored similarly, with a slightly lower mean for males than for females. The distribution approached a fairly normal curve.

Stereotypical Feminine Interests is a factor that showed substantial gender differences in the distribution of scores in the normative sample. Females scored substantially higher than males. The male distribution was negatively skewed, whereas the female curve was relatively normal. Notice that very few males (only 0.4 percent) obtained a score of 6.00, whereas only a few females (2.6 percent) obtained a score of 0.00. Once again, the

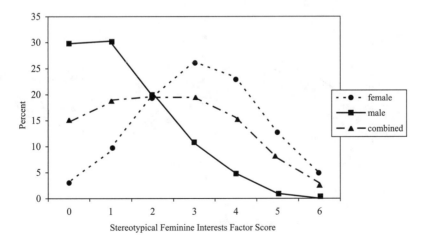

Figure 5.3. Distribution of Scores on the Stereotypical Feminine Interests Factor

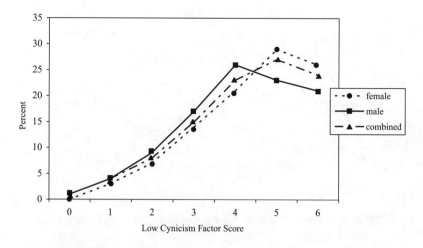

Figure 5.4. Distribution of Scores on the Low Cynicism Factor

combined data obscured the gender differences and produced a relatively flat curve.

Males and females performed similarly on the Low Cynicism factor, but the resulting distribution was linear and positively skewed. In fact, the factor seemed truncated, with scores accumulating at the high end of the distribution. It appears that more items would be needed to adequately capture the full range of variance on this trait. (Fortunately, there are other, better measures of cynicism on the MMPI-2.)

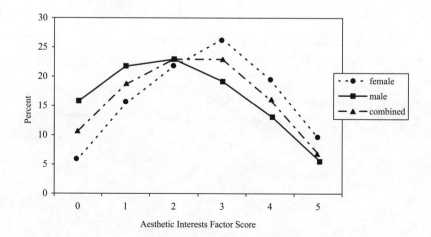

Figure 5.5. Distribution of Scores on the Aesthetic Interests Factor

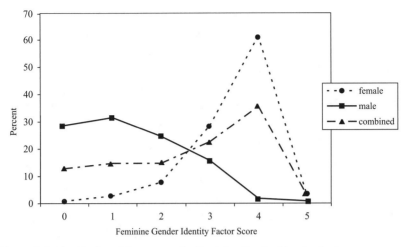

Figure 5.6. Distribution of Scores on the Feminine Gender Identity Factor

Males and females scored similarly on the Aesthetic Interests factor. The females had a slightly higher mean on the factor and thus appeared to have more interest in the arts. Notice the difference between this graph and the graph for Stereotypical Feminine Interests, where the gender differences were substantial. The difference perhaps suggests that, although some interests are truly gender-related, others, such as an interest in the arts, are not as gender-related.

The Feminine Gender Identity factor showed the largest gender differences of all the factors. Considering the genders combined, the curve for Feminine

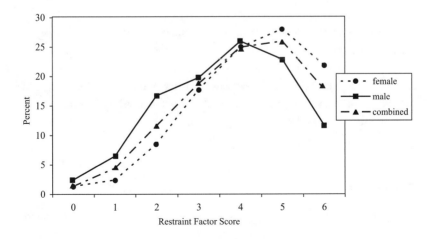

Figure 5.7. Distribution of Scores on the Restraint Factor

Gender Identity was odd. If we look at the distributions for males and females separately, we see that most males fall at one end of the scale and most females fall at the other. This supports the argument that we advanced earlier, namely, that there would be a bimodal distribution for this dimension, and it provides some construct validation of the Feminine Gender Identity factor.

On the Restraint factor, males and females scored similarly, with males exhibiting a slightly lower mean than females, indicating that they showed slightly less restraint than did females.

Test-Retest Reliability

We then examined the stability of the factors in the normative data, using the 193 subjects (82 males and 111 females) on which the MMPI-2 normative test-retest data were calculated. As reported in the MMPI-2 manual (Butcher, Dahlstrom, Graham, Tellegen, & Kaemmer, 1989), the average interval between test and retest was 8.58 days (median = 7 days). Pearson correlations (two-tailed) showed the following test-retest coefficients:

Denial of Stereotypical Masculine Interests	.93
Hypersensitivity/Anxiety	.78
Stereotypical Feminine Interests	.83
Low Cynicism	.68
Aesthetic Interests	.83
Feminine Gender Identity	.90
Restraint	.82

These results show that the factors were stable over a one-week interval. The Denial of Stereotypical Masculine Interests and Feminine Gender Identity factors reached coefficients in the .90 to .93 range, showing very strong resilience over the two testing periods. Furthermore, the Feminine Gender Identity factor showed high test-retest reliability (.90), suggesting that it is also a stable measure. The lowest test-retest score belonged to the Low Cynicism factor (.68). This result may reflect the previously mentioned low ceiling on the scale.

Conclusions

Thus, the augmented factors demonstrated improved internal consistency over their unaugmented counterparts, retained similar patterns in males and females (even enhancing the discrimination of males from females on

Table 5.4. Factor Structure of Scale 5 of the MMPI-2

1. **DENIAL OF STEREOTYPICAL MASCULINE INTERESTS** (alphas: combined = .77; males = .66; females = .63)

   (–) 001. Like mechanics magazines.
   (–) 069. Would like being a forest ranger.
   (–) 133. Would like to be in military.
   (–) 197. Would like to be a building contractor.
   (–) 199. Like science.
   (–) 201. Like hunting.
   (–) 417. Would like to race cars.
   (–) 465. Like to fix things.
   (–) 467. Like science.
   (–) 474. Prefer adventure stories to romances.
   (–) 477. Like to play football.

2. **HYPERSENSITIVITY/ANXIETY** (alphas: combined = .66, for males = .65, for females = .66)

   (–) 063. Feelings not hurt easily.
       166. Worry about sex.
   (–) 184. Seldom daydream.
   (–) 194. Never had worrisome skin rashes.
       196. Frequently worry.
       205. Habits of some family members very irritating.
       219. Disappointed in love.
   (–) 237. Don't mind not being better looking.
   (–) 239. Wholly self-confident.
       251. Often strangers look at me critically.
       256. Occasionally hate family members I love.
       268. Bothered by sexual thoughts.
       271. Feel more intensely than most.

3. **STEREOTYPICAL FEMININE INTERESTS** (alphas: combined = .61; males = .46; females = .43)

       004. Like library work.
       064. Like romances.
       074. Would like to be a florist.
       080. Would like being a nurse.
       119. Like collecting plants.
       236. Would like to be an artist who draws flowers.

4. **LOW CYNICISM** (alphas: combined = .52, males = .51, females = .51)

   (–) 026. Keep quiet when in trouble.
   (–) 027. Retaliate when wronged.
   (–) 076. Hard to convince people of truth.
   (–) 104. People honest because they don't want to be caught.
   (–) 193. I avoid stepping on sidewalk cracks.
   (–) 254. People have friends because they're useful.

5. **AESTHETIC INTERESTS** (alphas: combined = .55, males = .59, females = .49)

       025. Would like to be a singer.

(Continued)

Table 5.4. (*Continued*)

     067. Like poetry.
     112. Like theater.
     187. Would like to report theater news.
     191. Would like to be a journalist.

6. FEMININE GENDER IDENTITY (alphas: combined = .81; males = .43; females = .43)

     062. Wish was a girl or happy that am.
(–) 272. Never liked to play with dolls.
     371. Wished were member of opposite sex.[a]
        (– for females; + for males)
     384. Liked playing "house."
     426. Like to play hopscotch and jump rope.

7. RESTRAINT (alphas: combined = .46, males = .46, females = .43)

(–) 068. Tease animals.
(–) 086. Like loud parties.
(–) 019. On a new job, find out who is important.
(–) 207. Would like to be a member of clubs.
(–) 209. Like to talk about sex.
(–) 231. Like being with people who play jokes on one another.

Note. Test item numbers are included for each item along with the direction in which the item is scored (a minus sign in parentheses preceding the item number indicates that the item is scored when the response is "false"; the absence of a minus marker indicates that the item is scored when the response it "true").

Note. [a] denotes that this item is scored in opposite directions for males and females (in the Feminine Gender Identity Subscale).

constructs in which this was expected), retained similar relationships with other factors, demonstrated strong test-retest reliability, and showed reasonable distributions in the normative sample. With this evidence in mind, we adopted these augmented factors as the best markers of denial of stereotypical masculine interests and feminine gender identity in the MMPI-2. With this conclusion, we now had identified the seven dimensions that underlie Scale 5, including three factors that measure dimensions of masculinity-femininity. These dimensions are shown in Table 5.4.

Higher-Order Factor Structure of Scale 5

Given the substantial intercorrelations between several of the factors, we explored their higher-order structure, with hopes of identifying a dominant higher-order factor in Scale 5 that might be a good marker of masculinity-femininity. If identified, such a higher-order factor could help us understand masculinity-femininity and its relationship to other dimensions of personality.

So, we conducted principal components analyses of the Scale 5 factor intercorrelations for males and females separately, as well as for the combined normative MMPI-2 sample. We considered the unrotated principal components and orthogonal (varimax) and nonorthogonal (promax) rotated solutions. The scree plots suggested from two to four factors existed. As expected, the solutions for males and females separately did not result in a stable and comprehensible structure because of the reduced variance when only one sex/gender is considered.

In all solutions using the combined male and female data, a dominant first factor emerged that accounted for most of the variance in the factor scale correlations. This first factor was clearest in the three-factor unrotated principal components analysis and was defined by Feminine Gender Identity (.83 loading), Stereotypical Feminine Interests (.76), and Denial of Stereotypical Masculine Interests (.67), as well having as a lesser loading of Aesthetic Interests (.47). (See Appendix F.) We called this higher-order factor Femininity-Masculinity, because it clearly is a bipolar dimension capturing this trait. The Aesthetic Interests factor split and loaded higher on the third higher-order factor (.57), along with Low Cynicism (.57). This higher-order factor appears to be an openness to experience dimension. The second higher-order factor was defined by loadings on Restraint (.71), Hypersensitivity/Anxiety (reversed) (−.58), and Low Cynicism (.55) factors, which may reflect the higher order dimension of Constraint (calmness or a lack of emotional/behavioral engagement).

At this point, we could have computed factor scores for the higher-order factors using coefficients from this principle components analysis. However, research has shown that linear composites often do as well on cross-validation as weighted composites, especially when their components are correlated (Wainer, 1976). Thus, we elected to construct a marker of the underlying higher-order factor by simply combining the items on Denial of Stereotypical Masculine Interests, Stereotypical Feminine Interests, and Feminine Gender Identity. We did not include Aesthetic Interests in this composite because of its higher loading on the Openness to Experience factor and because it did not show the overlapping, bimodal gender distributions typified by the other factors. The resulting composite, Femininity-Masculinity, or FM, is shown in Table 5.5.

Table 5.5. Composite Femininity-Masculinity Marker (FM Scale)

(–) 001. Like mechanics magazines.
(–) 069. Would like being a forest ranger.
(–) 133. Would like to be in military.
(–) 197. Would like to be a building contractor.
(–) 199. Like science.
(–) 201. Like hunting.
(–) 417. Would like to race cars.
(–) 465. Like to fix things.
(–) 467. Like science.
(–) 474. Prefer adventure stories to romances.
(–) 477. Like to play football.
    004. Like library work.
    064. Like romances.
    074. Would like to be a florist.
    080. Would like being a nurse.
    119. Like collecting plants.
    236. Would like to be an artist who draws flowers.
    062. Wish was a girl or happy that am.
(–) 272. Never liked to play with dolls.
    371. Wished were member of opposite sex.[a]
    (– for females; + for males)
    384. Liked playing "house."
    426. Like to play hopscotch and jump rope.

Note. Test item numbers are included for each item along with the direction in which the item is scored (a minus sign in parentheses preceding the item number indicates that the item is scored when the response is "false"; the absence of a minus marker indicates that the item is scored when the response is "true").

Note. [a] denotes that this item is scored in opposite directions for males and females.

Parameters of the FM Marker

Mean and Standard Deviation

The mean for the FM marker in the combined normative data was 11.77, with a standard deviation of 4.47 (scored on male criteria). For males, the mean was 7.67, with a standard deviation of 2.79; for females, the mean was 15.73, with a standard deviation of 2.62. Gender comparisons demonstrated an effect size of 2.98.

Internal Consistency

We computed the internal consistency coefficients for the composite masculinity-femininity scale in the normative sample. In the combined data, the alpha was .82. In the male data, it was .52; in the female data, it was .53.

The average item correlations were .19 in the combined data and .05 in both the male and female data.

Distribution of FM Scores in the Normative Sample

The frequency distribution of the FM marker in the male, female, and combined normative sample is shown in Figure 5.8. The distribution of the FM marker is bimodal as a result of its strong association with gender. The modal score for females is 16; the mode for males is 8; and the distribution curves for males and females are clearly distinct. This bimodal distribution of the FM marker is what we would expect of a continuous bipolar measure of masculinity-femininity. This result provides significant evidence supporting the bipolar nature of masculinity-femininity.

Test-Retest

We then examined the temporal stability of the FM composite scale in the normative data, using the 193 subjects mentioned earlier, who were tested and then retested at approximately a one-week interval. These are the data used to calculate reliability estimates in the MMPI-2 normative sample (82 males and 111 females). Pearson correlations showed that the test-retest coefficient

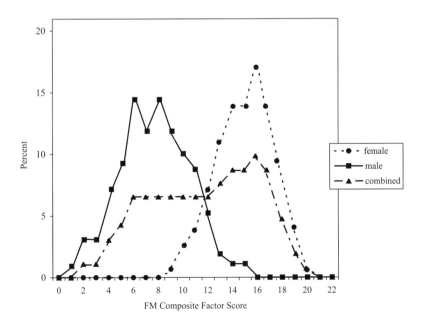

Figure 5.8. Distribution of Scores on the FM Composite Factor

for the FM composite marker was .96. This shows very strong reliability of the scores over a week's time and supports the conclusion that the underlying dimension represents a stable personality characteristic

Conclusions

Thus, the FM scale is promising as a composite marker of masculinity-femininity, and it isolates that part of the variance in the MMPI-2 that may be attributable to a core dimension of femininity-masculinity, without the noise of other more distantly related constructs (i.e., Hypersensitivity/Anxiety, Cynicism, Restraint). The psychometric properties of the FM marker suggest that it is sound for use in nomothetic comparisons. With a solid marker of masculinity-femininity in the MMPI-2, we can explore its relationship to other dimensions of personality. In the next chapter, we consider convergent and discriminant validity and what these tell us about the nature of masculinity-femininity.

Summary of the Scale 5 Factors

We determined that two of the three masculinity-femininity factors for Scale 5 could be enhanced by adding items from outside Scale 5. The augmented Denial of Stereotypical Masculine Interests factor and augmented Feminine Gender Identity factor were improved in their internal consistency and retained significant qualities of the unaugmented versions, at least in their relationship to the other factors. In these important ways, they were superior to the original factors. Of course, the addition of items from outside Scale 5 means that, technically, two of our factors were no longer true factors of the Scale 5. However, our aim was to identify the best markers of masculinity-femininity that we could, using the MMPI-2 item pool.

We next developed a higher-order factor scale of Femininity-Masculinity, by combining the three factors that defined the first principal component underlying the seven Scale 5 factors (i.e., the augmented Denial of Stereotypical Masculine Interests factor, the Stereotypical Feminine Interests factor, and augmented Feminine Gender Identity factor). We believe that this higher-order factor is a better indicator of masculinity-femininity than any other item set in the MMPI-2.

Chapter 6

Understanding the Dimensions of Scale 5 of the MMPI-2

Having identified the factor structure of Scale 5 and developed the composite marker of masculinity-femininity we call the FM marker, we arrived at the central task of understanding what these factors mean and what they reveal about masculinity-femininity. Obviously, it was essential to establish clearly what constructs the factors and the FM marker assessed before we could trust what they may tell us about masculinity-femininity. This entailed close examination of the factors' relationship to established measures of similar and dissimilar qualities.

In this chapter, we first assess the relationship of the Scale 5 factors to established scales in the MMPI-2, including the Clinical Scales, Content Scales, selected Supplementary Scales, and other purported MMPI measures of masculinity-femininity developed over the years. Then we explore the relationship of the factors with a broader range of instruments in two college samples. Finally, we examine the GM and GF scales in comparison to the Scale 5 factors.

As discussed in chapter 2, a difficulty in examining validity in the area of masculinity and femininity is that there is no universally acceptable measure of these constructs. The problem is intensified in that the construct validity of some widely used measures of masculinity-femininity is highly questionable because these measures show little discriminant validity from other well-established dimensions of personality (e.g., Lubinski, Tellegen, & Butcher, 1981). We believed it would be profitable to examine correlations of the Scale 5 factors with a variety of measures that purport to measure aspects of masculinity-femininity, as well as with measures that are conceptually distinct.

Before we look at the correlations that help us understand the Scale 5 factors and the FM marker, it is important to be aware that the Scale 5 factors, Scale 5, GM, and GF of the MMPI-2, and the F/M and Baucom masculinity and femininity scales of the CPI contain many items in common. This is because these measures were all developed from the same or similar item pools. Obviously, this item overlap, which is substantial in some cases, leads to an inflation of the correlations among certain measures. The highest overlap involving the Scale 5 factors occurs with GM and GF scales of the MMPI-2. Seven of the eleven items on the Denial of Stereotypical Masculine Interests factor and four of the five items composing the Feminine Gender Identity factor are also on the forty-six-item GF scale. Stereotypical Feminine Interests shows considerable overlap with GM, having four of its six items on the forty-seven-item GM scale.

There are various ways to address this problem, but none are without drawbacks. For example, we could have "corrected" for overlapping items by eliminating the overlapping items, or we could have performed statistical corrections in one way or another. These procedures may have provided a better sense of how the constructs interrelate, but the end result would tell little about how the two measures operate in conjunction. Unless otherwise noted, we scored each measure as it was originally constructed and did not attempt to adjust statistically for item overlap. However, we keep the item overlap in mind when considering the following correlations.

Discriminant and Convergent Validity of Scale 5 Factors with MMPI-2 Scales

Correlations with Validity, Clinical, and Selected Supplementary Scales

We computed Pearson correlations of raw scores on the Scale 5 factors with raw scores on the MMPI-2 Clinical scales, Validity scales, Content scales, selected Supplementary scales, Restructured Clinical scales, PSY5 scales, and other masculinity-femininity measures previously developed in the MMPI. We selected three supplementary scales that are thought to show good validity themselves: A, R, and Mt. We computed correlations combining the male and female data from the MMPI-2 normative sample data, as well as using the male and female data separately. We report here only the results from the combined data because, in general, the results by gender looked highly similar. For each table, we include the correlations computed separately for each gender in the appendices (Appendix G and H for females and males respectively).

Table 6.1 shows correlations of the Scale 5 factors with the MMPI-2 validity, clinical and selected supplementary scales.

Table 6.1. Intercorrelations of the Scale 5 Factors with Validity, Clinical, and Supplementary Scales Computed in the Combined Normative Sample

	DSMI	H/A	SFI	LC	AE	FGI	Rt	FM	5
L	.03	−.40	.01	.04	−.11	−.02	.27	.02	−.14
F	−.08	.34	−.14	−.35	−.02	−.12	−.16	−.14	−.03
K	.00	−.51	−.03	.51	−.02	−.03	.19	−.02	−.08
Fp	−.02	.12	−.02	−.34	.00	−.03	−.11	−.03	−.09
S	.03	−.60	.00	.54	−.08	.01	.25	.02	−.11
Hs	.11	.34	.07	−.31	.02	.06	−.01	.11	.12
D	.25	.35	.08	−.12	−.04	.10	.19	.20	.24
Hy	.14	.05	.03	.30	.08	.07	.13	.12	.20
Pd	.00	.44	−.06	−.19	.10	−.03	−.14	−.03	.12
Pa	.02	.33	.03	.09	.09	.01	−.04	.03	.22
Pt	.10	.66	.07	−.40	.07	.08	−.15	.10	.23
Sc	−.01	.60	−.01	−.42	.08	.00	−.21	−.01	.14
Ma	−.19	.27	−.02	−.28	.21	−.04	−.41	−.13	.00
Si	.20	.39	.02	−.30	−.21	.05	.31	.14	.14
A	.11	.63	.08	−.42	.06	.08	−.14	.12	.22
R	.45	−.19	−.05	.19	−.25	.04	.45	.27	.10
Mt	.09	.60	.02	−.40	.04	.04	−.12	.07	.18

Note. DSMI = Denial of Stereotypical Masculine Interests Subscale; H/A = Hypersensitivity/Anxiety Subscale; SFI = Stereotypical Feminine Interests Subscale; LC = Low Cynicism Subscale; AE = Aesthetic Interests Subscale; FGI = Feminine Gender Identity Subscale; Rt = Restraint Subscale; FM = Femininity-Masculinity Scale; 5 = Scale 5.

The Hypersensitivity/Anxiety factor showed the highest correlations with the validity, clinical, and selected supplementary scales. It correlated highly with Pt (.66), with Sc (.60), with Anxiety (A; .63), and with College Maladjustment (Mt; .60). It also correlated negatively with the Superlative validity scale (S; −.60). Thus, as already deduced, there is clearly a strong component of negative emotionality represented in the Hypersensitivity/Anxiety factor. In most instances, there is some item overlap between this Scale 5 factor and these MMPI-2 scales, which would heighten the correlations.

The Low Cynicism factor showed the next highest correlations. It correlated with K (.51) and the Superlative scale (.54). It also correlated negatively with Pt (−.40), Sc (−.42), A (−.42), and Mt (−.40). These correlations suggest that the Low Cynicism factor is related to downplaying problems and not endorsing negative emotionality. We might see this factor as capturing a tendency to put a good face on life and see the best in things. Thus, it is not surprising that the factor also shows some correlation with Hy (.30).

As expected, the Restraint factor correlated with the Repression scale (.45) and, to a lesser degree, with Si (.31). It also correlated negatively with Ma (−.41). Thus, Restraint appears to reflect a tendency toward behavioral and emotional constraint, as well as toward being less outgoing. These correlations support our naming this factor Restraint.

The Aesthetic Interests factor showed little correlation with any of the Validity, Clinical, or selected Supplementary scales. Its highest correlation was a negative one with Repression (−.25). These findings suggest that this factor is mildly related to expressiveness and that the variance it captures is otherwise not well represented on the MMPI-2, or at least not in the scales we examined here.

Those Scale 5 factors believed to represent core aspects of masculinity-femininity, including Denial of Stereotypical Masculine Interests, Stereotypical Feminine Interests, and Feminine Gender Identity, as well as their composite FM marker, showed low correlations with the Validity, Clinical, and Supplementary scales. Of the three masculinity-femininity factors, Denial of Stereotypical Masculine Interests showed the highest correlation. It correlated .45 with Repression scale. This correlation was .41 when females were considered separately and .53 in males. The implication is that there is a constrained quality to a lack of interest in masculine activities, especially for males but also in females. Conversely, one might speculate that stereotypical masculine interests are related to excitement-seeking. If we consider the interests included on this factor (i.e., forest ranger, soldier, building contractor, science, hunting, auto racer, adventure stories, rough sports), it makes some sense that the lack of interest in them would correlate moderately with Repression. From Table 5.3 in chapter 5, which shows the intercorrelations of the Scale 5 factors, we remember that Denial of Stereotypical Masculine Interests correlated .23 with the Restraint factor (.21 for males and .08 for females). We consider other correlations of the Denial of Stereotypical Interests factor to further enhance our understanding of this relationship.

The highest correlation of the Stereotypical Feminine Interests factor was negligible (−.14 with the F scale). The Feminine Gender Identity factor's highest correlation was even lower (−.12 with the F scale also). The FM marker yielded its highest correlation with the Repression supplementary scale (.27).

This correlation was surely influenced by the moderate correlation of its largest component, Denial of Stereotypical Masculine Interests, with Repression. With the exception of the correlation of the Denial of Stereotypical Masculine Interests factor with Repression, the pattern of correlations suggests that the masculinity-femininity dimension is not captured in existing scales of the MMPI-2. Thus, we see the first substantial evidence that these three Scale 5 factors tap something that existing scales of the MMPI-2 do not measure.

Correlations with the Content Scales

Next, we computed correlations of the factors with the Content scales of the MMPI-2. The results are shown in Table 6.2. Comparable tables with

Table 6.2. Intercorrelations of the Scale 5 Factors with the Content Scales Computed in the Combined Normative Sample

	DSMI	H/A	SFI	LC	AE	FGI	Rt	FM	5
ANX	.12	.63	.07	−.32	.05	.07	−.15	.12	.25
FRS	.38	.25	.27	−.26	.05	.31	.02	.42	.27
OBS	.08	.55	.10	−.40	.07	.08	−.15	.11	.18
DEP	.11	.55	.05	−.37	.06	.08	−.11	.11	.19
HEA	.08	.37	.09	−.27	.06	.05	−.05	.09	.15
BIZ	−.08	.32	.05	−.37	.10	.03	−.23	−.02	.02
ANG	−.05	.45	−.03	−.35	.03	−.01	−.23	−.04	.06
CYN	−.06	.27	−.01	−.71	−.02	−.04	−.19	−.06	−.14
ASP	−.21	.23	−.14	−.64	−.02	−.15	−.35	−.22	−.24
TPA	−.08	.36	−.07	−.45	.00	−.08	−.25	−.10	−.06
LSE	.12	.47	.08	−.37	−.02	.08	−.04	.13	.14
SOD	.07	.28	−.06	−.19	−.19	−.06	.28	.00	.08
FAM	.09	.57	.04	−.34	.08	.09	−.15	.10	.23
WRK	.12	.56	.07	−.38	.04	.09	−.10	.13	.19
TRT	.08	.45	.03	−.46	−.01	.02	−.08	.06	.06

Note. DSMI = Denial of Stereotypical Masculine Interests Subscale; H/A = Hypersensitivity/Anxiety Subscale; SFI = Stereotypical Feminine Interests Subscale; LC = Low Cynicism Subscale; AE = Aesthetic Interests Subscale; FGI = Feminine Gender Identity Subscale; Rt = Restraint Subscale; FM = Femininity Masculinity Scale; 5 = Scale 5.

correlations computed for females and males separately are displayed in Appendices I and J, respectively.

As was found with the clinical scales, the Hypersensitivity/Anxiety factor correlated highly with Content Scales that measure negative emotionality and the absence of positive emotionality. It correlated with ANX (.63), FAM (.57), WRK (.56), DEP (.55), and OBS (.55). Thus, it reflects feeling bad (i.e., anxious and depressed) and having negative feelings toward work and family. The Low Cynicism factor correlated highly in the negative direction with CYN (−.71), suggesting that it is aptly named. The item overlap is substantial with three of the six items on the Low Cynicism factor also included on the twenty-three-item CYN scale. The Low Cynicism factor also showed a strong negative correlation with ASP (−.64), implying that those who score high on Low Cynicism are not likely to engage in antisocial practices. Thus, it may reflect naïve trust and efforts to appear well-adjusted and to cause no problems. Three items on the Low Cynicism factor are also on the twenty-two-item ASP scale.

The highest correlation of the Restraint factor was a moderate negative relationship with ASP (−.35). As expected, someone scoring high on a factor measuring restraint in action would be unlikely to engage in antisocial practices. The Aesthetic Interests factor showed virtually no relationship to any of the Content scales. Again, this lack of significant correlations suggests that it captures a unique dimension on the MMPI-2.

The Denial of Stereotypical Masculine Interests factor showed low correlations with all the Content scales, except that it correlated moderately with FRS (.38). Stereotypical Feminine Interests also correlates highest with FRS, but only at the modest .27 level. Feminine Gender Identity also shows its highest correlations with FRS (.31). It may be that individuals with specific fears and phobias are more attracted to the sedentary interests reflected in Stereotypical Feminine Interests than to the adventuresome interests reflected in Denial of Stereotypical Interests. Alternatively, those with high masculine traits may be less fearful of specific objects than those who score high on the feminine dimension. Notice that the ANX Content Scale showed no such correlations, suggesting that general anxiety unrelated to specific fears is not associated with masculinity-femininity. Note also that FRS is known to tap a unique source of variance in the MMPI-2 and potentially add information not assessed elsewhere (Tonsager & Finn, 1992). However, we must remember that these correlations were, at best, moderate and that the three Scale 5 factors that we believe capture the dimension of masculinity-femininity showed substantial discriminant validity with the Content scales.

Correlations with the Restructured Clinical Scales

We compared the Scale 5 factors to the Restructured Clinical scales developed by Tellegen, Ben-Porath, McNulty, Arbisi, Graham, and Kaemmer (2003). Their aim in developing these restructured scales was to remove from the Clinical scales the pervasive negative emotionality that saturates them, thus resulting in more refined measures of the constructs that they purport to measure. In doing this, they developed a measure of "Demoralization" (RCd), which reflects the general, nonspecific negative emotionality and lack of positive emotionality that permeates the MMPI-2 scales. They then present revised Clinical scales with this variance removed: RC1 Somatic Complaints, RC2 Low Positive Emotions, RC3 Cynicism, RC4 Antisocial Behavior, RC6 Ideas of Malevolence, RC7 Dysfunctional Negative Emotions, RC8 Aberrant Experiences, and RC9 Hypomanic Activation. There is no restructured scale for Si because it is not as permeated with the demoralization factor as the other Clinical scales.

Correlations between the Scale 5 factors and the Restructured scales are shown in Table 6.3. The correlations for females and males separately are shown

Table 6.3. Intercorrelations of the Scale 5 Factors with Restructured Clinical Scales Computed in the Combined Normative Sample

	DSMI	H/A	SFI	LC	AI	FGI	Rt	FM	5
RCd	.12	.59	.06	−.32	.07	.08	−.11	.12	.23
RC1	.09	.31	.09	−.28	.05	.07	−.04	.11	.12
RC2	.12	.32	−.07	−.08	−.11	−.07	.21	.02	.13
RC3	−.05	.26	−.03	−.71	−.02	−.04	−.17	−.06	−.13
RC4	−.21	.29	−.17	−.22	.02	−.15	−.30	−.24	−.07
RC6	−.05	.23	−.01	−.38	.03	−.05	−.17	−.05	−.05
RC7	.11	.60	.12	−.42	.04	.13	−.15	.15	.22
RC8	−.08	.29	.05	−.34	.11	.03	−.22	−.02	.03
RC9	−.23	.34	−.05	−.38	.15	−.09	−.55	−.19	−.07

Note. DSMI = Denial of Stereotypical Masculine Interests Subscale; H/A = Hypersensitivity/Anxiety Subscale; SFI = Stereotypical Feminine Interests Subscale; LC = Low Cynicism Subscale; AI = Aesthetic Interests Subscale; FGI = Feminine Gender Identity Subscale; Rt = Restraint Subscale; FM = Femininity Masculinity Scale; 5 = Scale 5; RCd = Demoralization; RC1 = Somatic Complaints; RC2 = Low Positive Emotions; RC3 = Cynicism; RC4 = Antisocial Behavior; RC6 = Ideas of Malevolence; RC7 = Dysfunctional Negative Emotions; RC8 = Aberrant Experiences; and RC9 = Hypomanic Activation.

in Appendix K and Appendix L, respectively. Remember that the correlations in these tables are spuriously high because the factors and scales contain some of the same items.

Once again, the Hypersensitivity/Anxiety factor shows a number of interesting correlations. It correlates highly with the RCd scale (.59), which is the scale that Tellegen et al. (2003) developed to measure the combination of high negative emotionality and low positive emotionality, and with RC7 (.60), Dysfunctional Negative Emotions, which is the "core" of Pt (Scale 7), once variance associated with Demoralization has been removed. The Hypersensitivity/Anxiety factor correlations with the other Restructured Clinical scales were substantially lower than those observed with their counterpart original clinical scales. Specifically, the high correlation with Sc (Scale 8) observed in the original clinical scales dropped from .60 to .29 in the Restructured Clinical scales. These correlations support the contention by Tellegen et al. that the negative emotionality component has been reduced in the restructured version of the scale. Thus, given this new pattern of correlations, the label of Hypersensitivity/Anxiety for our factor seems to be an accurate one.

As expected, the Low Cynicism factor correlates strongly with RC3 (−.71). Of course, this is partially a result of the item overlap. Half of the six items on the Low Cynicism factor are also on the fifteen-item RC3 scale. Furthermore, the correlation is equally strong in males and females (−.71 in both). It correlated .30 with the original clinical Scale 3 (.22 in females and .30 in males). Tellegen et al. believe that Hy (Scale 3) with the negative emotionality removed is a purer measure of cynicism, the name they adopted for the restructured version. Thus, the high correlation of the Restructured Scale 3 with our Low Cynicism factor suggests that we are right on target, that our Low Cynicism factor captures just that.

The Restraint factor found its highest correlation (−.55) with RC9 (the restructured scale labeled Hypomanic Activation). This negative relationship suggests that our factor measures something moderately opposite the high activity level captured by RC9 and supports the moniker "restraint."

The rest of our factors show low correlations with all the Restructured Clinical scales. Overall, these correlations in the normative data between the Restructured Clinical scales and the new Scale 5 factors provide additional strong evidence for the convergent and divergent validity of the Scale 5 factors of the MMPI-2.

Correlations with the PSY-5 Scales

We next examined the correlations between the Scale 5 factors and the MMPI-2 PSY-5 scales developed by Harkness, McNulty, and Ben-Porath (1995). They identified scales for Aggression, Psychoticism, Disconstraint, Negative

Table 6.4. Intercorrelations of the Scale 5 Factors with the PSY-5 Scales Computed in the Combined Normative Sample

	DSMI	H/A	SFI	LC	AE	FGI	Rt	FM	5
AGG	−.26	.02	−.15	−.32	.07	−.18	−.35	−.27	−.25
PSY	−.06	.40	.03	−.45	.10	.00	−.23	−.03	.03
DISC	−.45	.07	−.29	−.12	.02	−.31	−.44	−.47	−.27
NEGE	.14	.65	.08	−.36	.06	.09	−.17	.14	.25
INTR	.14	.20	−.15	−.06	−.20	−.10	.42	.00	.08

Note. DSMI = Denial of Stereotypical Masculine Interests Subscale; H/A = Hypersensitivity/Anxiety Subscale; SFI = Stereotypical Feminine Interests Subscale; LC = Low Cynicism Subscale; AE = Aesthetic Interests Subscale; FGI = Feminine Gender Identity Subscale; Rt = Restraint Subscale; 5 = Scale 5; FM = Femininity-Masculinity Scale; AGG = Aggression; PSY = Psychoticism; DISC = Disconstraint; NEGE = Negative Emotionality; INTR= Introversion.

Emotionality, and Introversion (formerly called Low Positive Emotionality). The results for the combined sample are shown in Table 6.4, for females in Appendix M, and for males in Appendix N.

Consistent with emerging expectations, the Hypersensitivity/Anxiety factor correlated highly (.65) with NEGE (Negative Emotionality) and moderately (.40) with PSY (Psychoticism). Low Cynicism correlated moderately negatively (−.45) with PSY, suggesting that cynicism may be moderately related to disturbed thinking. The Aesthetic Interests factor had no substantial correlation with any of the PSY-5 scales, suggesting, again, that it captures some dimension that is not well-represented elsewhere in the MMPI-2. As expected, the Restraint factor was moderately negatively correlated (−.44) with DISC (Disconstraint). This correlation was lower than we might expect, but it confirmed the expectation that our Restraint factor is related to inhibition of action.

The Denial of Stereotypical Masculine Interests factor, Stereotypical Feminine Interests factor, Feminine Gender Identity factor, and the composite FM marker were not substantially correlated with any of the PSY-5 scales, except for DISC (Disconstraint). The highest correlation for each of these four factors was with DISC, with Denial of Stereotypical Masculine Interests (−.45), Stereotypical Feminine Interests (−.29), Feminine Gender Identity (−.31), and FM (−.47). This suggests that high scores on all these scales reflect a tendency to be more reflective than impulsive, perhaps even to stifle one's words and actions. Given that elevations on each of these masculinity-femininity factors indicate what we would call a feminine tendency, the implication of the correlations with DISC is that femininity carries with it more reserved, less aggressive behavior than masculinity.

Correlations with Other Measures of Masculinity-Femininity in the MMPI

We also wanted to consider the Scale 5 factors in comparison to past efforts to develop masculinity-femininity-related scales in the MMPI. Accordingly, we looked at correlations between our factors and those scales described in chapter 3 that were developed by Harris (Ap Scale), Panton (Hsx Scale; 1960), Althof, Lothstein, Jones, and Shen (Gd Scale; 1983), and McGrath, Sapareto, and Pogge (Mfp Scale; 1998). Table 6.5 shows the correlations of these four existing masculinity-femininity scales with the Scale 5 factors. The tables for females and males are shown separately in Appendices O and P, respectively.

The Ap and the Hsx scales showed low correlations with the Scale 5 factors. They therefore provide little insight into the dimensions identified by the Scale 5 factors. However, the Gd and Mfp scales showed more defined relationships to the factors. Gd and, to a lesser extent, Mfp had moderate to high correlations with the four masculinity-femininity factors and low correlations with the other Scale 5 factors. Gd correlated with Denial of Stereotypical Masculine Interests (.47), Stereotypical Feminine Interests (.55), Feminine Gender Identity (.66), and FM (.69), showing good convergent validity. It also correlated minimally with Hypersensitivity/Anxiety (−.08), Low Cynicism (.27), Aesthetic Interests (.25), and Restraint (.13), thereby showing good discriminate validity.

Table 6.5. Intercorrelations of the Scale 5 Factors with Other MMPI Measures of Masculinity-Femininity Computed in the Combined Normative Sample

	DSMI	H/A	SFI	LC	AE	FGI	Rt	FM	5
Ap	.27	.24	.21	.25	.12	.28	.15	.33	.39
Gd	.47	−.08	.55	.27	.25	.66	.13	.69	.54
Hsx	.14	−.35	.22	.31	.05	.13	.22	.21	.13
Mfp	.49	.43	.37	−.01	.09	.45	.27	.57	.54

Note. DSMI = Denial of Stereotypical Masculine Interests ; H/A = Hypersensitivity/Anxiety; SFI = Stereotypical Feminine Interests; LC = Low Cynicism; AE = Aesthetic Interests; FGI = Feminine Gender Identity; Rt = Restraint; FM = Femininity-Masculinity marker scale; 5 = Scale 5; Ap = Harris's Ap Scale; Gd = Althof et al. Gd Scale; Hsx = Panton's Hsx Scale; Mfp = McGrath et al. Mfp Scale.

The Mfp scale showed a similar pattern, but with lower convergent correlations and less clear discriminant correlations, especially with the Hypersensitivity/Anxiety factor (.43). This latter finding is not unexpected, in that Mfp was constructed as a measure of psychopathology. Thus, the Gd scale appears to be the best of the older scales in removing the negative emotionality and other confounding dimensions from the measurement of masculinity-femininity.

The conclusions that can be drawn from these correlations become clearer as we further explore the nature of the Scale 5 factors, but the early implication is that the Gd scale developed by Althof, Lothstein, Jones, and Shen (1983) is the best measure of masculinity-femininity developed to date from the MMPI item pool. Although the Gd scale presents a global measure of masculinity-femininity that is reasonably similar to the FM marker scale, we can speculate that the Gd scale does not provide the refinement of measurement possible with the three identified components of FM represented in the Scale 5 factors.

Summary of Intercorrelations with Other MMPI-2 Scales

Let us briefly summarize the correlations of the Scale 5 factors with other scales of the MMPI. In general, the highest correlations with other MMPI scales involve those factors that are not related to masculinity-femininity. We believe that this is largely because these factors measure other aspects of personality and that these constructs are better measured by other scales of the MMPI: Hypersensitivity/Anxiety by Pt (.66), 8 (.60), S (−.60), A (.63), Mt (.60), ANX (.63), RCd (.59), RC7 (.60), NEGE (.65); Low Cynicism by S (.54), CYN (−.71), ASP (−.64), RC3 (−.71); and Restraint by Ma (−.41), R (.45), RC9 (−.55), DISC (−.44), INTR (.42). The Aesthetic Interests factor does not correlate highly with any other MMPI-2 scale, again suggesting that its variance is not well-represented elsewhere on the MMPI-2.

The highest correlations of the Denial of Stereotypical Masculine Interests factor are with R (.45), FRS (.38), DISC (−.45), Gd (.47), and Mfp (.49). The Stereotypical Feminine Interests factor correlates with F (−.14), FRS (.27), DISC (−.29), Gd (.55), and Mfp (.37). The Feminine Gender Identity factor correlates with F (−.12), FRS (.31), DISC (−.31), Gd (.66) and Mfp (.45). The FM marker scale correlates with D (.20), R (.27), FRS (.42), APS (−.22), RC4 (−.24), DISC (−.47), AGG (−.27), Gd (.69), and Mfp (.57). These data suggest that masculinity-femininity has a moderately low association with specific fears (which captures a unique component of the MMPI-2) and with inhibition. As stated earlier, these correlations also suggest that the Gd scale is probably the best measure of masculinity-femininity that has been previously developed from the MMPI.

Convergent and Discriminant Validity with MMPI-2-RF Interest Scales

Finally, we also examined correlations between our Scale 5 factors and the two new interest scales of the MMPI-2-RF, AES (Aesthetic/Literary Interests) and MEC (Mechanical/Physical Interests). (See Table 6.6 for the combined data and Appendices Q and R for the females and males, respectively.) As discussed in chapter 3, these scales were developed by restructuring Scale 5, much as was done in developing the Restructured Clinical scales (Tellegen et al., 2003). In fact, as regards Scale 5, it can be said that the goals of our project and those of Tellegen and colleagues were highly similar, although we extracted a larger number of factors from Scale 5 than they did.

Our Aesthetic Interests factor correlated highly with AES (.93). This is to be expected, given that all five of the items on the Aesthetic Interest factor are also included on the seven-item AES factor. The Stereotypical Feminine Interests factor is also related to AES (.54), but this correlation is also inflated because the two remaining items on the AES factor are also included on the six-item Stereotypical Feminine Interests factor. This splitting of the AES items between the two factors reflects the relationship between Stereotypical Feminine Interests and Aesthetic Interests (.32) observed in the intercorrelations of our factors (see Table 5.3).

The Denial of Stereotypical Masculine Interests factor finds its highest correlation with MEC (−.91), which is not surprising, given that eight of its eleven items are on the nine-item MEC scale. The Feminine Gender Identity factor correlates with MEC (−.47) and has no item overlap with that factor. It correlates only .29 with AES, suggesting that aesthetic interests and feminine gender identity are only moderately related. Interestingly, this correlation drops when males and females are considered separately (see Appendices Q and R).

Table 6.6. Intercorrelations of the Scale 5 Factors with the MMPI-2-RF Interest Scales Computed in the Combined Normative Sample

	DSMI	H/A	SFI	LC	AE	FGI	Rt	FM	5
AES	.09	.20	.54	.05	.93	.29	−.06	.34	.56
MEC	−.91	−.13	−.27	−.14	−.08	−.47	−.28	−.79	−.59

Note. DSMI = Denial of Stereotypical Masculine Interests Subscale; H/A = Hypersensitivity/Anxiety Subscale; SFI = Stereotypical Feminine Interests Subscale; LC = Low Cynicism Subscale; AE = Aesthetic Interests Subscale; FGI = Feminine Gender Identity Subscale; Rt = Restraint Subscale; FM = Femininity-Masculinity Scale; 5 = Scale 5; AES = Aesthetic/Literary Interests; MEC = Mechanical/Physical Interests.

For males, the correlations between Feminine Gender Identity and AES is .20; for females, it drops to a negligible .06.

So, to summarize, two of our subscales are highly similar, although not identical, to AES and MEC. The Scale 5 variance captured in our subscales that was not located and refined when Tellegen et al. (2003) restructured Scale 5 is that related to feminine gender identity.

Discriminant and Convergent Validity in College Samples

Our next effort in exploring the discriminant and convergent validity of the Scale 5 factors involved collecting a broad range of data from samples of college students. These samples were collected in 1990 and 1992 at the University of Texas at Austin (henceforth called the UT90 and UT92 samples, respectively). The subjects were students in introductory psychology classes who were required to participate in research projects for class credit. In the comparisons that follow, the results from the UT90 data are computed using the unaugmented factors (i.e., Denial of Stereotypical Masculine Interests and Feminine Gender Identity), whereas the results from the UT92 sample are computed using the final augmented factors.

The UT90 Study

The UT90 study surveyed 817 college students (434 females and 383 males) in introductory psychology classes at the University of Texas at Austin during the Summer and Fall semesters of 1990. The average age of females was 20.5 years (standard deviation = 2.8; range 19 to 50). The average age of males was 20.8 years (standard deviation = 2.7; range 19 to 55).

The UT90 Questionnaire

The three hundred-item UT90 questionnaire, which we used to cross-validate the factors in chapter 4, also contained various measures of masculinity-femininity, gender identity, sexual orientation, and personality markers. The following "masculinity-femininity" scales were included on the questionnaire: Scale 5 of the Minnesota Multiphasic Personality Inventory-2 (MMPI-2; Butcher, Dahlstrom, Graham, Tellegen, & Kaemmer, 1989), the Extended Personal Attributes Questionnaire (EPAQ; Spence, Helmreich, & Holahan, 1979), the F/M scale from the California Personality Inventory (CPI; Gough, 1966), the Short-Form Sex Role Behavior Scale (SRBS; Orlofsky & O'Heron, 1987), and the Sex Role Identity Scale (SRIS; Storms, 1979). We considered including the widely used Bem Sex Role Inventory (BSRI; Bem, 1981b), but elected not to because of its very high correlations with the EPAQ. A detailed description of these measures is available in chapters 2 and 3.

We chose these existing measures of masculinity-femininity and related characteristics to be included on the questionnaire because they provided coverage of the broad domain of what had been considered masculinity-femininity at the time that we collected our data. These previous conceptualizations included personality traits (dominance-poise, nurturance-warmth, dependency, self-confidence, fearfulness, emotional sensitivity, tolerance of vulgarity, and exhibitionism), stereotypical interests, feminist values, as well as gender identity and sexual orientation.

The EPAQ contains items that cover the dominance-poise and nurturance-warmth dimensions of personality. The CPI F/M scale and the Short-Form Sex Role Behavior Scale represent the conventional gender-differentiating qualities of traditional masculinity-femininity measures. They likely are multidimensional measures of personality traits, including dependency, self-confidence, fearfulness, emotional sensitivity, and exhibitionism, as well as interests. The SRIS represents a direct self-rating of masculinity-femininity that likely is a good measure of gender identity.

Of the gender identity measures available, we selected the one constructed by Finn (1986a). The Finn scale was preferred over other measures of gender identity in that it is less intrusive, offensive, and threatening to college students (e.g., it does not ask males about wearing women's underwear, as does the Feminine Gender Identity Scale [Freund, Nagler, Langevin, Zajac, & Steiner, 1974]). Finn's scale also has more variance within gender as a result of its more subtle items. We selected eighteen items from the female version of the Gender Identity Scale (GIF) (Finn, 1986a; see Appendix S), and eighteen items from the male version (GIM) (see Appendix T).

Of possible measures to assess the sexual orientation of the subjects, the two items used by Bailey, Willerman, and Parks (1991) were selected. One of the questions measures the extent to which the subject's sexual fantasies involve the same and opposite gender (Fantasy); the other measures the extent of the subject's sexual experience with the same and opposite gender (Experience). This measure is brief, direct, and seems to address two major aspects of sexual orientation. More direct assessment of erotic interests is not essential to the present study and would present practical difficulties. In assessing college students whose sexual experience may be limited, in flux, or determined by outside factors, the Fantasy measure is likely to be the best marker of sexual orientation.

We also included twelve items selected from each of three higher-order personality dimensions measured by the Multidimensional Personality

Questionnaire (MPQ; Tellegen, 1982): Positive Emotionality (MPQP), Negative Emotionality (MPQN), and Constraint (MPQC). We believed that these abbreviated personality factors would provide reasonable markers of these major personality dimensions.

Results for the UT90 Study

The correlations of Scale 5 factors with various measures of masculinity-femininity, gender identity, sexual orientation, and personality in the UT90 sample are displayed in Table 6.7. Remember that the Denial of Stereotypical Masculine Interests factor and the Feminine Gender Identity factor are represented in their unaugmented form.

Stereotypical Interests. The Denial of Stereotypical Masculine Interests factor (unaugmented) correlated with measures of masculinity-femininity in such a way as to suggest that it taps the reverse of a traditional masculine attribute. It correlated .51 with female gender. The Stereotypical Feminine Interests factor correlated in a similar pattern as the Denial of Stereotypical Masculine Interests factor (unaugmented), suggesting that it measures a traditional feminine attribute. It correlated .63 with female gender. Both of these factors had low correlations with the MPQ marker scales, showing that they tap variance outside the major personality domains reflected in that instrument.

Hypersensitivity/Anxiety. Hypersensitivity/Anxiety showed its highest correlation (.55) with MPQ Negative Emotionality, although it also showed a small negative correlation with MPQ Positive Emotionality (−.21). In addition, Hypersensitivity/Anxiety had relatively low correlations with measures of masculinity-femininity, gender identity, and sexual orientation. The convergence and discrimination shown by these correlations suggest that Hypersensitivity/Anxiety is not primarily a measure of masculinity-femininity, but rather a measure of negative emotionality and to some extent of low positive emotionality.

Low Cynicism. Low Cynicism showed its highest correlation (.41) with the MPQ negative emotionality marker also. It showed even lower correlations with measures of masculinity-femininity, gender identity, and sexual orientation than did the Hypersensitivity/Anxiety factor. This suggests that Low Cynicism is also measuring an aspect of the higher-order personality trait negative emotionality.

Aesthetic Interests. Aesthetic Interests showed its highest correlation (.42) with the femininity scale of Orlofsky's (1981) SRBS. It did not correlate as highly with other measures of masculinity-femininity. Its correlation with female gender was .26. Orlofsky's instrument differs from other traditional

Table 6.7. Correlations of Scale 5 Factors with Measures of Masculinity-Femininity, Gender Identity, Sexual Orientation, and Personality in the UT90 Sample (Computed in Male, Female, and Combined Data)

	DSMI [unaug]	H/A	SFI	LC	AE	FGI [unaug]	Rt
Female gender	.51	.17	.63	.19	.26	.77	.15
(GIM)	(.15)	(.29)	(.36)	(−.01)	(.27)	(.48)	(.03)
GIF	**−.26**	**.06**	**−.10**	**−.09**	**−.05**	**−.33**	**.00**
SRIS	−.54	−.21	−.63	−.22	−.30	−.79	−.16
	(−.16)	(−.27)	(−.34)	(−.19)	(−.35)	(−.44)	(−.11)
	−.32	**.01**	**−.10**	**−.05**	**.04**	**−.25**	**−.01**
Fantasy	.03	.11	.05	−.01	.12	.10	−.01
	(.14)	(.19)	(.14)	(.11)	(.21)	(.33)	(.00)
	−.12	**.04**	**.04**	**−.12**	**.04**	**−.02**	**−.01**
Experience	−.06	.03	.02	−.02	.01	−.01	−.06
	(.03)	(.08)	(.19)	(.08)	(.11)	(.18)	(−.06)
	−.12	**.00**	**.03**	**−.09**	**−.07**	**−.06**	**−.04**
CPI F/M	.61	.38	.54	.09	.29	.65	.22
	(.47)	(.34)	(.16)	(−.04)	(.17)	(.28)	(.17)
	.34	**.41**	**.20**	**−.08**	**.14**	**.19**	**.14**
PAQM	−.31	−.33	−.33	−.12	−.10	−.43	−.27
	(−.10)	(−.31)	(−.10)	(−.06)	(−.13)	(−.23)	(−.20)
	−.13	**−.27**	**−.06**	**−.02**	**.13**	**−.08**	**−.26**
PAQF	.30	.36	.36	.01	.19	.38	.03
	(.12)	(.38)	(.15)	(−.07)	(.21)	(.14)	(−.08)
	.12	**.26**	**.14**	**−.08**	**.00**	**.10**	**.03**
SRBSM	−.51	−.16	−.38	−.14	−.07	−.60	−.35
	(−.25)	(−.09)	(−.09)	(−.04)	(.01)	(−.25)	(−.38)
	−.32	**−.02**	**.15**	**.01**	**.23**	**−.14**	**−.31**
SRBSF	.24	.20	.63	.17	.42	.56	.08
	(−.08)	(.13)	(.32)	(.14)	(.39)	(.21)	(.08)
	−.15	**.10**	**.45**	**.00**	**.30**	**.11**	**−.09**

(Continued)

Table 6.7. (*Continued*)

	DSMI [unaug]	H/A	SFI	LC	AE	FGI [unaug]	Rt
SRBSS	−.55	−.23	−.66	−.20	−.31	−.78	−.15
	(−.33)	(−.19)	(−.25)	(−.13)	(−.26)	(−.37)	(−.15)
	−.17	**−.11**	**−.33**	**.02**	**−.10**	**−.30**	**.05**
MPQP	−.05	−.21	.14	.12	.16	.07	−.10
	(−.12)	(−.23)	(.06)	(.02)	(.01)	(−.10)	(−.10)
	−.15	**−.24**	**.11**	**.18**	**.26**	**.03**	**−.13**
MPQN	.11	.55	−.04	−.41	.03	.00	−.21
	(.12)	(.54)	(−.03)	(−.42)	(.08)	(.07)	(−.23)
	.16	**.59**	**−.05**	**−.40**	**−.01**	**−.05**	**−.20**
MPQC	.16	.01	.17	.01	−.07	.16	.24
	(.00)	(−.07)	(−.03)	(.00)	(−.15)	(−.10)	(.16)
	.11	**−.01**	**.06**	**−.06**	**−.14**	**.00**	**.26**

Note. The correlation for the combined data is on the top of each cell, the correlation for the male data is in the middle in parentheses, and the female correlation is on the bottom in bold.

Note. DSMI = Denial of Stereotypical Interests (Unaugmented); H/A = Hypersensitivity/ Anxiety; SFI = Stereotypical Feminine Interests; LC = Low Cynicism; AE = Aesthetic Interests; FGI = Feminine Gender Identity (Unaugmented); Rt = Restraint; CPI = the masculinity-femininity scale of the California Psychological Inventory; PAQM = the M scale of the Personal Attributes Questionnaire; PAQF = the F scale of the Personal Attributes Questionnaire; SRBSM = the masculinity scale of the Sex Role Behavior Scale; SRBSF = the femininity scale of the Sex Role Behavior Scale; SRBSS = the sex-specific scale of the Sex Role Behavior Scale; SRIS = Sex Role Identity Scale; GIM= Gender Identity Scale-feminine gender identity in males; GIF=Gender Identity Scale-masculine gender identity in females; Fantasy = Fantasy measure of sexual orientation; Experience = Experience measure of sexual orientation; MPQP = Positive Emotionality from the MPQ; MPQN = Negative Emotionality from the MPQ; MPQC = Constraint from the MPQ.

masculinity-femininity measures in that he did not use gender differences in endorsement rates to construct scales. He also did not view male and female interests as mutually exclusive and therefore allowed a moderate positive correlation between the male-valued scale and the female-valued scale of the SRBS. The fact that Aesthetic Interests diverged from stereotypical masculine and feminine interests in our factor analyses suggests that it too may reflect common interests between the genders. Its correlation with female gender suggests a moderate predominance of female-valued interests, but it appears not to be as laden with traditional gender expectations as the other two interest scales.

This explanation is supported by the fact that gender differences appeared in the pattern of intercorrelations of this factor. For example, for males the score on Aesthetic Interests is negatively correlated (−.35) with their self-rating of masculinity (i.e., SRIS score), whereas for females the correlation is negligible (.04). Thus, males may see these interests as feminine, whereas females do not consider them to be gender-linked. Perhaps the most we can say about the Aesthetic Interests factor is that it is mildly related to traditional concepts of femininity, perhaps more so for males. It is also interesting to note that, for females, the Aesthetic Interests factor correlated moderately with Positive Emotionality (.26), whereas, for males, this correlation was negligible (.01).

Feminine Gender Identity. The Feminine Gender Identity factor (unaugmented) moderately to highly correlated with other measures of gender identity (e.g., SRIS = −.79; GIM = .48; GIF = −.33), suggesting that this factor is a reasonable measure of gender identity. It is also interesting to note that this factor correlated with sexual orientation for males (.33 with Fantasy), but not for females (−.02). (Remember: the higher the score is on Fantasy or Experience, the more the person's sexual fantasies or experiences involve members of one's own gender). Feminine Gender Identity (unaugmented) demonstrated the highest correlations of all the factors with external measures of masculinity-femininity. It was highly positively correlated with female gender (.77) and with traditional femininity (e.g., CPI F/M = .65), and it was also highly negatively correlated with traditional masculinity (SRBSS = −.78). The strength of these correlations supports Spence's (1985) assertion that gender identity may be the most important variable underlying traditional masculinity-femininity measures. Again, the extremely low correlations of this factor and the MPQ marker scales suggest that gender identity is quite independent of those more frequently researched dimensions of personality.

Restraint. Restraint was moderately negatively correlated with other measures of "masculine" personality traits (e.g., PAQM = −.27; SRBSM = −.35), confirming the overlap between these measures and broader gender-related personality traits (Tellegen & Lubinski, 1983). The Restraint factor was uncorrelated with gender identity or with sexual orientation. However, it showed a moderate correlation (.24) with the Constraint personality measure, suggesting that Restraint is related to the personality dimension of Constraint. It also showed a slightly lower negative correlation (−.21) with Negative Emotionality.

Conclusions from UT90 data

Thus, major personality dimensions appear to be represented in the Scale 5 factors. Hypersensitivity/Anxiety and Low Cynicism are clearly related to Negative Emotionality, and Restraint seems to be moderately related to Constraint and negatively related to Negative Emotionality. Hypersensitivity/Anxiety also shows some correlation with low Positive Emotionality. In females, Aesthetic Interests correlated somewhat with Positive Emotionality, but it did not for males. Sexual orientation showed a moderate correlation with the Feminine Gender Identity factor (unaugmented) in males (Fantasy = .33), but not in females (Fantasy = −.02).

The external correlates suggest that the Denial of Stereotypical Masculine Interests factor and the Stereotypical Feminine Interests factor are measures of traditional masculinity-femininity. Feminine Gender Identity (unaugmented) seems to be a measure of gender identity. We then gathered a second sample of students to further explore the convergent and discriminant patterns of the Scale 5 factors.

The UT92 Study

The second sample we collected to examine the construct validity of the Scale 5 factors was the UT92 sample. It allowed for refined comparisons between the Scale 5 factors and external correlates, this time including the augmented factors. Thus, we used the UT92 sample not only to cross-validate the factors that we developed in chapter 4, but also to corroborate the findings from the UT90 sample and to investigate the relationship of the new GM and GF scales to other measures.

The UT92 sample was collected during the Spring semester of 1992 at the University of Texas at Austin. It consisted of 402 subjects (258 males and 144 females) who were introductory psychology students. The average age of females was 20.2 years (standard deviation = 2.4; range 18 to 30). The average of males was 20.8 years (standard deviation = 2.3; range 19 to 30).

The UT92 Questionnaire

The UT92 questionnaire contained 398 items, including all Scale 5 items intermixed with other selected MMPI-2 items, other measures of masculinity-femininity, gender identity, sexual orientation, and personality. The masculinity-femininity measures included the following: GM and GF scales of the MMPI-2; the Personal Attributes Questionnaire (PAQ; Spence, Helmreich, & Holahan, 1979); the F/M scales and the Baucom scales for masculine qualities (BMS) and feminine qualities (BFM) from the California Psychological Inventory (CPI; Gough, 1987); the Sex Role Identity Scale (SRIS; Storms, 1979); and the Male-Female Relations Questionnaire (MFRQ; Spence, Helmreich, & Sawin, 1980). We included the MFRQ to reflect traditional sex-typed values and interests and feminist values. Detailed descriptions of these measures are provided in chapter 2. As in the UT90 questionnaire, we used the gender identity measures developed by Finn (1986a). The recommended twenty items from the male version of the Gender Identity Scale (GIM; Finn, 1986a) were included on the male UT92 questionnaire, and the suggested 14 items from the female version (GIF), on the female form. We also again used the two items measuring sexual orientation developed by Bailey, Willerman, and Parks (1991).

We included on the questionnaire items from each of the four higher-order personality dimensions of Positive Emotionality-communal (MPQPc), Positive Emotionality-agentic (MPQPa), Negative Emotionality (MPQN), and Constraint (MPQC), measured by the Multidimensional Personality Questionnaire (MPQ; Tellegen, 1982). These markers were refined from our use of MPQ personality markers in the UT90 study. This time we did not select the MPQ items used, but rather used the subset suggested by Tellegen and Waller (2008) to accurately measure these four higher-order dimensions.

A validity scale was also included to allow identification of potential invalid data. Pairs of items from the VRIN scale (Variable Response Inconsistency) of the MMPI-2 were selected to measure inconsistent responding and delete data of questionable validity (see Martin, 1993, for details).

Reliability of the Measures

We examined the reliability of the measures used, the parameters of Scale 5 in the UT92 sample, and the correlations of the Scale 5 factors with the various measures of masculinity-femininity, gender identity, sexual orientation, and personality. Our first task was to investigate the reliability of the UT92 data. First, we examined the validity indicators that we had included on the questionnaire. Using the same proportions recommended by Graham (1987) to detect invalid profiles (thirteen of sixty-seven items), we deleted subjects who scored above 4 on the subset of VRIN items. This led to the exclusion of eleven subjects (six males and five females). Furthermore, a subject's score on a particular measure was deleted if it was deemed that an insufficient number of items had been completed. Stringent criteria (i.e., at least 90 percent of a measure had to be completed in order for the score to be included) eliminated only a few subjects' scores.

Next, we compared the sample means to those presented as normative data for the measures. The mean scores of the UT92 sample on Scale 5, GM, and GF of the MMPI-2 compared favorably with the normative sample for the MMPI-2 (Butcher et al., 1989) and with norms on the MMPI-2 for college students (Butcher, Graham, Dahlstrom, & Bowman, 1990). Appendix U shows the comparison of the Scale 5, GM, and GF means found in the normative samples to those found in the UT92 sample. Additionally, means in the UT92 sample agreed closely with the normative data for the CPI, as shown in Appendix V, and the PAQ, as shown in Appendix W.

However, comparisons of the UT92 data to the Male-Female Relations Questionnaire (MFRQ) normative data based on college students showed substantial differences (displayed in Appendix X). The UT92 sample scored consistently lower on the MFRQ measures than those in the 1980 normative sample of that instrument (which was based on a sample of 250 male and 258 female college students, also from the University of Texas). One possible reason for this difference is that, in the twelve years between the samples, students may have become less traditional in their view of male-female roles. If this is true, it suggests a surprisingly rapid change in beliefs. However, the MFRQ is a measure of attitudes, which can change rapidly, rather than of traits, which are expected to be relatively stable.

We calculated the means and standard deviations of the Scale 5 factors on the UT92 data and found that they were similar to those obtained in the UT90 data. Then we computed the coefficients of internal consistency for the factors in the UT92 data. These results were also similar to those in the UT90 data. As in the UT90 sample, a few items detracted from alpha consistency in the college population. However, no item detracted from alpha in both the male and female data.

In summary, the reliability of the measures contained on the UT92 questionnaire seemed high. The data were groomed to exclude possible invalid protocols, resulting in only a few deletions. The measures generally paralleled expectations in terms of means and standard deviations compared to known parameters. We now examine the intercorrelations of the measures to glean information about the validity of the Scale 5 factors.

Intercorrelations of Various Measures in the UT92 Sample

Correlations between the Scale 5 factors and various measures of masculinity-femininity, gender identity, sexual orientation, and personality were calculated on the UT92 data. The results are shown in Table 6.8.

Table 6.8. Correlations of Scale 5 Factors with Measures of Masculinity-Femininity, Gender Identity, Sexual Orientation, and Personality in the UT92 Sample (Computed in Male, Female, and Combined Data)

	DSMI [Aug]	H/A	SFI	LC	AE	FGI [Aug]	Rt	FM
Female gender	.59	.21	.60	.18	.26	.83	.11	.82
(GIM)	(.15)	(,28)	(.29)	(.04)	(.26)	(.37)	(.18)	(.37)
GIF	**−.41**	**−.06**	**−.33**	**−.02**	**.03**	**−.50**	**−.01**	**−.59**
SRIS	−.58	−.24	−.59	−.22	−.29	−.77	−.14	−.79
	(−.13)	(−.20)	(−.27)	(−.18)	(−.22)	(−.24)	(−.15)	(−.30)
	−.35	**−.01**	**−.13**	**−.04**	**.02**	**−.29**	**.01**	**−.38**
Fantasy	.18	.15	.09	.03	.14	.13	.08	.18
	(.16)	(.11)	(.07)	(.06)	(.12)	(.15)	(.02)	(.21)
	.08	**.16**	**−.03**	**−.06**	**.10**	**−.08**	**.13**	**.03**
Experience	−.02	−.04	−.03	.07	.02	−.02	−.01	b
	(.03)	(−.07)	(.02)	(.10)	(.04)	(.06)	(.00)	b
	.03[a]	**.16**	**.06**	**.06**	**.04**	**.17**[a]	**.00**	b
GM	−.45	−.60	−.47	.08	−.27	−.51	−.02	−.63
	(−.20)	(−.64)	(−.17)	(.18)	(−.23)	(−.14)	(−.04)	(−.30)
	−.27	**−.57**	**−.15**	**.35**	**.00**	**−.12**	**.22**	**−.32**
GF	.60	.25	.56	.27	.26	.68	.29	.80
	(.45)	(.19)	(.20)	(.23)	(.16)	(.32)	(.40)	(.58)
	.29	**.06**	**.33**	**.17**	**−.01**	**.38**	**.08**	**.56**
CPI F/M	.73	.39	.50	.13	.30	.59	.21	.79
	(.59)	(.30)	(.14)	(.05)	(.23)	(.05)	(.30)	(.58)
	.51	**.46**	**.20**	**.05**	**.06**	**.19**	**−.05**	**.56**
BMS	−.30	−.61	−.22	.23	−.03	−.31	−.07	−.36
	(−.16)	(−.61)	(−.09)	(.23)	(.00)	(−.18)	(−.12)	(−.24)
	−.16	**−.54**	**.00**	**.41**	**.15**	**−.02**	**.10**	**−.16**
BFM	.66	.03	.35	.24	.05	.41	.37	.60
	(.47)	(−.06)	(−.02)	(.18)	(−.09)	(−.14)	(.41)	(.34)
	.37	**−.15**	**.19**	**.18**	**−.12**	**.22**	**.27**	**.44**
PAQM	−.22	−.45	−.17	.06	−.02	−.23	−.13	−.27
	(−.12)	(−.43)	(−.01)	(.10)	(−.04)	(−.07)	(−.17)	(−.14)
	−.04	**−.41**	**−.06**	**.13**	**.21**	**.00**	**.00**	**−.11**

(*Continued*)

Table 6.8. (*Continued*)

	DSMI [Aug]	H/A	SFI	LC	AE	FGI [Aug]	Rt	FM
PAQF	.16	.10	.30	.22	.20	.23	.07	.26
	(−.04)	(.02)	(.20)	(.24)	(.23)	(.03)	(.05)	(.05)
	.21	**.13**	**.21**	**.09**	**−.02**	**.13**	**.01**	**.24**
MFRQ	−.11	.12	−.15	−.34	−.22	−.18	−.28	[b]
	(−.15)	(.19)	(−.25)	(−.37)	(−.26)	(−.23)	(−.33)	[b]
	.12[a]	**.03**	**.08**	**−.24**	**−.11**	**−.07**[a]	**−.18**	[b]
MPQPc	.18	−.03	.13	.17	.20	.17	−.28	.20
	(.00)	(−.14)	(−.02)	(.14)	(.17)	(−.08)	(−.29)	(−.04)
	.21	**.05**	**.03**	**.14**	**.13**	**.14**	**−.35**	**.22**
MPQPa	−.17	−.18	.05	.14	.15	.00	−.08	−.08
	(−.23)	(−.17)	(.05)	(.07)	(.06)	(−.04)	(−.16)	(−.18)
	−.18	**−.23**	**.10**	**.25**	**.32**	**.07**	**.05**	**−.09**
MPQN	.05	.67	.11	−.32	.13	.10	−.21	.11
	(.01)	(.67)	(.07)	(−.39)	(.10)	(.00)	(−.18)	(.05)
	−.04	**.65**	**.04**	**−.28**	**.11**	**.08**	**−.30**	**.04**
MPQC	.27	.15	.15	−.08	−.14	.18	.15	.27
	(.24)	(.13)	(−.05)	(−.06)	(−.16)	(−.07)	(.13)	(.18)
	.13	**.09**	**.16**	**−.21**	**−.27**	**.20**	**.13**	**.24**

Note. The correlation for the combined data is on the top of each cell, the correlation for the male data is in the middle in parentheses, and the female correlation is on the bottom in bold.

Note. DSMI = Denial of Stereotypical Interests (Augmented); H/A = Hypersensitivity/Anxiety; SFI = Stereotypical Feminine Interests; LC = Low Cynicism; AE = Aesthetic Interests; FGI = Feminine Gender Identity (Augmented); Rt = Restraint; FM = Femininity-Masculinity scale; CPI = the masculinity-femininity scale of the California Psychological Inventory; PAQM = the M scale of the Personal Attributes Questionnaire; PAQF = the F scale of the Personal Attributes Questionnaire; GM = GM scale of the MMPI-2; GF = GF scale from the MMPI-2; MFRQ = Male-Female Relations Questionnaire; BMS = Baucom Masculine Scale; BFM = Baucom Feminine Scale; SRIS = Sex Role Identity Scale; GIM= Gender Identity Scale-feminine gender identity in males; GIF=Gender Identity Scale-masculine gender identity in females; Fantasy = Fantasy measure of sexual orientation; Experience = Experience measure of sexual orientation; MPQPa = Positive Emotionality-agentic from the MPQ; MPQPc = Positive Emotionality-communal from the MPQ; MPQN = Negative Emotionality from the MPQ; MPQC = Constraint from the MPQ.

Note. [a] denotes where values from the unaugmented scales (Denial of Stereotypical Masculine Interests and Feminine Gender Identity) have been used rather than from the augmented measures.

Note. [b] denotes correlations unavailable.

Stereotypical Interests. Similar to the UT90 data, Denial of Stereotypical Masculine Interests correlated highly with female gender (.59) and with several measures related to masculinity-femininity (i.e., .73 with the CPI F/M scale; .66 with the Baucom femininity scale; −.58 with SRIS). A correlation of only −.30 resulted with the Baucom masculinity score.

Furthermore, with the refinement of Positive Emotionality into the agentic and communal components, gender differences in its relationship to Denial of Stereotypical Masculine Interests were found. In females, a mild correlation existed between the Denial of Stereotypical Masculine Interests factor and MPQ Positive Emotionality-communal (.21), but this correlation did not exist in males (.00). Thus, the Denial of Stereotypical Masculine Interests factor may show a slight relationship to personality for females but not for males.

Again, Stereotypical Feminine Interests generally correlated in a similar fashion to Denial of Stereotypical Masculine Interests (i.e., .50 with the CPI F/M scale; −.59 with SRIS), suggesting that it measures a traditional feminine attribute. Correlations with the Baucom scales were relatively low (−.22 with masculinity and .35 with femininity). Stereotypical Feminine Interests correlated .60 with female gender.

Hypersensitivity/Anxiety. As in the UT90 sample, the Hypersensitivity/Anxiety factor showed the highest correlation in the UT92 sample with MPQ Negative Emotionality (.67) and a low correlation with Positive Emotionality-agentic (−.18). It also showed high negative correlations with GM (−.60), the Baucom masculinity scale (−.61), and the PAQ (−.45). These correlations held up when males and females were considered separately. The results corroborate the idea that Hypersensitivity/Anxiety is not primarily a measure of masculinity-femininity, but rather a measure of negative emotionality. Also, negative emotionality (reversed) appears to be a substantial component of some traditional measures of masculinity.

Low Cynicism. Low Cynicism showed its highest correlations with MPQ Negative Emotionality (−.32) and with the MFRQ (−.34). It showed low correlations with measures of masculinity-femininity, gender identity, and sexual orientation. This corroborates the suggestion that Low Cynicism shows some relationship to the higher-order personality dimension of negative emotionality and that this dimension may be reflected to some degree in the conventionality measured by the MFRQ.

Aesthetic Interests. As with the UT90 results, Aesthetic Interests in the UT92 sample correlated in the .20 to .30 range with traditional measures of femininity (.30 with the CPI F/M scale; .20 with the PAQF scale; −.29 with the SRIS).

Its correlation with female gender was, again, .26. As in the UT90 data, Aesthetic Interests correlated moderately with MPQ Positive Emotionality (this time with the agentic subdivision) in females (.32), but not in males (.06). Also, in females only, it correlated negatively with MPQ Constraint (−.27). Traditional feminine measures generally correlated positively with Constraint. This suggests that, although Aesthetic Interests is mildly related to traditional concepts of femininity, it reflects a more agentic, less constrained quality than traditional femininity.

Feminine Gender Identity. The Feminine Gender Identity factor (this time the final augmented version) correlated highly with female gender (.83). It also correlated highly with SRIS (−.77), a measure that seems to reflect gender identity, but it correlated lower with Finn's GIM (.37) and GIF (−.50). Its correlations with more traditional measures of masculinity-femininity were moderate to high (e.g., GM, −.51; GF, .68; BMS, −.31; PAQF, .23). Interestingly, its correlation with sexual orientation (i.e., Fantasy) was low (.13). This correlation broke out slightly differently between the genders, with males showing a higher correlation (.15) than females (−.08).

Restraint. With the subdivision of MPQ Positive Emotionality into agentic and communal aspects, a moderate negative correlation arose between the communal dimension and the Restraint factor (−.28 for the combined data, −.29 in males, and −.35 in females). Furthermore, the mild correlation of the Restraint factor with the MPQ Constraint marker seen in the UT90 sample (.24) was smaller in the UT92 sample (.15). Also, a mild correlation with MPQ Negative Emotionality appeared (−.21), which was even stronger in females (−.30). The correlations with traditional measures of masculinity-femininity, gender identity, and sexual orientation remained negligible. Thus, although there were indications that the Restraint factor is related to communal Positive Emotionality, Negative Emotionality, and Constraint, the relationships were small and inconclusive in the two samples examined here.

The FM Factor. The FM factor showed high correlations with female gender (.82) and a range from moderate to high correlations with traditional measures of masculinity-femininity (e.g., .79 with CPI F/M; −.27 with PAQM; .26 with PAQF; −.36 with BMS; .60 with BFM). Correlations with measures of gender identity were high: .37 with GIM (computed in males only, therefore restricted variance); −.57 with GIF (computed in females only, therefore restricted variance); and −.79 with SRIS. The FM factor did not correlate highly with sexual orientation (.18 with Fantasy), although in males it showed a moderate correlation (.21 with Fantasy), whereas, in females, the relationship was negligible (.03 with Fantasy). It displayed low correlations with personality dimensions: .20

with Positive Affectivity-Communal; −.08 with Positive Affectivity-Agentic; .11 with Negative Affectivity; and .27 with Constraint.

Conclusions from Discriminant and Convergent Measures

Thus, with some modifications, the major findings in the correlations of the UT90 data were confirmed in the UT92 data. Hypersensitivity/Anxiety is a measure of negative emotionality and is minimally related to masculinity-femininity. Low Cynicism is primarily related to negative emotionality rather than to masculinity-femininity. The relationship of Restraint to the higher-order personality dimensions is hazy, but it was not strongly related to the key measures of masculinity-femininity. In females, Aesthetic Interests captured some of the personality dimension of Positive Emotionality, but this did not hold true for males. The Denial of Stereotypical Masculine Interests and Stereotypical Feminine Interests factors appeared to be reasonable measures of masculine and feminine interests. Denial of Stereotypical Masculine Interests displayed small gender differences in the relationship to personality. The Feminine Gender Identity factor seemed to be a viable measure of gender identity. Sexual orientation has no substantial correlate among the factors.

With accumulating evidence bearing on construct validity, we can finally identify with some confidence the construct tapped by each of the Scale 5 factors. Table 6.9 provides a brief description of what each factor measures.

Age, Education, and Ethnicity and the Scale 5 Factors

Our curiosity then turned to the relationship of the new Scale 5 factors to various demographic variables. Are there significant differences in factor scores among different age groups, education levels, or ethnicities? And, if so, what do these differences tell us about the expression of masculinity-femininity in various groups? To explore these questions, we examined the MMPI-2 normative data for males and females separately, by computing separate one-way analyses of variance and Scheffe's tests of significance ($p < .01$). As independent variables, we used the same categories presented in the MMPI-2 Manual for Administration and Scoring (Butcher, Dahlstrom, Graham, Tellegen, & Kaemmer, 1989) for age, ethnicity, and education. The seven Scale 5 factor scores and FM composite score all entered the calculations as dependent variables. Subjects missing items on one of these factors were excluded from these calculations. T scores were used in the calculations. Following the lead of Greene (2000) in his discussion of demographic variables and MMPI-2 scores, we also opted to consider scale differences of less than 5 T score points to be clinically insignificant.

Table 6.9. Summary of Scale 5 Factor Scales of the MMPI-2

1. DENIAL OF STEREOTYPICAL MASCULINE INTERESTS

A factor reflecting lack of interest in activities typically considered male or masculine (e.g., mechanics, hunting, soldiering, playing rough sports)

2. HYPERSENSITIVITY/ANXIETY

A factor reflecting self-focused worry and sensitivity (e.g., feelings easily hurt, worry about sex, believing one feels more intensely than others)

3. STEREOTYPICAL FEMININE INTERESTS

A factor reflecting activities and interests typically considered female or feminine (e.g., love stories, flowers, nursing)

4. LOW CYNICISM

A factor reflecting a lack of cynicism and suspiciousness about human motivations (e.g., people are honest because they are afraid of being caught)

5. AESTHETIC INTERESTS

A factor reflecting interest in the arts and written expression (e.g., dramatics, poetry, journalism)

6. FEMININE GENDER IDENTITY

A factor reflecting the wish to be female and of interests and activities traditionally associated with feminine gender (e.g., wishing to be a girl, playing with dolls as a child)

7. RESTRAINT

A factor reflecting a lack of interest in and pleasure from loud and aggressive activities (e.g., loud fun, playing jokes, teasing animals, talking about sex)

FM: COMPOSITE FEMININITY-MASCULINITY SCALE

A bipolar marker of core masculinity-femininity (combining Denial of Stereotypical Masculine Interests, Stereotypical Feminine Interests, and Feminine Gender Identity)

The results of the one-way analysis of variance with Scheffe's Test of Significance using Scale 5 and the Scale 5 factors with age ranges are shown in Appendices Y (males) and Z (females). The results for level of education are shown in Appendices AA (males) and BB (females). Appendices CC (males) and DD (females) show the results for ethnicity.

Age

In spite of the often repeated clinical lore that men become "softer" and more feminine as they age, researchers have yet to find significant differences in MMPI-2 Scale 5 scores among men of different ages. Butcher, Aldwin, Levenson, Ben-Porath, Spiro, and Bossé (1991) compared scores on the Basic and Content scales of four age groups from forty to ninety-one years of age in two separate samples: the Boston Normative Aging Sample (N = 1,242; Bossé, Ekerdt, & Silbert, 1984) and 519 men in the MMPI-2 Restandardization sample (Butcher et al., 1989). They found no difference in Scale 5 scores between the four age groups in either sample.

Greene (2000) analyzed the complete MMPI-2 normative group (N = 2,589), as well as Caldwell's (1997) clinical dataset of 52,543 MMPI-2s of inpatients and outpatients collected from his scoring service. Greene found minimal age effects on Scale 5 T scores in either group. The average Scale 5 T score decreased slightly in a linear fashion over the seven intervals of years used (eighteen- to nineteen-year-olds, mean = 50.9 for normals and 52.1 for patients; seventy and over age group, mean = 49.1 for normals and 50.8 for patients). However, Greene did not compute these scores separately by gender, which makes these analyses difficult to interpret

We examined the differences in Scale 5 scores by different age groups separately by gender. As stated earlier, the age categories used in our calculations are the same as those included in the MMPI-2 *Manual for Administration and Scoring* (Butcher et al., 1989) and similar to those in the Butcher et al. study (1991) and the Greene study (2000) previously mentioned: eighteen to nineteen years of age, twenty to twenty-nine years, thirty to thirty-nine years, forty to forty-nine years, fifty to fifty-nine years, sixty to sixty-nine years, seventy to seventy-nine years, and eighty to eighty-four years.

Although overall Scale 5 scores do not appear to change much with age (no significant differences among age group for males [Appendix X] or for females [Appendix Y]), there were some significant differences between age groups for some of the Scale 5 factors. Before we discuss these, it is important to keep in mind that the analyses involve cross-sectional, not longitudinal, data. Thus, the results may reflect cohort (i.e., generational) differences, not simply the effects of age/development.

In our analyses, neither males nor females showed any significant differences by age on the three factors that correlate highest with other measures of masculinity-femininity: Denial of Stereotypical Masculine Interests, Stereotypical Feminine Interests, and Feminine Gender Identity. There was also no significant difference among age groups for males on the composite FM factor when scores were considered by age.

On the Hypersensitivity/Anxiety factor, both males and females showed a general linear decline with age. This was not entirely surprising, in that Greene

(2000) had previously reported that Scales Pt, A, and Mt—all of which correlate substantially with Hypersensitivity/Anxiety— showed moderate declines across age groups in both the restandardization and the Caldwell (1997) clinical samples. Also, McCrae, Martin, and Costa (2005) and others have documented a cross-sectional decline with age on neuroticism and other variables related to negative affectivity. However, for males, this decline was minimal and included no statistically significant T score differences by age category (51.0 in eighteen- to nineteen-year-olds to 42.9 in eighty- to eighty-four-year olds). For females, the decline with age of Hypersensitivity/Anxiety score was striking, going from a high T score of 58.3 for eighteen- to nineteen-year-olds to a T score of 37.3 for eighty- to eighty-four-years olds. Even if one eliminates the oldest and youngest age groups (because of their relatively small sample size), there still was a clinically significant decline from age twenty to seventy-nine, from a mean T score of 51.5 for the youngest women to 45.7 in the older women. It seems reasonable to expect that hypersensitivity would decline with age, as we perhaps begin to master our own fates and care less about the opinions of others. We can only speculate why that decline was greater for women than for men. It may be that women generally start adulthood with greater sensitivity than men and that they are more likely to develop "thicker skins" as they age.

Low Cynicism showed a few statistically significant differences between age groups for each gender, but none of these exceeded our 5 T-score point criterion and hence do not appear to be practically or clinically significant. These results parallel that found by Greene (2000) when he examined the Cynicism (CYN) Content Scale in the combined MMPI-2 normative sample. We suspect that cynicism is a relatively enduring personality trait.

Neither males nor females showed any significant differences on the Aesthetic Interests factor. This finding suggests that aesthetic interests are probably lifelong interests that are set by late adolescence. It is slightly surprising that these interests do not change as one matures through life, especially given that the last factor, Restraint, changes significantly.

The Restraint factor showed many effects of age, as expected. For females, Restraint increased linearly from a T score of 39.4 for eighteen- to nineteen-year-olds to 58.4 for eighty- to eighty-four-year-olds. Males also followed this pattern, with twenty- to twenty-nine-year-old males being significantly less restrained than thirty- to thirty-nine-year-olds, fifty- to fifty-nine-year-olds, and sixty- to sixty-nine-year-olds. The trend for males after fifty-nine was slightly downward in restraint. These results suggest that, as we age, we become more restrained, at least until older age, when we lose some restraint.

Again, however, we must remember that these results may reflect cohort/generational (or sampling) differences rather than actual changes in personality across the life span.

In summary, the age differences in the Scale 5 factor scores support the construct validity of the factors. Those that reflect what we see as more central aspects of masculinity-femininity do not vary by age, whereas those that reflect other dimensions of personality vary fairly predictably. This suggests that core masculinity-femininity is a relatively constant phenomenon over the life span.

Education

As discussed in chapter 3, MMPI-2 Scale 5 scores do appear to show a modest relationship with education, especially for men, although it is less than the association found with the original MMPI. We were interested in the relationship of level of education with each of the Scale 5 factors. The results of the one-way analysis of variance with Scheffe's Test of Significance that we computed for Scale 5 and the Scale 5 factors with level of education are shown in Appendices Z (males) and AA (females).

The education categories used in our calculations reflect the highest attained education and are the same as those in the MMPI-2 *Manual for Administration and Scoring* (Butcher et al., 1989): completed part of high school, high school graduate, completed part of college, college graduate, and postgraduate education. We first examined those factors most closely related to the core of masculinity-femininity—Denial of Stereotypical Masculine Interests, Stereotypical Feminine Interests, and Feminine Gender Identity—separately by gender. In both males and females, only Denial of Stereotypical Masculine Interests showed significant differences by education. Male T scores increased from 47.7 for men with less than a high school degree to 53.5 for males with postgraduate education. This result suggests that higher-educated men endorse fewer stereotypical masculine interests than less-educated men. This fits with the notion that men with less education are more gender-stereotyped in their interests.

A similar pattern was found for women. The mean female T score on the Denial of Stereotypical Masculine Interests factor decreased from 52.1 for women with less than a high school diploma to 48.5 for women with postgraduate education. This result indicates that less-educated women endorsed fewer masculine interests than did more-educated women. In other words, as with men, less-educated women adhered more closely to traditional gender stereotypes regarding interests that are considered to be stereotypically masculine. Interestingly, however, this result was limited to traditional masculine interests: neither males nor females showed significant differences in Stereotypical Feminine Interests by education level. Also, neither males nor females showed a difference in Feminine Gender Identity regardless of level of education. This last result fits with our conception of gender identity as being a fairly stable trait that is established early in life and is less influenced by adult environment. (See also Spence, 1985.)

There are several possible explanations for the findings concerning masculine and feminine interests. As noted in chapter 5, the distribution of Stereotypical Feminine Interests scores was highly skewed among normal men, with very few men in the restandardization sample endorsing any of the six items on the factor. (The mean raw score among men was 1.35, with a standard deviation of 1.25.) We suspect these types of interests (e.g., in romantic stories, flowers, and nursing) are so eschewed by men, because of their social undesirability, that their educational level matters little. This same kind of restricted range was not found for men regarding masculine interests; we suspect that the lack of masculine interests is not as socially sanctioned for men as the endorsement of feminine interests. Hence, education is able to exert an influence in this area.

Among women, the opposite may be true. Stereotypical feminine interests (e.g., reading love stories, growing house plants) may be so de rigueur that many women endorse a number of these items, regardless of education. Thus, the relevant Scale 5 factor has a fairly low ceiling (i.e., the highest obtainable linear T score would be 70). We suspect stereotypical masculine interests (e.g., in science, adventure stories, and football) are not generally proscribed for women, and thus, once again, education can have an effect by exposing women to such interests.

Finally, regarding masculine interests and education, one must consider the possibility of a causal effect in the other direction. Perhaps, traditional males who like mechanic magazines, being a soldier, and playing rough sports pursue vocational, military, or athletic careers and, thus, do not seek higher education. Similarly, women who have these traditional masculine interests may be less likely to stay home as traditional mothers and more likely to compete with men, which might mean attaining more education than their traditional peers.

The factors less central to masculinity-femininity showed predictable relationships with educational level. For both males and females, scores on the Hypersensitivity/Anxiety factor showed no clinically significant differences with highest education attained. Scores on the Restraint factor also showed no differences with education for either males or females.

T scores on the Low Cynicism factor showed a strong linear relationship to education level for both males and females, with the more-educated individuals being less cynical than the less-educated. In fact, the Low Cynicism factor scores showed virtually no gender difference. For males, the average Low Cynicism T scores increased from 42.3 for men with less than a high school diploma to 53.5 for those with a postgraduate education. For females, these means were 42.8 and 54.7, respectively. This finding was not unanticipated, in that Greene (2000) showed that Cynicism (CYN) was the MMPI-2 Content Scale that was most associated with education in both the MMPI-2 normative (Butcher et al., 1989) and Caldwell's (1997) clinical samples (with correlations of −.334 and −.271, respectively). This finding may indicate that the more educated one becomes, the fewer impediments and setbacks one may encounter, leading to a sense that life is fair. Of course, it may equally be true that those with less cynicism are those who pursue the rigors of higher education. They may at least perceive fewer obstacles to success than those with high cynicism.

Differences in T scores by education on the Aesthetic Interests factor are as expected, with a linear positive relationship between education level and aesthetic interests. Because aesthetic interests are often a component of higher education (e.g., dramatics, poetry, journalism), it follows that those with higher education would score higher on this factor. The mean T score for males increased from 47.6 for men with less than a high school degree to 52.7 for males with postgraduate education. Similarly, the mean T score for women with less than a high school education was 47.5 and for those with postgraduate education, 52.5.

Finally, the composite FM factor did show differences by education for men in the normative sample, with those with less than a high school education obtaining an average T score of 52.0 and those with postgraduate training averaging 57.9. Similarly, females showed significant differences on the FM factor between those whose highest education was high school graduate (T = 53.42) and college graduates (51.05) and those with postgraduate education (49.01). This result is likely primarily a result of the previously discussed differences on the component Denial of Stereotypical Masculine Interests, because this factor comprises half of the items in the FM Composite. Again, males and females score less gender-typed (i.e., males more like females and females more like males) as they attain more education.

So what can we conclude about the relationship between MMPI-2 Scale 5 and educational level, and how should this affect our interpretation of Scale 5 scores in individual cases? First, as shown by Dahlstrom and Tellegen (1993) and discussed in chapter 3, there are significant differences among educational groups with respect to Scale 5 scores, with an average 11-point T score difference between the highest- and lowest-educated men in the normative sample. Among women, these mean differences are less, but it still is true that women with less education are most likely to have Scale 5 as the highest in their protocols. Furthermore, for both men and women, Scale 5 is the Basic scale that is most correlated with education.

However, the Scale 5 factors provide more fine-tuned interpretation than old rules of thumb or "mental adjustments" allowed. The results of our analyses show that traditional masculine interests, aesthetic interests, and cynicism do covary with education level, for both men and women, whereas traditional feminine interests, feminine gender identity, hypersensitivity, and restraint do not, in either gender. This understanding allows more precise interpretations of Scale 5 scores to be made. Whereas, in the past, one needed to be careful not to make assumptions about a highly educated man's gender identity from an elevated Scale 5 alone, now one can understand that highly educated men endorse more aesthetic interests and fewer stereotypical masculine interests on Scale 5 than do lesser-educated men. Differences on these two dimensions could by themselves produce an elevation on Scale 5 that has little to do with gender identity.

Ethnicity

Finally, we looked at differences in Scale 5 and Scale 5 factor scores as a function of ethnicity. Once again, we used the MMPI-2 normative data and its "ethnic" categories: Asian, Black, Hispanic, Native American, and White (Butcher et al., 1989). As we have mentioned, the MMPI-2 normative sample was patterned after the 1980 U.S. Census. Thus, there were limited numbers in some categories, especially Asian. For females, only thirteen Asians and, for males, only five to six Asians are included in our calculations. (These numbers may vary between factors because we excluded subjects from a calculation if they did not answer all the questions scored on that particular scale or factor.) These small numbers suggest that we should be careful in any conclusions we draw about Asians. For females there were at least 168 Black, 37 Hispanic, 36 Native American, and 1,088 White subjects in our calculations. For males, there were at least 111 Black, 32 Hispanic, 35 Native American, and 872 White subjects. These numbers offer more confidence in the results for these ethnic groups.

Previous research has shown that the question of ethnic differences on MMPI-2 scales is quite complicated. First, there are issues of accurately identifying distinct ethnic groups. Often biological heritage (i.e., race) is considered, but culture (including levels of acculturation) is not. This complexity makes results questionable. We refer to "ethnicity" but recognize that these categories may be more complex than that one word suggests. Second, there are a number of studies with conflicting results. One potential confounding variable is education level, which, as we discussed previously, seems to be a variable that affects Scale 5 scores. Because level of education may vary by ethnicity, it may be important to control for education when we compare Scale 5 scores by ethnic group. Finally, to understand any potential construct variance that may exist between ethnicities (i.e., that is, to better understand whether the derived constructs are equivalent across the cultures), it may be important to do separate factor analytic studies for each ethnic group independently. In this way, we could determine whether the constructs themselves vary among different cultures.

With the potential complications in mind, let us refer you to a thorough presentation of the evidence in Greene (2000, pp. 480–89). Briefly, he cited nine studies that looked at Black-White differences on Scale 5 of the MMPI-2 (including three normal sample studies, two forensic sample studies, and four psychiatric sample studies). Of those studies, none found significant differences between Blacks and Whites on Scale 5 scores. (Differences of less than 5 T-score points between the two groups were not reported, regardless of statistical significance.) At least three of these studies did consider males and females separately. A more recent study by Arbisi, Ben-Porath, and McNulty (2002) found no differences on Scale 5 of the MMPI-2 between Black and White psychiatric inpatients. (See also Munley, Morris, & Murray, 2001.)

Greene (2000) reported seven studies that investigated differences between Hispanics and Whites on Scale 5 of the MMPI-2 (four normal samples, two psychiatric samples, one forensic sample). None of these studies found significant differences, although, once again, differences of less than 5 T-score points between the two groups were not reported, regardless of statistical significance. A more recent study by Scott and Pampa (2000) developed MMPI-2 norms on a Peruvian sample. They found that Peruvian women scored significantly higher on Scale 5 than women in the U.S. normative sample. (See also Lucio et al. 2001.)

Greene found three normal sample studies (representing at least four different tribes) comparing Native Americans and Whites on MMPI-2 Scale 5 scores. None of these studies reported significant differences between Native Americans and Whites on Scale 5. Finally, Greene analyzed the results of two normal sample studies comparing Asian Americans to Whites on Scale 5 of the MMPI-2. Neither of these studies showed significant differences.

Thus, the only suggestion of ethnic differences on Scale 5 scores comes from the study by Scott and Pampa (2000), which showed significantly higher Scale 5 scores in Peruvian women than women in the U.S. normative sample. It is important to note that a number of older studies using the original MMPI reported significant differences in Scale 5 scores among ethnicities. The fact that only one of numerous MMPI-2 studies has shown ethnic differences on Scale 5 scores may reflect that the revised version is less sensitive to ethnic diversity.

The results of the one-way analysis of variance with Scheffe's Test of Significance that we computed for Scale 5 and the Scale 5 factors with ethnicity are shown in Appendices BB (males) and CC (females). We found no significant differences ($p > .01$) in overall Scale 5 scores in males among the different ethnic groups, but there was one ethnic difference among the female ethnic groups. Black females scored significantly higher on Scale 5 (T = 53.1) than White females (T = 48.7). We ran an analysis of covariance to control for education level to determine whether this difference was an artifact of level of education achieved. The results of this analysis not only confirmed significant differences between Whites and Blacks but also showed differences on Scale 5 between Whites and Native Americans. If one interprets Scale 5 traditionally, this difference suggests that Black and Native American females are more "rejecting of a very traditional female role, or . . . likely to be interested in sports, hobbies, and other activities that are stereotypically more masculine than feminine," whereas White females have more "stereotypically feminine interests, are likely to derive satisfaction from their roles as spouses or mothers; or may be traditionally feminine or more androgynous" (Graham, 2000, p. 74).

However, our analysis of the factors indicated that neither males nor females showed differences on the core masculinity-femininity factors: Denial of Stereotypical Masculine Interests, Stereotypical Feminine Interests, Feminine Gender Identity, and the composite FM factor. Thus, there were no significant differences between Black and White females on those dimensions that reflect traditional femininity.

Similarly, there were no significant differences among ethnic groups on the Hypersensitivity/Anxiety factor or on the dimension of Restraint. On the Aesthetic Interests factor, females showed no differences by ethnic group, but males did. Black males scored significantly higher (mean T = 53.7) than White males (mean T = 49.5) on the Aesthetic Interests factor. An analysis of covariance controlling for highest level of education achieved did not alter this result. Thus, Black males might be seen as having more interest than their White counterparts in the arts and written expression, such as dramatics, poetry, and journalism.

However, both males and females showed large differences on the Low Cynicism factor by ethnic group. For females, Black (mean T = 44.3), Hispanic (mean T = 44.6), and Native American (mean T = 41.3) groups all scored significantly lower than the White female group (mean T = 51.3) on the Low Cynicism factor. The males of these ethnic groups followed a similar pattern: Black (mean T = 45.4), Hispanic (mean T = 44.6), and Native American (mean T = 43.3) males all scored significantly lower than the White male ethnic group (mean T = 51.1). Only the Asian group, both male and female, showed no difference from their White counterparts. There were no significant differences on the Low Cynicism factor among the Black, Hispanic, and Native American groups.

We computed an analysis of covariance to determine whether these differences were influenced by education level. Controlling for highest education attained did not significantly alter these results for either males or females. This result may not be surprising in U.S. culture, where it is often noted that Whites enjoy advantages over other ethnic groups and thus may be naïve to the bias that may exist, whereas minority ethnic groups are personally affected by these biases or at least believe them to be true.

Overall, these results suggest that there are no differences among ethnic groups in the United States on dimensions that tap core masculinity-femininity. Thus, the traditional interpretation offered by Graham (2000) appears to be misleading. There is a large difference in cynicism among the various ethnic groups, but this difference is not attributable to education differences, and it affects the total Scale 5 score and probably underlies the ethnic differences on that scale that have been noted at times. These findings provide another important reason to consider the Scale 5 factors when interpreting an MMPI-2 profile.

GM and GF

A look at efforts to measure gender-related phenomena in the MMPI-2 led to an examination of the GM and GF scales. Table 6.10 displays the correlations of GM and GF with the measures of masculinity-femininity, gender identity, sexual orientation, and personality dimensions in the combined data and in the male and female data separately from the UT92 sample.

In this sample, GM and GF were negatively correlated with each other in the combined data (−.57), although this correlation decreased when the genders were considered separately (−.28 in males and −.19 in females). Not surprisingly, the GM and GF scales seemed to relate to external measures in

Table 6.10. Correlates of GM and GF in the UT92 Sample

	Combined		Male		Female	
	GM	GF	GM	GF	GM	GF
Female Gender	−.61	.70				
GF	−.57		−.28		−.19	
DSMI	−.45	.60	−.20	.45	−.27	.29
H/A	−.60	.25	−.64	.19	−.57	.06
SFI	−.47	.56	−.17	.20	−.15	.33
FGI	−.51	.68	−.14	.32	−.12	.38
FM	−.63	.80	−.30	.58	−.32	.56
CPI F/M	−.73	.76	−.53	.61	−.59	.44
CPI-BMS	.73	−.38	.76	−.29	.69	−.16
CPI-BFM	−.37	.78	−.07	.67	−.12	.71
PAQM	.54	−.34	.50	−.24	.53	−.26
PAQF	−.24	.33	−.09	.24	−.16	.26
PAQM-F	.63	−.48	.54	−.35	.60	−.34
SRIS	.59	−.71	.22	−.30	.16	−.32
GIM/**GIF**	—	—	−.32	.25	**.18**	**−.56**
Fantasy	−.17	.12	−.13	.09	−.11	.00
MFRQ	−.11	−.20	−.10	−.29	−.37	.01
MPQPa	.29	−.10	.29	−.15	.47	−.14
MPQPc	−.07	.15	.14	−.07	−.03	.12
MPQN	−.53	.00	−.62	−.04	−.56	−.25
MPQC	−.36	.38	−.30	.32	−.31	.39

Note. DSMI = Denial of Stereotypical Masculine Interests; H/A = Hypersensitivity/ Anxiety; SFI = Stereotypical Feminine Interests; FGI = Feminine Gender Identity; FM = Femininity-Masculinity scale.

Note. See Table 6.8 for additional abbreviations used.

the opposite direction; that is, when the correlation of one with an external measure was positive, the correlation of the other to that measure was likely to be negative. Furthermore, as expected given the method of using differential endorsement of items by gender to construct GM and GF, GM correlated highly negatively with female gender (−.61), whereas GF correlated highly positively with female gender (.70).

Construct Validity of GM

GM showed high correlations with broad measures of traditional masculinity (.73 with Baucom masculinity factor; −.73 with the CPI F/M factor), as well as high correlations with the M factor and the M-F factor of the PAQ (.54 and .63, respectively), and a strong negative correlation with the composite FM factor (−.63). It also correlated with gender identity (i.e., .59 with the SRIS and −.51 with Feminine Gender Identity).

However, GM also showed a strong negative relationship to negative emotionality (−.53 with MPQN and −.60 with Hypersensitivity/Anxiety), a moderate negative relationship to Constraint (−.36), and a moderate relationship with Positive Emotionality-agentic (.29). Thus, it appears that, although GM reflects traditional masculinity-femininity, including its gender identity component, it also reflects negative emotionality (reversed) and, to some extent, Constraint (reversed) as well as agentic Positive Emotionality. Clearly, it is a multidimensional measure.

Many GM items "deal primarily with the denial of fears, anxieties, and somatic symptoms" (Graham, 2000, p. 180), which is likely why GM shows the negative correlation with negative emotionality. GM also includes content dealing "with denial of excessive emotionality and presentation of self as independent, decisive, and self-confident" (Graham, 2000, p. 180). The correlation with Positive Emotionality-agentic and Constraint may be based in this content. Other substantial components of GM include stereotypical masculine activities and denial of stereotypical feminine occupations (Graham, 1990). This content would contribute to the correlations observed with traditional measures of masculinity-femininity.

Construct Validity of GF

GF showed a clearer pattern of convergent and discriminant validity than GM. It showed a clear relationship to comprehensive femininity measures (.76 with the CPI F/M factor; .78 with the Baucom femininity factor). It also correlated with Denial of Stereotypical Masculine Interests (.60), Stereotypical Feminine Interests (.56), and the composite FM factor (.80) (see chapter 5). In addition, it correlated with gender identity (.25 with GIM; .56 with GIF; and .68 with Feminine Gender Identity). The only personality dimension reflected in GF was Constraint (.38). Thus, GF appears to be related to femininity, but with a moderate influence from Constraint.

An examination of the content of GF reveals that the largest components are denial of antisocial acts, endorsement of stereotypical feminine activities, and denial of masculine activities (Graham, 2000). This content would likely lead to correlations with Constraint and with femininity measures. There are also several items involving gender identity that would contribute to the moderate correlations with the gender identity measures. (See also Peterson, 1991.)

Conclusions Regarding GM and GF

The results of these analyses suggest that GM and GF are multidimensional. Neither is a clear measure of a single construct. Thus, interpretation of scores on these two factors is problematic. It is likely that GM and GF may be most useful as a screening measure: elevations on either of these factors may signal that something is unusual in the protocol and that further examination is warranted. One might then look at other measures, such as the Scale 5 factors, to gain insight into what significance the elevations carry.

When the GM score is significantly elevated, one might look at the composite FM factor as well as the Feminine Gender Identity factor. One should also examine measures of negative emotionality, such as the Hypersensitivity/Anxiety factor, to determine whether this dimension underlies the elevated GM score. It may also be helpful to check measures of Constraint, such as the Restraint factor, and Positive Emotionality-agentic to determine their significance in the elevation. To interpret an elevated GF score, one might look at the Scale 5 factors to note elevations on the Stereotypical Feminine Interests or Feminine Gender Identity factors. One could also look at measures of Constraint, such as the Restraint factor. Either or both of these dimensions could be elevating the GF score. Thus, it is important to look further to more unidimensional measures on the MMPI-2 to determine what significance an elevated GM or GF score may suggest.

Summary of the Reliability and Validity of the Scale 5 Factors

Thus, we have successfully established the reliability and validity of the newly developed Scale 5 factors through the course of these studies. The internal consistency coefficients suggest that the factors are reasonably cohesive when males and females are combined, as well as when they are considered separately. For reasons consistent with the construct, the Feminine Gender Identity factor shows greater internal consistency when the genders are considered together.

The stability of the Scale 5 factors across samples argued for their reliability and construct validity. The factors appeared to apply equally well to a representative sample of the U.S. population and a sample of college students. Although there were mean differences between the two samples, the differences were generally predictable, given the constructs that we believe they tap. The internal consistencies of the factors were similar in both samples. The test-retest reliability of the factors was high, ranging from .68 for Low Cynicism to .93 for Denial of Stereotypical Masculine Interests, with the Feminine Gender Identity factor at .90 and the Stereotypical Feminine Interests factor at .83

The pattern of correlations found among the factors—both with other MMPI-2 scales as well as with various other measures of masculinity-femininity, gender related measures, and personality markers—supported their construct validity as well. The patterns of correlations were similar in both the normative sample and samples of college students. The pattern of correlations showed that the Hypersensitivity/Anxiety factor consistently captured negative emotionality and, to some extent, low positive emotionality. The Restraint factor aligned with constraint. The Low Cynicism factor was related to negative emotionality, although to a lesser degree than the Hypersensitivity/Anxiety factor. The Aesthetic Interests factor was separate from but related to Stereotypical Feminine Interests. Feminine Gender Identity provided a solid measure of gender identity. Furthermore, the Denial of Stereotypical Interests, Stereotypical Feminine Interests, and Feminine Gender Identity factors form a higher-order dimension of masculinity-femininity. The higher-order factor was supported by its correlations with the various other measures of masculinity-femininity, gender-related characteristics, sexual orientation, and markers of other personality dimensions. Thus, the pattern of correlations across a range of measures and samples clarified the constructs measured by each factor.

We then looked at Scale 5 factors parameters in different social groups to gauge the characteristics of the factors across various social dimensions. Using the normative data, we looked for differences in factor scores among age groups, education levels, and ethnicities. The results of these analyses showed few differences among those social parameters on those factors that reflect central aspects of masculinity-femininity (Denial of Stereotypical Masculine Interests, Stereotypical Feminine Interests, and Feminine Gender Identity). We did observe differences in scores on the Denial of Stereotypical Masculine Interests factor, depending on education level achieved. We discussed possible reasons that both men and women with less education have more gender-typed masculine interests. Overall, these results reflect the stability of masculinity-femininity across age, education level, and ethnicity. There were predictable differences in other factors, particularly Low Cynicism, which varied among education level and ethnicity in predictable ways.

Overall, the Scale 5 factors demonstrate substantial reliability and validity through a number of examinations. They appear to greatly increase our understanding of what is being measured by Scale 5 of the MMPI-2.

Chapter 7

Dimensions of Scale 5 of the MMPI-A

The MMPI-A, the adolescent version of the MMPI, was developed subsequent to the MMPI-2. Similar to the MMPI-2, it includes a Scale 5, referred to as the Masculinity-Femininity scale, as one of its ten Clinical scales. We believe it offers another opportunity to explore masculinity-femininity, potentially providing insight into questions about the development of the trait. In this chapter, we replicate our efforts to clarify the dimensions of Scale 5, following procedures similar to those used with the MMPI-2 (see chapter 4). We had some skepticism that cohesive and stable factor dimensions could be identified because of the reduction of items in the MMPI-A Scale 5.

The MMPI-A contains 478 items, many of which are the same or similar to the 567 items contained in the MMPI-2. Items were added to assess new dimensions (e.g., eating disorders), and, obviously, items were deleted. Scale 5 is similar to but not identical to the Scale 5 of the MMPI-2. The MMPI-A Scale 5 has only forty-four items, a significant reduction from the fifty-six on Scale 5 of the MMPI-2. There are no new items on MMPI-A Scale 5. The twelve items on Scale 5 of the MMPI-2 not included on Scale 5 of the MMPI-A are indicated in Table 7.1 with the item number included as well as what MMPI-2 Scale 5 factor the item is on (if any).

Several of the Scale 5 factors developed in chapter 4 for the MMPI-2 suffered substantial loss of items in the MMPI-A. Half of the six items on the Stereotypical Feminine Interests factor of the MMPI-2 were dropped in the MMPI-A, four of the five items on the Aesthetic Interests factor were omitted, two of thirteen items on the Hypersensitivity/Anxiety factor were deleted, and one item of six on the Restraint factor is no longer in the item pool of

Table 7.1. Items on Scale 5 of the MMPI-2 Not Included on Scale 5 of the MMPI-A

4. Like library work.

(On MMPI-2's Stereotypical Feminine Interests factor)

25. Would like to be a singer.

(On MMPI-2's Aesthetic Interests factor)

74. Would like to be a florist.

(On MMPI-2's Stereotypical Feminine Interests factor)

112. Like theater.

(On MMPI-2's Aesthetic Interests factor)

187. Would like to report theater news.

(On MMPI-2's Aesthetic Interests factor)

191. Would like to be journalist.

(On MMPI-2's Aesthetic Interests factor)

236. Would like to be an artist who draws flowers.

(On MMPI-2's Stereotypical Feminine Interests factor)

19. On a new job, find out who is important.

(Not on any MMPI-2 Scale 5 factor)

121. Don't engage in unusual sex.

(Not on any MMPI-2 Scale 5 factor)

184. Seldom daydream.

(On MMPI-2's Hypersensitivity/Anxiety factor)

194. Never had worrisome skin rashes.

(On MMPI-2's Hypersensitivity/Anxiety factor)

207. Would like to be a member of clubs.

(On MMPI-2's Restraint factor)

the adolescent Scale 5. Given that all but one item from the Aesthetic Interests factor was deleted, we knew it was unlikely that this dimension would appear in the MMPI-A Scale 5 factor structure. Also, the deletion of half of the Stereotypical Feminine Interests factor items made it questionable that it would be represented on the MMPI-A version.

Thus, with some doubt that cohesive structure would be identified, we subjected the MMPI-A normative data to the same scrutiny we had the MMPI-2 data. Our procedure was very similar to that outlined in the previous three chapters. The overall strategy we followed to identify Scale 5 dimensions for the MMPI-A included the following steps:

Step 1. Factor development (see chapter 4)

Step 2: Augmentation of the factors using items outside Scale 5 (see chapter 5)

Step 3: Creation of a composite masculinity-femininity marker (see chapter 5)

Step 4: Consideration of convergent and discriminant validity (see chapter 6)

Factor Development

Factor Analytic Procedure

The normative sample for the MMPI-A included 805 males and 815 females from eight states. They ranged in age from fourteen to eighteen years, with the mean male age 15.5 and the mean female age 15.6. In ethnic composition, the sample represents a "reasonable match" (Archer, 2005) to the U. S. Census figures (76 percent white, 12 percent black, 3 percent Asian, 3 percent Native American, 2 percent Hispanic). Although the Hispanic population seems particularly underrepresented, this is the best sample available; therefore, we used it in our analyses.

We first calculated principle components analyses of the forty-four items on Scale 5 for the male and female data separately. We selected a range of most likely solutions, using scree plots and Cattell's rule, and then factor analyzed the correlation matrices for these possible solutions. In both males and females, an oblique rotation did not converge, but an orthogonal rotation did and was thus selected as the best solution.

Similar to development of the adult factors, we assigned items to factors if the item loaded .35 or more with that factor but also loaded less than .25 with any other factor. We also selected items that loaded .30 or more on a factor and at least .10 less on any other factor. The resulting solutions contained some factors that were similar to those derived from the MMPI-2. As we had observed in the adult factor development, the solutions were very similar for males and females. Thus, as we had done for the MMPI-2, we combined the male and female data and repeated the same analyses on the combined data. In the male, female, and combined data, the same five stable factors emerged in various versions. The six-factor solution in the combined data best clarified these five factors. Thus, we selected the six-factor solution as the basis for factor development.

Next, we correlated all Scale 5 items not on a resulting factor with composite scores derived for each factor in the six-factor solution. We added any item to a factor that correlated at least .20 with that factor and at least .10 less with any other factor. This resulted in the addition of two items to factor 1 and one item to factor 2. The resulting factors had seven, nine, five, three, three, and one items, respectively. We dropped the sixth factor because it had only one item. Cronbach alpha internal consistency coefficients were then calculated for each of the remaining five factors. They ranged from 0.65 for factor 1 to 0.34 for factor 5. We then dropped any factor with an alpha less than .40 or with less than five items. This left only factors 1, 2, and 3.

Next, we repeated our principle components and factor analytic procedure on the twenty-three items that were not then on one of the retained three factors. With orthogonal rotation, the four-factor solution was the most comprehensible. We added these four factors to the original three factors. Then we correlated all items that were not then on any of those seven factors with the composite scores for each factor. No item was sufficiently correlated with a composite score to warrant addition to that factor. We then dropped factors 6 and 7 because they contained too few items.

Last, we correlated these dropped items with the five remaining factors and found that for one item (#254 "Never liked to play with dolls"), its negative correlation with factor 1 was sufficiently high to be added to it. We then calculated stepwise alpha coefficients on the five factors. Dropping one item from factor 1, one from factor 3, and one from factor 4 increased the cohesiveness of each of those factors. We discovered that then dropping an additional item from factor 1 further enhanced that factor's cohesiveness. With the deletion of these detracting items, we arrived at the following alpha consistency coefficients: factor 1 = .69 (six items), factor 2 = .60 (nine items), factor 3 = .58 (four items), factor 4 = .43 (three items), and factor 5 = .38 (four items).

Because the items in factor 5 were similar to those in the Restraint factor of the adult test and because it was very close to the .40 cutoff for retaining factors we had used previously, it was kept. Also, factor 4 was kept because of its similarity to the Low Cynicism factor in the adult test. Furthermore, it seemed possible that additional items from the MMPI-A outside Scale 5 could strengthen these factors (to be explored later in this chapter).

Naming the Factors

Considering the item content of the remaining factors and their similarity to the adult factors, we derived names that captured the dimension ostensibly reflected in each factor. Factor 1 contained items from the adult Stereotypical Feminine Interest and Feminine Gender Identity factors. Remember that half the items from the adult Stereotypical Feminine Interest factor were deleted in the adolescent Scale 5. Remember too that these two dimensions were closely correlated in adults. A similar underlying correlational structure may have led to their combination in the adolescent solution. Because it contains items reflecting feminine interests and gender identity, the name Stereotypical Femininity seemed most appropriate for this adolescent factor. We adopted that name for this factor.

Adolescent factor 2 contained many items from the adult Hypersensitivity/ Anxiety factor and seemed to reflect this dimension. Thus, we adopted that name for factor 2. Factors 3, 4, and 5 were very similar to the adult Denial of Stereotypical Masculine Interests, Low Cynicism, and Restraint factors, respectively, so those labels were used for these factors.

Because factor 1 in the adolescent analysis paralleled factor 3 in the adult analysis and because factor 3 in the adolescent analysis paralleled factor 1 in the adult analysis, we switched the order of these two factors in the adolescent outcome in order to align the two sets of factors. Additionally, we stayed consistent with the adult factors by also reverse-scoring some of the adolescent factors. Thus, we converted masculine interests to Denial of Stereotypical Masculine interests, cynicism to Low Cynicism, and boisterousness to Restraint. The resulting factors were adopted as provisional factors for Scale 5 of the MMPI-A and are shown in Table 7.2. In order to differentiate these Scale 5 factors from the MMPI-2 Scale 5 factors, we used the prefix "Adolescent" with each of the MMPI-A Scale 5 factors.

Discussion

Two of the factors that we have developed, Adolescent-Stereotypical Femininity and Adolescent-Denial of Stereotypical Masculine Interests, appear to represent at least in part the stereotypical interests dimension of the bipolar masculinity-femininity factor that we discussed earlier. However, Stereotypical Femininity may be a combination of two of the underlying dimensions of this factor: stereotypical gender interests and gender identity. We suspect this because, in the adult version of the test, several of these items were included in the Feminine Gender Identity factor. The collapsing of these two content areas into one factor here may be the result of lost items in the MMPI-A pool, or it may reflect differences between adolescents and adults in this gender identity/interests area. Adolescent-Denial of Stereotypical Masculine Interests is a representation of the stereotypical gender interests component. The three other factors appear to be modified versions of three adult Scale 5 factors. Thus,

Table 7.2. Provisional Factors for Scale 5 of the MMPI-A

Subscale 1: Adolescent-Denial of Stereotypical Masculine Interests

- (–) 001. Like mechanics magazines.
- (–) 127. Would like to be in military.
- (–) 186. Would like to be a building contractor.
- (–) 190. Like hunting.

Subscale 2: Adolescent-Hypersensitivity/Anxiety

- (–) 060. Feelings not easily hurt.
- 159. Worry about sex.
- 185. Frequently worry.
- 194. Habits of some family members very irritating.
- 206. Disappointed in love.
- (–) 221. Don't mind not being better looking.
- (–) 223. Wholly self-confident.
- 235. Often strangers look at me critically.
- 240. Occasionally hate family members I love.

Subscale 3: Adolescent-Stereotypical Femininity

- 059. Wish was a girl or happy that am.
- 061. Like romances.
- 064. Like poetry
- 114. Like collecting plants.
- 131. Kept a diary.
- (–) 254. Never liked to play with dolls.

Subscale 4: Adolescent-Low Cynicism

- (–) 072. Hard to convince people of truth.
- (–) 100. People honest because they don't want to be caught.
- (–) 238. People have friends because they're useful.

Subscale 5: Adolescent-Restraint

- (–) 082. Like loud parties.
- (–) 099. Betting enhances a race.
- (–) 197. Like to talk about sex.
- (–) 217. Like being with people who play jokes on one another.

Note. Test item numbers are included for each item along with the direction in which the item is scored (a minus sign in parentheses preceding the item number indicates that the item is scored when the response is "false"; the lack of a minus marker indicates that the item is scored when the response is "true").

representations of some of the adult factors emerged in the adolescent data. However, three of the factors contain fewer than five items, and some have weak internal consistency. As we expected, the adult Aesthetic Interests factor did not appear in the adolescent analysis; four of its five items were deleted in the MMPI-A. We next turned our attention to enhancing the weak factors with items from the wider MMPI-A item pool.

Augmentation of the Factors Using MMPI-A Items outside Scale 5

Adolescent-Stereotypical Femininity and Adolescent-Denial of Stereotypical Masculine Interests Factors

Our initial reason for turning to the entire MMPI-A item pool was to lengthen the two adolescent factors that might be included in a higher-order masculinity-femininity marker scale as they were with adults (i.e., Adolescent-Stereotypical Femininity and Adolescent-Denial of Stereotypical Masculine Interests). In searching for the MMPI-A items that might augment these scales, we first considered items that showed a pattern of differential endorsement by males and females in the normative sample. Our reasoning was as follows: differential endorsement by males and females partly underlay the selection of items for the original MMPI Scale 5 (see chapter 3) and may be a necessary but not sufficient characteristic of any scale measuring masculinity-femininity (see chapter 2). Also, nine of the ten items on the Adolescent-Stereotypical Femininity and Adolescent-Denial of Stereotypical Masculine Interests factors showed at least a 20 percent differential endorsement between males and females in the normative sample (Butcher, Williams, Graham, Archer, Tellegen, Ben-Porath, & Kaemmer, 1992). Differential endorsements of the ten items on Adolescent-Stereotypical Femininity and Adolescent-Denial of Stereotypical Masculine Interests factors are listed in Table 7.3 and generally show substantial differences between males and females.

Table 7.3. Differential Endorsement Rates between Males and Females on Items from the Adolescent-Stereotypical Femininity Factor and the Adolescent-Denial of Stereotypical Masculine Interests Factor

Item	Differential Endorsement Rate
61	58.8%
131	54.2%
59	51.2%
254	37.5%
64	32.5%
1	30.5%
114	28.0%
190	24.9%
186	21.1%
127	18.9%

Note. The differential endorsement rate denotes the absolute difference in the percentage of males and females that endorsed the indicated item (in the MMPI-A normative sample).

Furthermore, of the eight MMPI-A items in the entire item pool that had a 30 percent or greater differential endorsement between males and females, six of those are on the Adolescent-Stereotypical Femininity and Adolescent-Denial of Stereotypical Masculine Interests factors. The other two items (#21 "Uncontrollable laughing and crying" and #139 "Cry easily") are not included on Scale 5, so they did not have the chance yet to be included on the factors.

Thus, we considered seventy-three non-Scale 5 items with gender differences of at least 10 percent in item endorsement rates for addition to the Adolescent-Stereotypical Femininity or Adolescent-Denial of Stereotypical Masculine Interests factor. These items were correlated with the item totals for these factors to determine whether any item correlated at least .20 with either of the provisional factor scores. We computed these associations for each gender separately and for the genders combined. The Adolescent-Stereotypical Femininity factor gained one item, "Love going to dances" (#319). The Adolescent-Denial of Stereotypical Masculine Interests factor gained no new items. We examined the alpha consistency coefficient for the expanded Adolescent-Stereotypical Femininity factor and found that the added item detracted from the internal consistency of the factor; hence it was dropped. Finally, we computed the correlations of scores on the Adolescent-Stereotypical Femininity and Adolescent-Denial of Stereotypical Masculine Interests factors with all other MMPI-A items that were not included in Scale 5 or previously considered. As expected, none of these remaining items revealed sufficient correlations to warrant their inclusion on either the Adolescent-Stereotypical Femininity or Adolescent-Denial of Stereotypical Masculine Interests factors.

Adolescent-Hypersensitivity/Anxiety, Adolescent-Low Cynicism, and Adolescent-Restraint Factors

We decided not to augment the Adolescent-Hypersensitivity/Anxiety factor because it already had nine items and demonstrated sufficient internal consistency (.60). Also, given the likelihood that this factor is a measure of negative affectivity, we suspected that it would correlate highly with many items outside Scale 5. Our suspicion proved correct, in that we found fifteen items outside Scale 5 that correlated greater than .30 with the Adolescent-Hypersensitivity/Anxiety factor.

Scores on the Adolescent-Low Cynicism and Adolescent-Restraint factors were correlated with all MMPI-A items that were not on Scale 5. We selected items that correlated at least .30 with the factor and at least .10 less with any other factor. This led to the addition of two items to the Adolescent-Low

Cynicism factor and one item to the Adolescent-Restraint factor. These items added to the internal consistency of their respective factors and thus were retained. The final augmented factors and their alpha consistency coefficients are listed in Table 7.4.

Table 7.4. Final Augmented Factors for Scale 5 of the MMPI-A

Adolescent-Denial of Stereotypical Masculine Interests (four items, alpha = .58)

- (−) 001. Like mechanics magazines.
- (−) 127. Would like to be in military.
- (−) 186. Would like to be a building contractor.
- (−) 190. Like hunting.

Adolescent-Hypersensitivity/Anxiety (nine items, alpha = .60)

- (−) 060. Feelings not easily hurt.
- 159. Worry about sex.
- 185. Frequently worry.
- 194. Habits of some family members very irritating.
- 206. Disappointed in love.
- (−) 221. Don't mind not being better looking.
- (−) 223. Wholly self-confident.
- 235. Often strangers look at me critically.
- 240. Occasionally hate family members I love.

Adolescent-Stereotypical Femininity (six items, alpha = .69)

- 059. Wish was a girl or happy that am.
- 061. Like romances.
- 064. Like poetry
- 114. Like collecting plants.
- 131. Kept a diary.
- (−) 254. Never liked to play with dolls.

Adolescent-Low Cynicism (five items, alpha = .58)

- (−) 072. Hard to convince people of truth.
- (−) 100. People honest because they don't want to be caught.
- (−) 238. People have friends because they're useful.
- (−) 77. Most would lie to succeed.
- (−) 118. Suspect motives of those nice to me.

Adolescent-Restraint (five items, alpha = .47)

- (−) 082. Like loud parties.
- (−) 099. Betting enhances a race.
- (−) 197. Like to talk about sex.
- (−) 217. Like being with people who play jokes on one another.
- (−) 323. Enjoy small stakes gambling.

Note. Test item numbers are included for each item along with the direction in which the item is scored (a minus sign in parentheses preceding the item number indicates that the item is scored when the response is "false"; the lack of a minus marker indicates that the item is scored when the response is "true").

Characteristics of the Factors

Our next step was to explore thoroughly the new factors to determine their characteristics in the combined normative data as well as in the data for males and females separately. We examined the intercorrelations among the factors; we calculated means and standard deviations and compared these by gender; we considered internal consistency in the combined data and by gender; and we explored the amount of variance in Scale 5 scores explained by the factors.

Intercorrelation among the Factors

First, we examined the intercorrelations among the factors. These results are shown in Table 7.5.

Remember that, in the adult data, the factors reflecting the higher-order dimension of masculinity-femininity were more highly intercorrelated than the other dimensions of Scale 5. Although only two components of the masculinity-femininity dimension are represented in the adolescent factors, these two factors showed the highest correlation (.32) in the intercorrelation matrix for the combined data. This correlation is higher than that observed between the two similar dimensions in the adult data (.19) but lower than the correlation between Stereotypical Feminine Interests and Feminine Gender Identity in the adult data (.47). This difference likely reflects the combination of feminine interests and gender identity in the adolescent factor. It may also

Table 7.5. Intercorrelation Matrix of Scale 5 Factors

	A-Stereotypical Femininity	A-Hypersen/ Anxiety	A-Denial of Masculine Interests	A-Low Cynicism	A-Restraint
A-Stereotypical Femininity	—	.29	.32	.05	.19
A-Hypersen/ Anxiety	.15/.07	—	.21	(−.20)	.06
A-Denial of Masculine Interests	(−.07)/.04	.09/.10	—	.09	.22
A-Low Cynicism	(−.01)/.07	(−.19)/(.25)	.10/.09	—	.17
A-Restraint	.06/.02	.00/(−.02)	.13/.15	.18/.16	—

Note. Combined data above the diagonal in plain text; the genders separately below the diagonal: females shown in bold text; males underlined.

Note. Adolescent is abbreviated as A.

support the argument that gender roles are more rigid in adolescents than in adults (Spence, 1985).

Interestingly, when males and females are considered separately, these two factors exhibit very low correlations with each other (.04 for females and −.07 for males). This may be explained by the loss of variance in these factors when considered in only one gender. With the variance attributed to gender removed, these factors are quite independent of each other.

The next highest correlations were between these two factors (i.e., Adolescent-Stereotypical Femininity and Adolescent-Denial of Stereotypical Masculine Interests) and the Adolescent-Hypersensitivity/Anxiety factor (.29 and .21, respectively). These correlations are higher than those between corresponding factors in the adult data (.14 and .13, respectively). This suggests that, among adolescents, traditional masculinity-femininity is moderately related to negative affectivity and perhaps more so than among adults. The latter point cannot be made with certainty because of the different composition of the adult and adolescent factors.

Thus, the pattern of intercorrelations supports our belief that the Adolescent-Stereotypical Femininity and Adolescent-Denial of Masculine Stereotypical Interests factors parallel the two similar adult factors that are part of the higher-order masculinity-femininity dimension.

Means and Standard Deviations Compared by Gender

Next, we calculated the means and standard deviations of the factors in the combined data as well as for males and females separately. These are shown in Table 7.6.

These results are consistent with those observed in the development of factors for adults. When males and females are considered separately on the two factors that reflect the higher-order masculinity-femininity factor in adults (i.e., Adolescent-Stereotypical Femininity and Adolescent-Denial of Stereotypical Masculine Interests), we see a general reduction in variance, but we do not see that reduction on the three factors that are not part of the masculinity-femininity factor. Also, when the means of males and females are compared, the effect size is greater than 1.00 on the two masculinity-femininity factors but much lower than 1.00 on the non-masculinity-femininity factors. This is exactly what we observed in the adult data. These findings support the contention that these are similar scales, but, more important, they confirm that the two masculinity-femininity factors are closely related to gender and support our sense that these are core components of masculinity-femininity.

Table 7.6. Means and Standard Deviations of the Scale 5 Factors of the MMPI-A

	Combined Mean (St. Dev.) n = 1,620	Males Mean (St. Dev.) n = 805	Females Mean (St. Dev.) n = 815	Effect Size[a] Male/Female
A-Denial of Stereotypical Masculine Interests	3.27 (1.03)	2.79 (1.14)	3.75 (0.59)	1.11
A-Hypersen/ Anxiety	5.35 (2.10)	4.72 (2.09)	5.97 (1.93)	0.62
A-Stereotypical Femininity	2.79 (1.81)	1.47 (1.20)	4.09 (1.30)	2.09
A-Low Cynicism	2.15 (1.48)	2.10 (1.41)	2.19 (1.54)	0.06
A-Restraint	2.50 (1.35)	2.20 (1.37)	2.80 (1.26)	0.46

Note. Adolescent is abbreviated A.

Note. [a] Cohen's (1988) *d*.

Internal Consistency of the Factors

Next we computed Cronbach alpha internal consistency coefficients of the factors for males and females separately. These results are shown in Table 7.7. In the combined data, the correlation coefficients are sufficiently high to argue that we have useful factors, as we have discussed previously. When considered separately by gender, the internal consistency decreases for the two factors that show the greatest gender differences and that, we believe, reflect the higher-order masculinity-femininity, Adolescent-Stereotypical Femininity and Adolescent-Denial of Stereotypical Masculine Interests. This is predictable, given the reduction of variance in these two factors when males and females are considered separately.

Variance in Scale 5 Explained by the Factors

Finally, we explored how much of the variance in Scale 5 is explained by the factors. The results of the multiple regression analyses are shown in Table 7.8.

The multiple regression results show that the factors are effective in explaining a significant part of the variance in Scale 5. In each instance, all factors contribute significantly to predicting Scale 5 scores. Even though only twenty-six items of the forty-four-item Scale 5 are included in the factors and

Table 7.7. Internal Consistency of Scale 5 Factors for Males and Females

	Combined Cronbach's alpha n =1,620	Males Cronbach's alpha n = 805	Females Cronbach's alpha n = 815
A-Denial of Masculine Interests	.58	.47	.43
A-Hypersensitivity/Anxiety	.60	.56	.55
A-Stereotypical Femininity	.69	.37	.35
A-Low Cynicism	.58	.53	.62
A-Restraint	.47	.48	.43

Note. Adolescent is abbreviated A.

although three factor items are not from Scale 5, 83 percent of the variance in Scale 5 is accounted for by using the factors in the combined data (74 percent when used with males only and 70 percent when used with females only).

Discussion

Sufficiently reliable factors were developed for Scale 5 of the MMPI-A. There are some differences between the adolescent and adult factors; however, these are predictable given the differences in item pools. The means and

Table 7.8. Percent of Variance in Scale 5 Captured by the Scale 5 Factors

Males	Adjusted R2
Adolescent-Hypersensitivity/Anxiety	.35
Adolescent-Denial of Stereotypical Masculine Interests	.48
Adolescent-Stereotypical Femininity	.62
Adolescent-Low Cynicism	.70
Adolescent-Restraint	.74
Females	Adjusted R2
Adolescent-Stereotypical Femininity	.25
Adolescent-Denial of Stereotypical Masculine Interests	.43
Adolescent-Hypersensitivity/Anxiety	.57
Adolescent-Low Cynicism	.66
Adolescent-Restraint	.70

intercorrelations of the adolescent factors are in line with theoretical predictions and knowledge gained from developing adult factors for Scale 5.

Although we must be cautious in comparing results from the adult and adolescent samples, because the resulting factors have different compositions, it is interesting to note that the Adolescent-Stereotypical Femininity factor correlates higher with Adolescent-Hypersensitivity/Anxiety (i.e., negative affectivity) than the roughly equivalent factors do in adults. Furthermore, this correlation is higher for males than for females. It may suggest that adolescent males with a feminine character are less secure and more anxious than those with a masculine character. Perhaps this insecurity diminishes as males age and find social groups more accepting of their interests. These suggested differences may also reflect Spence's (1985) contention that younger people are more rigid in their gender structures than adults. Thus, an adolescent male who is not congruent with stereotypical gender expectations may experience and fear a lack of acceptance by his peers.

Before we examine the validity of the relatively reliable factors that we have developed, we explore development of a composite higher-order masculinity-femininity scale that is similar to the one developed in the adult data.

Higher-Order Factor Structure of Scale 5 in the MMPI-A

The evidence so far strongly suggests that there is a higher-order factor structure in the simple factor structure that we have identified. As we did following the development of factors for Scale 5 for the MMPI-2, we explored this possibility using a factor analytic procedure similar to that used in the MMPI-2. Our hope was to understand the nature of masculinity-femininity in adolescents and how these constructs relate to other dimensions of personality.

Similar to our work with the MMPI-2, we conducted principal components analyses of the Scale 5 factor intercorrelations for males and females separately, as well as for the combined normative MMPI-A sample. We computed unrotated principal components of the intercorrelation matrix as well as orthogonal varimax and non-orthogonal promax rotated solutions. We used the scree plots from the combined data to decide that two to three higher-order factors might exist. As we found in the adult data, solutions computed separately for males and females did not yield reliable structure; again, this was likely because of reduced variance.

In the combined data, a dominant first factor consistently emerged that accounted for the preponderance of the variance in the factor correlations. We found the clearest solution in the three-factor promax solution, which included the Stereotypical Femininity factor (.81) and the Denial of Stereotypical Masculine Interests factor (.75) with a lesser loading of the Hypersensitivity/Anxiety factor (.51). (See Appendix EE). This factor clearly represents a bipolar higher-order masculinity-femininity dimension of Scale 5, and we designated it the Adolescent Femininity-Masculinity (A-FM) marker scale, similar to the designation of the adult marker. The Hypersensitivity/Anxiety factor split, loading higher on the second factor (−.57), along with Low Cynicism (.91), to capture what might be identified as a Lack of Concern factor. The third higher-order factor was defined by the single Restraint factor (1.00), which likely reflects the personality dimension often referred to as Constraint.

As with the analysis of Scale 5 of the MMPI-2, we constructed a marker of the underlying masculinity-femininity higher-order factor by combining the items on the two relevant scales, Stereotypical Femininity and Denial of Stereotypical Masculine Interests. We did not include the Hypersensitivity/Anxiety factor items because that factor loaded higher on the Lack of Concern factor. We also reasoned that hypersensitivity and anxiety may be a by-product of masculinity-femininity in adolescents, because teenagers are working to feel comfortable in the world, even in the face of peer pressures. The resulting composite, Adolescent Femininity-Masculinity, or A-FM, is shown in Table 7.9.

We then computed the parameters of this Adolescent-FM scale, as shown in Table 7.10. The difference in means for males and females on this Adolescent-FM higher-order factor shows a large effect size of 2.35. This is not surprising, given that we are combining two factors that themselves showed significant gender differences. The internal consistency of the Adolescent-FM scale is high in the combined data but much lower when males and females are considered separately. Again, this may be understood as a

Table 7.9. Composite Marker of Adolescent Femininity-Masculinity in the MMPI-A

    (−) 001. Like mechanics magazines.
    (−) 127. Would like to be in military.
    (−) 186. Would like to be a building contractor.
    (−) 190. Like hunting.
        059. Wish was a girl or happy that am.
        061. Like romances.
        064. Like poetry.
        114. Like collecting plants.
        131. Kept a diary.
    (−) 254. Never liked to play with dolls.

Table 7.10. Parameters of the Adolescent-FM Marker in the MMPI-A Normative Sample

	Mean	Stand Dev[a]	Alpha	Items that detract
COMBINED (n = 1,620)	6.06	2.35	.71	None
MALES (n = 805)	4.26	1.60	.31	127, 114, 59
FEMALES (n = 815)	7.83	1.45	.35	1

Note. [a] indicates standard deviation.

Note. Alpha denotes the Cronbach Alpha correlation coefficient.

result of the reduced variance when considering males and females separately. Note that one item detracts from factor consistency when considered in females alone (#1 "Like mechanics magazines") and that three items detract from alpha when considered in males alone (#127 "Would like to be in military," #114 "Like collecting plants," #59 "Wish was a girl or happy that am"). It is in the combined data that the items contribute to defining this gender-related characteristic.

We then explored the variance explained by the composite Adolescent-FM scale, using the augmented factors and the composite scale to predict Scale 5 scores. These results are shown in Table 7.11. As expected, the Adolescent-FM

Table 7.11. Variance Explained by Adolescent-FM and Augmented Scale 5 Factors

Male Data

Adolescent-FM Scale	.38
Adolescent-Hypersensitivity/Anxiety	.62
Adolescent-Low Cynicism	.70
Adolescent-Restraint	.74

Females

Adolescent-FM Scale	.33
Adolescent-Hypersensitivity/Anxiety	.44
Adolescent-Low Cynicism	.57
Adolescent-Restraint	.64
Adolescent-Stereotypical Femininity	.65

composite score supplanted the two factors from which it was composed. In the combined data, the Adolescent-FM scale accounted for 62 percent (adjusted R2) of the variance in Scale 5. It accounted for 38 percent and 33 percent of the variance for males and females, respectively. This explained the bulk of variance in Scale 5 in each instance, and, in each instance, it was followed by the Adolescent-Hypersensitivity/Anxiety factor in explanatory power.

Distribution of Scores in the Normative Sample

We computed the frequency distributions of the factors in the normative sample and plotted them as percentage of total cases. The results are shown in Figures 7.1 through 7.5.

The Adolescent-Denial of Stereotypical Masculine Interests factor appears substantially truncated, with 81 percent of the females endorsing all the items (36 percent of males endorsed all items). The addition of more items with a range of difficulty would improve this factor, but those items do not exist on the current version of the MMPI-A.

The Adolescent-Hypersensitivity/Anxiety factor shows greater gender differences than the adult version. Adolescent females score higher than males on this factor (effect size for male-female difference is .62 from Table 7.6).

There is clearly a very large gender difference on the Adolescent-Stereotypical Femininity factor producing a bimodal distribution, with females scoring at the high end of the range on the scale and males scoring at the low end. The effect

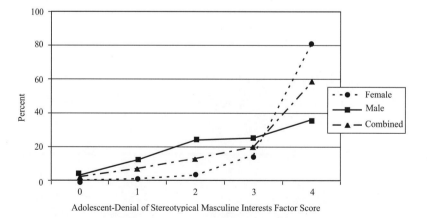

Figure 7.1. Distribution of Scores on the Adolescent-Denial of Stereotypical Masculine Interests Factor

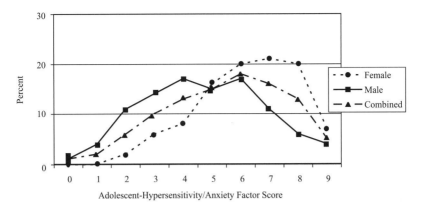

Figure 7.2. Distribution of Scores on the A-Hypersensitivity/Anxiety Factor

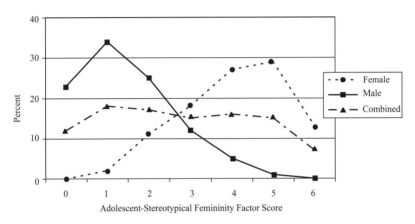

Figure 7.3. Distribution of Scores on the Adolescent-Stereotypical Femininity Factor

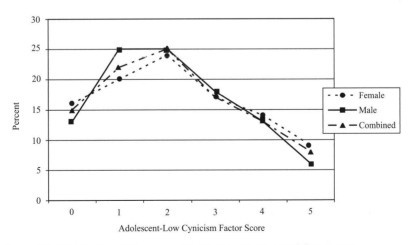

Figure 7.4. Distribution of Scores on the Adolescent-Low Cynicism Factor

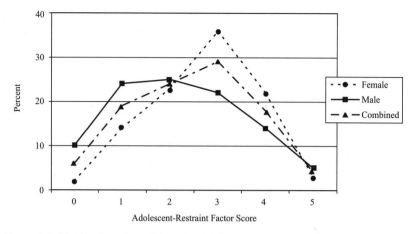

Figure 7.5. Distribution of Scores on the Adolescent-Restraint Factor

size of male-female differences on the Adolescent-Stereotypical Femininity from Table 7.6 is 2.09.

Males and females score similarly on the Adolescent-Low Cynicism factor. The scale seems to spread the samples out across its short range. More items could enhance this factor by spreading the subjects out across a broader range.

The distribution of the Adolescent-Restraint factor appears similar in males and females, and a normal distribution begins to appear in the normative sample. Females tend to score higher on restraint than males (see Table 7.7; effect size for male-female difference = .46).

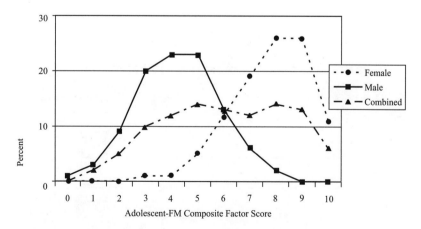

Figure 7.6. Distribution of Scores on the A-FM Composite Factor

The distribution of scores on the Adolescent-FM marker scale shows a clear bimodal distribution, with males scoring low and females scoring high. This is not surprising, given the distribution of its components (Adolescent-Denial of Stereotypical Masculine Interests Factor and Stereotypical Femininity).

Convergent and Discriminant Validity

Having established psychometrically sound factors and a composite Adolescent-FM marker, we next examined their convergent and discriminant validity. We did this by correlating the factors with other measures on the MMPI-A, including the Clinical scales, the Validity scales, the adolescent Content scales, and the Supplementary scales (A, R, ACK, PRO, IMM). The results of these analyses are shown in Tables 7.12 (combined data), Table 7.13 (male data), and Table 7.14 (female data).

These results provide some insight into what each factor is measuring. The three factors we have that tap the masculinity-femininity concept (i.e., Adolescent-Stereotypical Femininity, Adolescent-Denial of Stereotypical Masculine Interests, and the Adolescent-FM scale) show low correlations with all other scales, suggesting that they represent a dimension that is not captured by other scales of the MMPI-A. The highest correlation involving the Adolescent-FM composite scale is with the IMM supplementary scale (combined = −.26). This correlation is higher for females (−.33) than for males (−.17). The Adolescent-Stereotypical Femininity factor also correlates highest with the IMM supplemental scale (combined = −.21). The correlation is, again, higher in females (−.30) than in males, where it is negligible (−.01). The Adolescent-Denial of Stereotypical Masculine Interests factor found its highest correlation with the F scale (−.27). In the combined data, it correlates −.23 with IMM, but this time the correlation is higher for males (−.22) than for females (−.15). This suggests, again, that there may be a slightly different structure of masculinity-femininity for males than for females.

The highest correlation in the data is between the Adolescent-Low Cynicism factor and the CYN Content scale (combined = −.79; males = −.77; females = −.81). This factor also correlates moderately (.40 to .53) with an array of other scales reflecting anxiety and alienation. The factor thus appears to be a valid measure of low cynicism

The Adolescent-Hypersensitivity/Anxiety factor correlates highly with many scales including Scale 7/Pt (.62), A (.62), ANX (.58), OBS (.55), DEP

Table 7.12. Correlations of Scale 5 Factors with Other Measures on the MMPI-A (Combined Male and Female Data)

	A-Denial of Masc. Int.	A-Hyper/ Anxiety	A-Stereo. Femininity	A-Low Cynicism	A-Restraint	A-FM Scale
Scale 5	.56	.62	.70	.17	.34	.79
Hs	.01	.33	.13	−.22	−.00	.11
D	.11	.35	.10	−.09	.17	.13
Hy	.09	.14	.12	.24	.11	.13
Pd	−.05	.37	.03	−.28	−.07	.01
Pa	−.10	.26	.08	−.12	−.06	.02
Pt	.04	.62	.16	−.44	−.08	.14
Sc	−.11	.45	.06	−.44	−.14	.00
Ma	−.15	.24	.10	−.39	−.35	.02
Si	.05	.47	.03	−.36	.26	.04
L	−.17	−.37	−.13	.17	.17	−.18
F-1	−.28	.01	−.10	−.25	−.15	−.20
F-2	−.24	.04	−.05	−.28	−.12	−.14
F	−.27	.03	−.08	−.28	−.14	−.18
K	−.03	−.53	−.13	.53	.11	−.12
A	.03	.62	.16	−.45	−.06	.14
R	.18	−.21	−.11	.19	.28	−.00
ACK	−.21	.15	−.04	−.30	−.29	−.12
PRO	−.09	.19	−.03	−.22	−.33	−.06
IMM	−.23	.17	−.21	−.47	−.22	−.26
A-ANX	.03	.58	.14	−.39	−.05	.12
A-OBS	.01	.55	.17	−.45	−.11	.14
A-DEP	.01	.51	.14	−.37	−.03	.11
A-HEA	−.07	.24	.09	−.23	−.03	.04
A-ALN	−.13	.32	−.04	−.42	−.04	−.09
A-BIZ	−.16	.23	.06	−.39	−.16	−.03
A-ANG	−.05	.38	.07	−.38	−.21	.03
A-CYN	−.09	.30	.01	−.79	−.20	−.03
A-CON	−.24	.14	−.15	−.40	−.46	−.22
A-LSE	−.02	.44	.10	−.34	−.02	.07
A-LAS	.00	.18	−.09	−.19	−.07	−.07
A-SOD	−.09	.20	−.13	−.22	.20	−.14

(*Continued*)

Table 7.12. (*Continued*)

	A-Denial of Masc. Int.	A-Hyper/ Anxiety	A-Stereo. Femininity	A-Low Cynicism	A- Restraint	A-FM Scale
A-FAM	−.08	.39	.06	−.35	−.13	.01
A-SCH	−.20	.17	−.09	−.36	−.23	−.16
A-TRT	−.12	.33	−.01	−.48	−.08	−.06

Note. A-Denial of Masc. Int.= Adolescent-Denial of Masculine Interests Subscale; A-Hyper/Anxiety = Adolescent-Hypersensitivity/Anxiety Subscale; A-Stereo. Femininity = Adolescent-Stereotypical Femininity Subscale; A-FM = Adolescent-FM Scale

Table 7.13. Correlations of Scale 5 Factors with Other Measures on the MMPI-A (Male Data)

	A-Denial of Masc. Int.	A-Hyper/ Anxiety	A-Stereo. Femininity	A-Low Cynicism	A- Restraint	A-FM Scale
Scale 5	.41	.59	.43	.22	.31	.61
Hs	−.08	.30	.15	−.12	.02	.05
D	.04	.26	.12	.04	.21	.12
Hy	.04	.08	.08	.31	.14	.08
Pd	−.11	.37	.07	−.22	−.04	−.03
Pa	−.16	.28	.21	−.09	.00	.04
Pt	−.07	.63	.15	−.39	−.07	.06
Sc	−.19	.47	.18	−.37	−.09	.00
Ma	−.25	.24	.12	−.41	−.36	−.09
Si	.02	.48	.07	−.28	.32	.07
L	−.08	−.33	.05	.25	.23	−.02
F-1	−.27	.06	.18	−.19	−.06	−.06
F-2	−.27	.06	.19	−.20	−.04	−.05
F	−.28	.07	.19	−.20	−.06	−.06
K	.05	−.49	−.06	.54	.15	−.01
A	−.07	.61	.15	−.42	−.06	.06
R	.26	−.20	−.07	.23	.34	.13
ACK	−.28	.17	.11	−.26	−.25	−.12
PRO	−.17	.19	.02	−.19	−.31	−.11
IMM	−.22	.22	−.01	−.40	−.15	−.17
A-ANX	−.06	.57	.16	−.35	−.04	.08

(*Continued*)

Table 7.13. (*Continued*)

	A-Denial of Masc. Int.	A-Hyper/ Anxiety	A-Stereo. Femininity	A-Low Cynicism	A- Restraint	A-FM Scale
A-OBS	−.09	.54	.12	−.42	−.11	.03
A-DEP	−.11	.47	.15	−.33	−.00	.03
A-HEA	−.15	.21	.16	−.11	.01	.01
A-ALN	−.15	.37	.12	−.35	.01	−.02
A-BIZ	−.22	.25	.21	−.34	−.13	.00
A-ANG	−.15	.38	.07	−.37	−.24	−.05
A-CYN	−.12	.29	.04	−.77	−.23	−.06
A-CON	−.22	.23	.06	−.37	−.43	−.12
A-LSE	−.12	.41	.16	−.27	.01	.03
A-LAS	−.02	.14	−.08	−.15	−.02	−.07
A-SOD	−.02	.29	.08	−.15	.31	.04
A-FAM	−.19	.38	.11	−.31	−.12	−.05
A-SCH	−.24	.21	.06	−.31	−.18	−.13
A-TRT	−.20	.31	.06	−.41	−.03	−.09

Note. A-Denial of Masc. Int.= Adolescent-Denial of Masculine Interests Subscale; A-Hyper/Anxiety = Adolescent-Hypersensitivity/Anxiety Subscale; A-Stereo. Femininity = Adolescent-Stereotypical Femininity Subscale; A-FM = Adolescent-FM Scale.

Table 7.14. Correlations of Scale 5 Factors with Other Measures on the MMPI-A (Female Data)

	A-Denial of Masc. Int.	A-Hyper/ Anxiety	A-Stereo. Femininity	A-Low Cynicism	A- Restraint	A-FM Scale
Scale 5	.41	.40	.45	.30	.36	.58
HS	−.07	.30	−.09	−.32	−.09	−.11
D	.05	.38	−.17	−.22	.06	−.13
HY	−.04	.11	−.09	.16	−.01	−.09
PD	−.07	.35	−.12	−.34	−.15	−.14
PA	−.12	.23	−.07	−.14	−.15	−.11
PT	−.03	.58	−.04	−.49	−.17	−.04
SC	−.14	.43	−.10	−.51	−.22	−.15
MA	−.12	.22	.04	−.38	−.38	−.02

(*Continued*)

Table 7.14. (*Continued*)

	A-Denial of Masc. Int.	A-Hyper/ Anxiety	A-Stereo. Femininity	A-Low Cynicism	A- Restraint	A-FM Scale
SI	.04	.47	−.11	−.44	.18	−.09
A	−.01	.61	−.00	−.50	−.14	−.01
R	.09	−.24	−.23	.14	.24	−.17
ACK	−.11	.17	−.12	−.33	−.34	−.15
PRO	−.02	.18	−.14	−.25	−.38	−.14
IMM	−.15	.22	−.30	−.54	−.25	−.33
L	−.18	−.37	−.12	.10	.20	−.18
F-1	−.23	.05	−.22	−.32	−.20	−.29
F-2	−.21	.05	−.23	−.37	−.20	−.290
F	−.23	.05	−.24	−.37	−.21	−.31
K	−.01	−.56	−.05	.55	.13	−.05
A-ANX	.00	.56	−.03	−.44	−.13	−.02
A-OBS	−.01	.53	.07	−.49	−.19	.053
A-DEP	−.03	.52	−.06	−.42	−.14	−.06
A-HEA	−.13	.22	−.09	−.33	−.12	−.13
A-ALN	−.10	.34	−.13	−.49	−.08	−.16
A-BIZ	−.16	.23	−.06	−.43	−.21	−.12
A-ANG	−.02	.36	−.05	−.41	−.24	−.06
A-CYN	−.06	.34	−.01	−.81	−.18	−.03
A-CON	−.12	.19	−.11	−.44	−.44	−.15
A-LSE	−.03	.43	−.11	−.41	−.10	−.11
A-LAS	.01	.21	−.23	−.23	−.14	−.21
A-SOD	−.06	.22	−.18	−.28	.16	−.18
A-FAM	−.09	.39	−.12	−.40	−.20	−.15
A-SCH	−.10	.19	−.17	−.40	−.26	−.19
A-TRT	−.07	.36	−.14	−.54	−.13	−.15

Note. A-Denial of Masc. Int.= Adolescent-Denial of Masculine Interests Subscale; A-Hyper/Anxiety = Adolescent-Hypersensitivity/Anxiety Subscale; A-Stereo. Femininity = Adolescent-Stereotypical Femininity Subscale; A-FM = Adolescent-FM Scale.

(.51), and K (−.53). This factor thus measures anxiety and depression and reflects the large loading of negative affectivity contained in the MMPI-A. It might best be considered a measure of negative affectivity.

The Adolescent-Restraint factor correlates highest with the CON content scale in the negative direction (combined = −.46; males = −.43; females = −.44), reflecting the lack of restraint that underlies problems in conduct in adolescence. It also correlates with the Clinical Scale 9 (combined = −.35), suggesting that it may also reflect energy level, grandiosity, and impulsivity. Additionally, A-Restraint correlates moderately in the negative direction with the substance use supplemental scales (PRO = −.33 and ACK = −.29). This factor appears to reflect the variance in Scale 5 that Hathaway and Monachesi (1957) termed an inhibitory factor to acting-out behavior.

Table 7.15 presents briefly what each factor measures. Because the two masculinity-femininity factors and the Adolescent FM scale are bipolar, it is appropriate to interpret both high and low scores. Adolescent-Low Cynicism and Adolescent-Restraint are reversed-scored, so low scores are interpretable. Those factors and Adolescent-Hypersensitivity/Anxiety reflect constructs, for which both high and low levels tell us something about the test-taker.

Table 7.15. Summary of Factors for Scale 5 of the MMPI-A

1. ADOLESCENT-DENIAL OF STEREOTYPICAL MASCULINE INTERESTS

A factor reflecting a lack of interest in activities typically considered male or masculine (e.g., mechanics, hunting, soldiering, work of building contractor)

2. ADOLESCENT-HYPERSENSITIVITY/ANXIETY

A factor reflecting self-focused worry and sensitivity (e.g., feelings easily hurt, worry about sex, concern about appearance, lack of self-confidence, irritation at family)

3. ADOLESCENT-STEREOTYPICAL FEMININITY

A factor reflecting activities and interests typically considered female or feminine (e.g., love stories, poetry, collecting flowers, keeping a diary, playing with dolls) as well as being satisfied being a girl or wishing to be a girl

4. ADOLESCENT-LOW CYNICISM

A factor reflecting lack of cynicism and suspiciousness about human motivations (e.g., people are honest because they are afraid of being caught, believing people would lie to get ahead, suspecting hidden selfish motives in others)

5. ADOLESCENT-RESTRAINT

A factor reflecting lack of interest in and pleasure from loud and aggressive activities (e.g., loud fun, talking about sex, gambling)

ADOLESCENT COMPOSITE FEMININITY-MASCULINITY SCALE (FM)

A bipolar marker scale of core masculinity-femininity (combining Denial of Stereotypical Masculine Interests and Stereotypical Femininity)

Therefore, we believe that, in general, both high and low scores on the Scale 5 factors are interpretable.

Discussion

In summary, the three masculinity-femininity markers represent a dimension that is not reflected in other MMPI-A scales. The Adolescent-Hypersensitivity/ Anxiety factor reflects negative affectivity. The Adolescent-Low Cynicism factor measures cynicism, and the Adolescent-Restraint factor is a measure of inhibition. The correlations with other scales suggest that the names given to the factors are accurate reflections of their content.

The differences between adolescents and adults in the structure of Scale 5 were intriguing to us. Were these a result of developmental issues or the restricted set of items retained for Scale 5 of the MMPI-A? Or has the structure of masculinity-femininity changed across time so that different cohorts show different intercorrelations of Scale 5 items? With these questions, we wondered how the adult normative data for the MMPI-2 would have factor analyzed if it were limited to only those items included on the MMPI-A. Would it provide factors similar to those developed in the adolescent normative data for the MMPI-A? We next undertook a set of analyses to help us answer these questions.

Factor Analyzing the Adolescent Items in the Adult Data

To explore the nature of the differences between adolescent and adult factors, we factor analyzed the adult normative data using only the restricted set of forty-four Scale 5 items that are available on the MMPI-A. First, we calculated the same range of orthogonal solutions as when we were developing simple factors at the beginning of this chapter. The results looked very similar in adolescents and adults. We looked closely at the results of the six-factor orthogonal analysis, as shown in Table 7.16, which we chose as the best solution for adolescents.

There are several notable differences between the solutions for adolescents and adults. First, there is a difference in the relative coherence of factors. In the factor analysis of adolescent data, the factor with the highest eigenvalue— hence the most coherent factor—is the feminine factor, whereas, with adults, the masculine factor is the most coherent. The masculine factor is also primary in the MMPI-2 Scale 5 factors. This difference may mean that stereotypic feminine interests are more salient and have more variance in adolescents, whereas stereotypic masculine interests show more variability among adults.

Table 7.16. Six-Factor Solution of MMPI-A Items in the Adult Normative Data

Factor 1:

> 001/001. Like mechanics magazines.
> 069/066. Would like being a forest ranger.
> 197/186. Would like to be a building contractor.
> 199/188. Like science.

Factor 2:

> (−) 063/060. Feelings not easily hurt.
> 166/159. Worry about sex.
> 196/185. Frequently worry.
> 205/194. Habits of some family members very irritating.
> 219/206. Disappointed in love.
> (−) 237/221. Don't mind not being better looking.
> 251/235. Often strangers look at me critically.
> 256/240. Occasionally hate family members I love.

Factor 3:

> 067/064. Like poetry.
> 080/076. Would like being a nurse.
> 119/114. Like collecting plants.

Factor 4:

> 026/023. Keep quiet when in trouble.
> 027/024. Retaliate when wronged.
> 076/072. Hard to convince people of truth.
> 104/100. People honest because they don't want to be caught.
> 193/183. I avoid stepping on sidewalk cracks.
> 254/238. People have friends because they're useful.

Factor 5:

> 086/082. Like loud parties.
> 209/197. Like to talk about sex.
> 231/217. Like being with people who play jokes on one another.

Factor 6:

> None

Note. The MMPI-2 item number is given first, and the MMPI-A number is given second.

Note. (−) indicates that the item is scored if answered "false."

Second, there are changes in items that make up the feminine and masculine factors for adults and adolescents. Although there are substantial similarities in the factors' items, there are also some noteworthy differences. For example, the adult feminine factor added an item reflecting interest in nursing; this could reflect a generational difference, given that nursing is less exclusively a female occupation now than it was in the past. Also, the adult feminine factor did not include items #62 "Wished was a girl or happy that am," #61 "Like romances," #131 "Kept a diary," or #254 "Never liked to play with dolls," all of which appeared on the corresponding adolescent factors. Three of these four items are included on the MMPI-2's Feminine Gender Identity factor, which may not have emerged here as a result of the omission of its other item on the MMPI-A (#241 "Would like to be a sports reporter"). It is interesting that these items do not covary as highly with feminine interests in adults as in adolescents. It seems possible that feminine interests and gender identity become more differentiated as one ages. As Spence (1985) suggested, adolescents may have broader, less refined concepts of masculinity-femininity.

The masculine factor exhibited some differences also. The adult version included interests in being a forest ranger and in science, whereas the adolescent version did not. Again, these differences might reflect a cohort effect. Both of these interests are more acceptable now for females than they have been in the past. "Would like to be in military" (#127) and "Like hunting" (#190) were included on the adolescent masculine interest factor but did not appear on the adult factor using the same data. Again, this may reflect adolescents' tendency to "paint" the domain of masculinity and femininity with broader strokes than do adults.

Finally, the cynicism factor emerged earlier in the adult data than in the adolescent data and seemed more inclusive and cohesive than in the adolescent analyses. Several Scale 5 items loaded on this scale for adults that did not load highly on it in the adolescent data. These included "Keep quiet when in trouble" (#23), "Retaliate when wronged" (#24), and "I avoid stepping on sidewalk cracks" (#183). In examining frequency data for these items, we noted that many more adolescents in the MMPI-A normative sample endorsed these items than did adults in the MMPI-2 normative sample. For example, for the item "Retaliate when wronged," 52 percent of male adolescents and 34 percent of female adolescents said "True," as opposed to 27 percent of males and 14 percent of females in the adult normative sample. Possibly, a certain degree of cynicism is typical of adolescents, and only later in life do complex individual differences occur on this aspect of personality.

These structural differences between adults and adolescents, which emerged when we factor analyzed the same items, suggest some intriguing possibilities. Clearly, the differences between adults and adolescents in Scale 5 factor structures are not due solely to the more restricted set of items among adolescents. The differences highlight the possibility of generational, developmental, and perhaps cultural differences in masculinity and femininity.

Summary

In spite of the loss of twelve items from Scale 5 of the MMPI-2, a successful analysis of Scale 5 of the MMPI-A was accomplished. Five factors paralleling some derived from the MMPI-2 were developed. The resulting factors include Adolescent-Denial of Masculine Interests, Adolescent-Hypersensitivity/Anxiety, Adolescent-Stereotypical Femininity, Adolescent-Low Cynicism, and Adolescent-Restraint. They demonstrated sufficient cohesiveness as well as convergent and discriminant validity.

As predicted (because of the loss of four of the five items comprising this factor), a factor parallel to the adult Aesthetic Interest factor did not emerge. Additionally, the Stereotypical Feminine Interest factor from the MMPI-2 (which lost half of its items in the MMPI-A) combined with remnants (three of the four items) of the Feminine Gender Identity factor of the MMPI-2 to form a blended factor: Adolescent-Stereotypical Femininity. Subsequent investigation of the MMPI-A Scale 5 items in the adult sample indicated that the structural differences were not solely an artifact of the restricted item set available for the MMPI-A. It seems likely the structural differences reflect a less differentiated conceptualization of masculinity and femininity among adolescents.

The fact that neither the Adolescent-Stereotypical Femininity factor nor the Adolescent-Denial of Stereotypical Masculine Interests factor correlate highly with other MMPI-A scales suggests that they may be useful indicators, representing variance that is not otherwise captured in existing scales of the MMPI-A. Adolescent-Stereotypical Femininity and Adolescent-Denial of Stereotypical Masculine Interests appear to reflect the higher-order masculinity-femininity factor, which was also seen in the MMPI-2 analyses. Considered in combination (i.e., the A-FM scale), they may represent the best marker of this higher-order bipolar factor in the MMPI-A.

The limited set of items on Scale 5 of the MMPI-A may limit the test's effective measurement of the higher-order construct of masculinity-femininity. Just as the dimension of sexual orientation is not represented in the MMPI-2, so too it is not represented on the MMPI-A. Although it is possible that gender identity is not as well-defined in adolescents as in adults, it also may be that a paucity of items on the MMPI-A prevented the gender identity dimension from appearing on the MMPI-A. A future study could involve scoring adolescent subjects on the MMPI-2 (larger item pool) to determine whether the gender identity dimension distinguishes itself from feminine interests, as it does with adults. Given the evidence that gender roles are more pronounced in earlier life than later, it may be that the gender identity dimension would be pronounced in adolescents with the added items.

Finally, the differences between males and females and between adults and adolescents suggest that working definitions of masculinity and femininity may vary somewhat with gender, age, and generation. They may also vary with culture. These possible differences might be fruitful to study further in the effort to better understand the concept of masculinity-femininity. However, with our studies, masculinity-femininity becomes a higher-order construct that is circumscribed as well as empirically derived. This may yield a more precise and productive definition of the terms than has been available in the past and may offer new scientific life to terms that are constant in the vernacular.

Chapter 8

Summary and Conclusions: Masculinity-Femininity and the MMPI

In this final chapter, we look back on our exploration of masculinity-femininity through the MMPI-2 and MMPI-A and highlight the meaning and implications that can be derived from our work. We start by reviewing the major steps in our studies of masculinity-femininity. Then we apply what we have learned to those bigger questions that require informed answers. Finally, we point out areas for future research.

Historical Context of this Book

We have discussed the history and some of the issues involving masculinity-femininity and have seen that masculinity and femininity are poorly understood concepts. We traced conceptualizations of masculinity-femininity from a unidimensional bipolar construct to the notion of two separate, independent dimensions, to the idea of multidimensional correlated components, to proposals to abandon the terms altogether. Our work points in the direction of a circumscribed, multidimensional bipolar construct that includes the subcomponents of gender identity and stereotypical interests.

We gleaned some understanding of one contributory source of confusion about masculinity-femininity from considering the development of the MMPI, a major measure of masculinity-femininity for over fifty years. When Scale 5 was first constructed, it was assumed that those characteristics that differentiated men from women would be equivalent to those that differentiated homosexuals from heterosexuals (of both genders) and that these characteristics would define masculinity-femininity. Other measures were subsequently developed that correctly challenged these assumptions, but, in their own ways, they failed to clarify the illusive constructs and only muddied the water further. We examined the debate about the foundations of masculinity and femininity. Are these concepts rooted in nature or nurture? Another major question concerns their relationship to homosexuality and transsexualism.

Given the tortured history of the constructs of masculinity and femininity, it is tempting to conclude that they are encumbered with too much baggage and too many seemingly unanswerable questions and therefore should be abandoned as topics of scientific study or applied measurement. However, these constructs are still prevalent in everyday conversation in most if not all languages and cultures, and most laypersons seem to believe that the terms convey clear and useful information. It is evident that the terms *masculine* and *feminine* are not going away, at least any time soon.

Thus, we undertook our study with no illusions that clarifying the concepts would be simple or uncontroversial. We do hope that our work is a start in a fruitful direction that will lead to a better understanding of masculinity and femininity. We hope, at the very least, that the measurement of masculinity-femininity and related concepts will improve and that the concepts will become less susceptible to inaccurate, wasteful, and sometimes harmful applications.

What We Have Learned

MMPI-2

Using factor analytic methods, we identified seven dimensions of Scale 5 of the MMPI-2: Denial of Stereotypical Masculine Interests, Hypersensitivity/ Anxiety, Stereotypical Feminine Interests, Low Cynicism, Aesthetic Interests, Feminine Gender Identity, and Restraint. In spite of concerns that there might be substantial structural differences between men and women in the area of masculinity-femininity, we discovered that one set of factors was appropriate for both males and females. These factors accounted for 86 percent of the variance in MMPI-2 Scale 5 among males and 80 percent among females.

The factors demonstrated satisfactory internal consistency in the MMPI-2 normative sample in which they were identified as well as in two college samples to which they were applied. The one exception was the original Feminine Gender Identity scale, which was not a cohesive factor when the genders were considered separately. This may have been the result of the lack of variance in gender identity in the normal population represented by the normative sample. Nonetheless, by using the broader MMPI-2 item pool, we augmented two of the factors with items that improved their psychometric properties. In fact, by augmenting the Feminine Gender Identity factor and then deleting two original items, the low internal consistency of this factor was raised to acceptable levels when the genders were considered independently.

An ensuing abundance of correlations supported the validity of the Scale 5 factors. We examined the relationship of the factors to other MMPI scales and to an array of measures of masculinity-femininity, gender identity, sexual orientation, and personality. We used the normative sample and two college samples to study these relationships. By identifying the components of Scale 5, we discovered that some dimensions appear to measure personality dimensions that are already represented on the MMPI-2 and probably have little to do with the core concept of masculinity-femininity (e.g., cynicism). The measurement of such traits seems better left to other scales that more fully represent the domain of those constructs. We believe that this conclusion is sensible and that including other dimensions in a scale that is alleged to measure masculinity and femininity only clouds its interpretation.

The Hypersensitivity/Anxiety factor is strongly related to negative emotionality, which is a major dimension underlying variance in MMPI-2 scores. Negative emotionality is better captured by Pt, A (Anxiety scale), NEGE (negative emotionality scale in the PSY-5 scales), RCd (Restructured Demoralization), and by the RC7 (Restructured Dysfunctional Negative Emotions) scale. The Low Cynicism factor correlated moderately in the negative direction with negative emotionality, but it is better captured by the CYN Content scale, with which it correlated highly, and the Restructured Scale 3 (RC3), which Tellegen, Ben-Porath, McNulty, Arbisi, Graham, and Kaemmer (2003) call Cynicism. The Aesthetic Interests factor correlates moderately with the Stereotypical Feminine Interests factor, but it clearly represents a separate factor in adults. It has few correlates in other MMPI-2 scales and probably reflects a unique dimension in the MMPI item pool. This item content was retained and is captured in the AES scale of the MMPI-2-RF. The Restraint factor is related to the broader personality dimension of Constraint. It is captured in R (Repression scale) and in RC9 (the Restructured Hypomanic Activation scale).

We also discovered three dimensions of Scale 5 related to what we believe are core aspects of a higher-order dimension of masculinity-femininity: Denial of Stereotypical Masculine Interests, Stereotypical Feminine Interests, and Feminine Gender Identity. None of these scales correlated highly with any other MMPI-2 scale except GM and GF, with which they share many items. All of them show large gender differences, with effect sizes exceeding 1.0. Furthermore, patterns of correlations with an assortment of measures outside the MMPI-2 support the idea that these factors are related to masculinity-femininity. The Denial of Stereotypical Masculine Interests factor correlates highly with the Masculinity/Femininity scale of the California Psychological Inventory and the Baucom Femininity scale, both of which are traditional measures of femininity. The Stereotypical Feminine Interests factor correlates highly with these same measures and also the Sex Role Identity Scale (Storms, 1979). The Feminine Gender Identity factor correlated highly with the traditional measures as well, but it showed the strongest correlations with the sex-specific scale of Orlofsky's Sex Role Behavior Scale, with the Sex Role Identity Scale, and with female gender.

Furthermore, these three factors showed moderate to strong intercorrelations in the samples that we analyzed. They also represent constructs recognized by many as central to masculinity-femininity, unlike negative emotionality and cynicism. We factor analyzed the intercorrelation matrix of the factors and found a dominant first factor that included these three factors. Thus, we concluded that the three factors together reflect the higher-order construct of masculinity-femininity as it exists in the MMPI-2 item pool, and we combined these three factors to form a composite marker of femininity-masculinity, the FM Scale.

Correlations involving the FM marker computed in the MMPI-2 normative data and in two college samples indicated that it is a strong measure of masculinity-femininity. As expected, FM correlated highly but not completely with female gender (.82). It also correlated highly with the Sex Role Identity Scale (−.79), the California Psychological Inventory Masculinity/Femininity scale (.79), GF (.80) and GM (−.63) of the MMPI-2, and with two little-known MMPI scales, Gd (.69) and Mfp (.57). Importantly, it did not correlate substantially with other dimensions of personality, thus demonstrating discriminant validity. We believe that the FM marker is the best index of masculinity-femininity available from the MMPI-2.

Next, we explored the stability of the Scale 5 factors across a range of ages, levels of education, and ethnicities in the MMPI-2 normative sample. Although the non-masculinity-femininity factors, especially Low Cynicism, showed some predictable variations, those factors central to masculinity-femininity did not vary among different demographic groups in the normative sample. The one exception to this pattern concerned education level and Denial of Stereotypical Masculine Interests; less-educated respondents endorsed more masculine interests than did respondents with more education. This finding makes sense, given that many traditional masculine interests (e.g., sports, hunting) compete with formal academic education. The stability of core components of masculinity-femininity across age and ethnic groups suggests that these variables are fairly consistent and enduring aspects of personality. This conclusion is supported by Finn's (1986b) finding that thirty-year retest correlations of a masculine interests and a feminine interests scale were quite sizeable in two samples of college-aged and middle-aged men.

The convergence of all these data provides substantial evidence of the construct validity of the Scale 5 factors for the MMPI-2. Although more evidence is important in the ultimate validation of the factors, we have a good start that should instill enough confidence to begin to use the scales in research settings.

MMPI-A

We obtained similar results when we turned our attention to the MMPI-A, but we found less robust factors, and we have less information to support their validity. The evidence that we do have revealed that Scale 5 of the MMPI-A contains fewer dimensions than Scale 5 of the MMPI-2. Without a doubt, this result is partly due to the reduced item pool in the MMPI-A: there are only forty-four items on Scale 5 of the MMPI-A, whereas there are fifty-six items on Scale 5 of the MMPI-2. The lesser number of dimensions found for MMPI-A Scale 5 also relates to differences in masculinity-femininity between adolescents and adults. By factor analyzing the adolescent items in the adult data, we confirmed that the differences between adolescents and adults go beyond the reductions in the item pool. There appear to be differences in the structure of masculinity-femininity between adolescents and adults, with adolescents making fewer distinctions between different subcomponents of masculinity-femininity (e.g., considering aesthetic interests to be similar to stereotypical feminine interests).

Nonetheless, five seemingly viable variants of the MMPI-2 Scale 5 factors emerged in our analyses of the MMPI-A: Denial of Stereotypical Masculine Interests, Hypersensitivity/Anxiety, Stereotypical Femininity (a combination of Stereotypical Feminine Interests, Aesthetic Interests, and Feminine Gender Identity), Low Cynicism, and Restraint. Among males in the normative sample, these factors accounted for 74 percent of the variance in Scale 5; among females, they accounted for 70 percent. Two of these factors, Denial of Stereotypical Masculine Interests and Stereotypical Femininity, showed large gender differences and are combined into an adolescent version of the FM scale, which we believe is the best marker of masculinity-femininity available on the MMPI-A. Correlations with other MMPI-A scales provided convergent and discriminant validity that is strikingly similar to that observed in the MMPI-2.

Important Questions about Masculinity-Femininity

The studies presented in this book finally provide some answers to a number of questions arising from current knowledge about masculinity-femininity and the MMPI. Much of what we say here is based on evidence accumulated for the MMPI-2, but, because of the substantial similarity of the two inventories, we believe that our conclusions are applicable to the MMPI-A as well. We point out instances where substantial differences exist for the MMPI-A.

Is There Such a Thing as Masculinity-Femininity?

Our work shows that there is a set of correlated characteristics that captures a unique part of the variance present in the MMPI and that is independent of the traditional personality dimensions. This unique dimension has been identified by others and, because of its face validity, has been called masculinity-femininity (Dahlstrom, Welsh, & Dahlstrom, 1975; Johnson, Null, Butcher, & Johnson, 1984). One could call the construct comprised by this unique variance anything, but we know that it is strongly related to gender differences and that test items capturing it closely reflect lay conceptions of masculinity-femininity. Some might propose that we call the construct gender identity, but it seems to be multidimensional, with gender identity being only a part of it. In our study of the MMPI-2, masculine interests, feminine interests, and gender identity cohered in a higher-order factor that differentiated itself from other factors. In the MMPI-A, the gender identity dimension combined with feminine interests into a single factor, which then joined with masculine interests to form the higher-order factor. In both adults and adolescents, this higher-order factor was most visible when the genders were considered together, maximizing the variance, but it was also apparent when males and females were considered separately.

When we combined gender identity, feminine interests, and masculine interests (reversed), the resulting composite measure correlated with various existing measures of masculinity-femininity in such a way as to suggest that it tapped similar aspects of human experience. Thus, we called this dimension Femininity-Masculinity and were able to demonstrate its construct validity in other analyses. Our operational definition of the masculinity-femininity construct is more limited than has been advocated in the past, but the evidence suggests that it captures unique variance in individual differences in personality.

Thus, in spite of what Spence (1984), Deaux (1984), and others have argued, there is enough agreement between individuals in how they conceive of and express masculinity-femininity that it is possible to create a viable measure of the construct. However, this measure would be more limited in scope than has been reflected in traditional measures of masculinity-femininity. Although we agree that each person is unique, as feminist philosophy underscores, and can never be fully captured by assessment instruments designed for nomothetic comparisons, we also believe that nomothetic constructs and their operational definitions have much to contribute to our understanding of humanity. Our studies give hope for the nomothetic measurement of masculinity-femininity.

Are Gender Differences Viable Criteria for Establishing Masculinity-Femininity?

Historically, differences between males and females have been central in defining what is masculine and what is feminine. This is natural given our definition of masculine as "characteristics of a man" and feminine as "characteristics of women" (Merriam-Webster Collegiate Dictionary, 1993). Accordingly, efforts to develop measures of masculinity-femininity have generally considered differential endorsement of items by males and females as the central demonstration of construct validity.

In our opinion, it is important to differentiate gender differences, which can exist on a broad spectrum, from masculinity-femininity, which may be only a subset of overall gender differences. As we discussed in chapter 1, gender identity, sexual orientation, interests, personality traits, cognitive abilities, and rates of psychopathology have all been identified as areas in which gender differences are evident (Willerman, 1991). However, we don't believe—just because males generally exhibit better visual-spatial abilities than females or because females typically show better verbal fluency than males—that most people would consider these abilities to be core aspects of masculinity-femininity. Helgeson (1994) and Deaux (1999) contended that using gender differences as the sole criteria for determining masculinity-femininity is a mistake, and we agree.

The GM and GF scales of the MMPI-2 demonstrate the dangers of considering any and all male-female differences in personality test responses to be indicative of masculinity-femininity. GM and GF were developed solely on the basis of gender differences in the endorsement frequency of MMPI-2 items. As discussed in chapter 3, previous studies had already called the wisdom of this strategy into question. In our investigations, summarized in chapter 6, GM proved to be multidimensional in a college sample (UT92). It showed high correlations with traditional measures of masculinity-femininity but also a strong negative correlation with negative emotionality, as well as moderate positive correlations with Constraint (reversed) and Positive Emotionality-Agentic. GF correlated strongly with traditional measures of femininity and with gender identity, but it also correlated moderately with the personality dimension of Constraint. Thus, both GF and GM appear to be multifaceted, which makes their interpretation quite difficult. The most accurate conclusion that may be derived from GM and GF scores is whether a respondent has endorsed MMPI-2 items in a way typical of his or her gender.

The bottom line is that males and females differ on many dimensions, only part of which we consider to fall in the arena of masculinity-femininity. Thus, gender differences are important in defining masculinity-femininity, but they are not the only important criteria. Masculinity-femininity as a personality construct may be founded on gender differences, but it must also accommodate within-gender variance. We have empirically delineated a circumscribed definition of masculinity-femininity that we think has great promise in clarifying the construct, defining it in line with common understanding, and making it useful to the scientific community.

What Is Masculinity-Femininity?

Given substantial evidence that masculinity-femininity exists, the next question is "What is it?" This question raises the long debate about the nature of masculinity-femininity. The findings of our studies argue against Constantinople's assertion that masculinity-femininity does not exist as a single bipolar factor (1973). This study also does not support Bem's (1974) and Frable's (1989) contention that masculinity and femininity are two independent dimensions reflected in expressivity and instrumentality. This latter conclusion is not surprising, in that this theory had been discredited previously (Lubinski, Tellegen, & Butcher, 1981; Tellegen & Lubinski, 1983).

Our studies do confirm the obvious: Scale 5 is multidimensional (as have been many alleged measures of masculinity-femininity). It is also clear from our work that not all those dimensions represented in previous measures are masculinity-femininity. For example, we found a large portion of negative emotionality in Scale 5 of both the MMPI-2 and the MMPI-A. This was not at all surprising, given the way Scale 5 was developed, and it is in keeping with the work of Tellegen, Ben-Porath, McNulty, Arbisi, Graham, and Kaemmer (2003), who found that Scale 5 was highly correlated with Demoralization. Only three of the seven dimensions that we identified in Scale 5 of the MMPI-2 (and two of five in Scale 5 of the MMPI-A) seem closely related to masculinity-femininity. However, those three or two dimensions clearly imply that masculinity-femininity, as we have identified it, is itself multidimensional, but those dimensions are limited to a higher-order factor that is defined by a pattern of empirical intercorrelations and conceptual links.

In line with Spence and Buckner's (1995) thinking, we assert that the construct of masculinity-femininity revolves around gender identity. Although gender identity is highly correlated with gender in a normal sample, it still has enough variance to be measured within gender. Greater variance on gender identity is found in homosexual and transsexual samples. However, gender identity alone, although central, does not seem to be the whole of masculinity-femininity. Our studies support the notion that there is a higher-order bipolar trait of masculinity-femininity. In our work, which is limited to the measures used in our various studies, masculinity-femininity was shown to include stereotypical masculine and feminine interests as well as gender identity.

Thus, our work supports a multidimensional bipolar model of masculinity-femininity. Females and males tend to score at opposite ends of the continuum, but there is within-gender variance as well. Perhaps the best perspective that we can represent at this time is one of concentric circles and surrounding circles at various distances from the core dimensions (see Figure 8.1). The inner circles are sex and its almost indistinguishable partner, gender. The next circle is gender identity, which is highly correlated with gender but not identical to it. Following this come masculine and feminine interests, which are correlated with gender identity but, again, are conceptually distinct. This is where we propose that the demarcation be drawn between what is masculinity and femininity and what are simply correlated traits.

The close surrounding but independent circles contain characteristics moderately related to masculinity-femininity. These include sexual orientation (at least for men), followed by personality dimensions such as nurturance-warmth, dominance-poise, and so on. From the work of Wiggins and Holzmuller (1978) on the BSRI discussed in chapter 2, we closely align instrumental and expressive with dominance-poise and nurturing-warmth, respectively. More distant circles might represent abilities that tend to show gender differences, such as spatial abilities and verbal skills. Still further from the core dimension of masculinity-femininity are characteristics that have little to no correlation with masculinity-femininity, such as negative emotionality and other major dimensions of personality.

There may be other related aspects of behavior related to masculinity-femininity that cannot be captured by self-report measures but might only be identified by O data (i.e., observational data). These potential dimensions of masculinity-femininity might include movement or speech patterns, which demonstrate some promise in identifying high-masculine or high-feminine individuals.

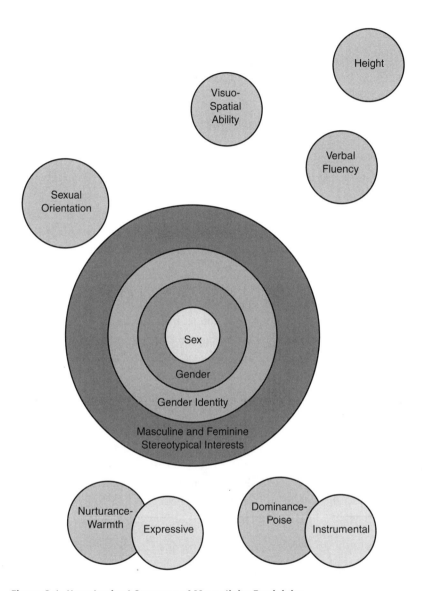

Figure 8.1. Hypothesized Structure of Masculinity-Femininity

The major source of data for this model of masculinity-femininity is from adult samples, and the data are clearer for men than for women. The data we have from adolescents are much more limited and raise interesting questions about the structure of masculinity-femininity in adolescents. It is important to gather additional data from adolescents and, perhaps, from children to determine the accuracy of this conceptualization for younger ages.

Furthermore, such data could provide insight into how these personality characteristics develop.

Are There Gender Differences in the Structure of Masculinity-Femininity?

Potential gender differences could manifest in differences in the characteristics that compose masculinity-femininity, the relative importance of those characteristics, and the relationship among them. In our studies, there were indications of some subtle differences in the structure of masculinity-femininity between males and females. We did not observe significant variations between males and females in the characteristics that compose masculinity-femininity. There was some evidence that some items (e.g., "Like cooking") related to masculinity-femininity for one gender but not the other; however, these instances were limited. We did see slight differences in the relative importance of the components (e.g., factor structure), but these also were minimal. We saw some differences in the relationships among components of masculinity-femininity (e.g., intercorrelations), but, again, these were small. The one area where our data suggest some difference between males and females was in the relationship of sexual orientation to other aspects of masculinity-femininity. More research is needed to explore this suggested gender difference.

The similarity of the factors in males and females that emerged, including the items identified, the interrelationship of these factors, and the apparent valence of these factors, was clearly sufficient to allow us to develop one set of factors for both genders and to consider the structure of masculinity-femininity to be substantially similar in males and in females. Thus, there is enough nomothetic commonality in the masculinity-femininity construct to overcome gender differences, at least in this society at this time.

Does Masculinity-Femininity Change over the Course of the Life Span?

We have two pieces of information that bear on this question, and they indicate somewhat different directions, although, when considered developmentally, they seem compatible. First, the study of adolescents, detailed in chapter 7, suggested that the structure of masculinity-femininity in adolescents differs from that in adults. This statement is based on the results of our efforts to score adults on the adolescent test item pool. We used this technique as a way to control for the number of items on the adolescent version of Scale 5 being substantially fewer from the number of items on the adult version. The results showed that adolescents and adults responded differently, suggesting that adolescents may construe and experience masculinity-femininity differently than do adults and, specifically, appear to make fewer distinctions between different aspects of masculinity-femininity.

The second piece of information that we generated compared different age groups in the adult normative MMPI-2 sample on their Scale 5 factors scores. The most important result was that there were no significant changes with age on any of the three factors related to masculinity-femininity or the FM composite scale. We did see differences among age groups on some of the other factors. We considered males and females separately and observed that both cynicism and restraint significantly increase with age. For females, we also noted a significant decrease in hypersensitivity/anxiety. These changes are not surprising, but they stand in contrast to the unchanging masculinity-femininity factors.

Along with these data are indications from other sources that stereotypical masculine and feminine interests are exceptionally stable. Finn (1986b) reported high retest coefficients for stereotypical feminine and masculine interests over a period of thirty years in males (from college age to middle adulthood). Spence (1985) and others (Ruble & Martin, 1998) have observed that there is a developmental aspect to gender identity but that, once it is established, it guides one's interests and behaviors. Gender identity begins to develop around the age of two and becomes an organizing principle that increasingly structures one's life.

We interpret these data to suggest that masculinity-femininity has a developmental aspect but that, once it is established, it remains relatively stable over the life span.

Are There Cultural Differences in Masculinity-Femininity?

If masculinity-femininity is at least partly socially determined, there likely would be some differences in its expression among individuals who grow up in different social contexts. The MMPI-2 could be useful in investigating cultural differences in masculinity-femininity, because it has been translated into many languages, and normative samples have been collected in a variety of countries.

Initially, we planned to use such existing data and compare mean MMPI-2 Scale 5 scores for males and females in the different extant normative samples (e.g., Sweden, the Netherlands, Israel, Mexico). As our work proceeded, however, it became clear that such comparisons would shed very little light on cultural differences in masculinity-femininity, because only a portion of the variance in Scale 5 has to do with this dimension. For example, if Swedish men showed a higher mean raw score on Scale 5 than did Israeli men, it could indicate a difference in masculinity-femininity, or it could mean that the Swedish men were more restrained or less cynical. Now that the Scale 5 factors are available, it is possible to sort out such confounds, and we encourage future researchers to use them in exploring possible cultural differences in masculinity-femininity. As discussed in chapter 1, it will be interesting to explore potential cultural differences at several levels: in mean factor scores, in the intercorrelation of items in a factor (e.g., by comparing alpha reliabilities across different samples), in the patterns of correlation between the different Scale 5 factors, and in the correlation of those factors with external variables (such as sexual orientation).

All the subjects used in our studies (i.e., the MMPI-2 and MMPI-A normative samples, UT90 and UT92 samples) come from the United States. However, some of our analyses are relevant to cultural differences in masculinity-femininity, in that we did explore differences between ethnic groups within the MMPI-2 normative sample. As discussed in chapter 6, there are significant limitations to conclusions that can be drawn from these analyses. For one, we know nothing about the acculturation levels of different ethnicities in the samples. It is likely that the samples reflect a fairly homogenous U.S. culture.

With this understood, our exploration of ethnic differences in chapter 6 showed no significant differences on total Scale 5 scores for men. However, the mean Scale 5 score of White females was significantly lower than that of either Black females or Native American females (when controlled for level of education). However, we traced this effect to differences on those Scale 5 factors that are not related to the core construct of masculinity-femininity. We found large differences between Whites and other ethnic groups (except Asian males and females) on Low Cynicism. It seems that Black, Hispanic, and Native American males and females, regardless of education, are substantially more cynical than White males and females. Furthermore, Black males scored significantly higher on the Aesthetic Interests factor than did White males, again regardless of education level. This is a difference masked in the overall Scale 5 score.

These results suggest that there are no ethnic differences, at least within the limited variance contained in a sample from the United States, on those dimensions of Scale 5 that we believe reflect masculinity-femininity: Denial of Stereotypical Masculine Interests, Stereotypical Feminine Interests, Feminine Gender Identity, and the composite FM scale. These results also underscore the critical importance of considering the multidimensionality of Scale 5 in any conclusions to be drawn from comparing mean scores of different ethnic or cultural groups. Clearly, more research with the Scale 5 factors would be helpful in pursuing further the question of whether there are ethnic or cultural differences in the expression of masculinity-femininity.

To What Extent Are Masculinity and Femininity Biologically or Socially Determined?

Many of us have probably heard mothers talk about what seem to be the unalterable interests of their children. For example, a young boy finds a stick to serve as a gun, when he has been diligently protected from anything that would encourage aggressive behavior, or a young girl turns with intensity to playing "house" in the absence of any encouragement (or in spite of discouragement) to do so. We are also aware of how powerful and subtle social influences can be. These are clear in the young boy who pretends to shave, as he has observed his father do, or in the young girl above who plays house, as she has observed women characters on TV or the mothers of her friends do. Given the complexities of development, it is indeed difficult to tease apart what influences are determinative.

Of course, the relative influence of biological and social determinants on behavior is a central debate in psychology, philosophy, and medicine, as well as in many grandmothers' kitchens. In chapter 1, we mentioned two recent books that advocate opposite answers to the question of whether nature or nurture produces gender differences. Barnett and Rivers (2004) argue that social influences are most salient in development of male-female differences, whereas Rhoads (2004) believes that biological influences play the major role. Both books argue persuasively that a particular influence trumps others and that each is able to gather substantial evidence to support their beliefs.

Through studies of intersex individuals (those with physical aspects of both sexes), we see the importance of biological influences. Case studies have revealed that gender identity is rooted in biology and central in guiding development and behavior, although social influences clearly also play a role. The hard lessons learned through Money and Ehrhardt's (1972) insistence that nurture was the only factor that mattered in determining a child's gender identity are memorable and instructive, and there are a number of individuals still living with the results of this erroneous conceptualization. At the same time, we also value the feminist position that we are all unique individuals who should be understood as such, that gender is an imperfect predictor of almost any characteristic one can imagine, and that males and females are highly similar in many aspects and, perhaps, more similar than different (Hyde, 2005).

Hopefully, the tension between the biological and social perspectives is beneficial to greater understanding. We believe that there is likely a combination of biological and social influences on masculinity-femininity. Clearly, however, the debate will outlive us.

Our studies have little to add to this debate concerning nature versus nurture. What we can glean from our work is that masculinity-femininity seems to be a coherent and enduring personality trait in adults. We found no mean differences in adults in the core dimensions of masculinity-femininity across ages or ethnicities. We also found no differences between genders in the lower- and higher-order factor structure of Scale 5. These results support the view that masculinity-femininity, at least once established, is not significantly affected by social influences.

The question about social influence in the *development* of masculinity-femininity is a different question. We did find differences in the structure of masculinity-femininity between adolescents and adults that were in line with those anticipated by developmental theory. Masculinity-femininity in adolescents was less differentiated, and it was painted with broader brush strokes than it was among adults. Whether such differences reflect a social training process or a biological unfolding is unknown. Thus, the relative influence of nature and nurture in the development of gender differences remains unclear.

One advance from our work that is more than trivial is the enhanced understanding and measurement of masculinity-femininity possible with the Scale 5 factors. It is clear that in order to study a construct effectively, one must have a reasonably valid and sensitive operational definition. Much research in the past thirty years has been misguided in using measures of masculinity-femininity such as the Bem Sex Role Inventory, which are not valid measures of the purported construct. Spence and others have recognized this fact but have all but abandoned the construct of masculinity-femininity rather than search for more accurate measures. It is hoped that our studies and the work that may follow will allow for more precise investigations of biological and social underpinnings than were possible before.

Are There Viable Markers of Masculinity-Femininity in the MMPI?

Our research indicates that there are valid measures of gender identity and stereotypical interests in the MMPI-2. The FM scale and its components, Denial of Stereotypical Masculine Interests, Stereotypical Feminine Interests, and Feminine Gender Identity, are reliable and valid measures of masculinity-femininity in the MMPI-2. We draw this conclusion from the pattern of correlations that we observed throughout our studies. The FM scale provides a better measure of masculinity-femininity than the GM or GF scales or any other MMPI scales examined here, with the possible exception of the Gd scale developed for the original MMPI by Althof, Lothstein, Jones, and Shen (1983). However, the Gd scale does not provide components, so it offers a less useful measure than the Scale 5 factors do.

In the MMPI-A, the A-FM scale is composed of only Denial of Stereotypical Masculine Interests and Stereotypical Femininity, which is a blend of stereotypical interests and gender-related characteristics. We believe that A-FM still serves as a viable marker of the masculinity-femininity construct, but, clearly, it is more limited than its adult counterpart. The MMPI-A has been researched much less than the MMPI and MMPI-2, so we have fewer efforts to establish measures of masculinity-femininity or gender-related characteristics than in the older MMPI and MMPI-2. For example, the MMPI-A does not have a GM or GF scale that identifies items that exhibit differential rates of responding in males and females. Thus, the Scale 5 adolescent factors have little competition on the MMPI-A. However, we can judge from their similarity to the adult scales and the similar pattern of correlations with other MMPI-A scales that they represent reasonable markers of masculinity-femininity.

In the MMPI-2-RF, much of the content related to masculinity-femininity was dropped from the test, with the exception of the sixteen items that comprise the two interest scales, AES (Aesthetic/Literary Interests) and MEC (Mechanical/Physical Interests). Although the published guidelines for interpreting these two scales deliberately avoid mention of masculinity or femininity, their published external correlates suggest that they may be related to traditional conceptions of masculinity and femininity. Further research is needed to clarify what AES and MEC actually measure.

An entirely different question is whether the masculinity-femininity factors that we have identified for the MMPI-2 and MMPI-A adequately encompass this personality dimension. Some people believe that sexual orientation is a component of, or at least a close cousin to, masculinity-femininity. However, there are no items in either the MMPI-2 or the MMPI-A that tap this dimension. The one item in the original MMPI that tapped sexual orientation was dropped in the test's revision, ostensibly because of its potential misuse. Furthermore, as we discussed previously, the evidence from our studies for including sexual orientation as a core component of the construct is less than compelling. Nevertheless, there may prove to be other critical dimensions of masculinity-femininity, but, until these are elucidated, the factors that we present here appear to capture the major variance associated with the core of masculinity-femininity.

Are the Factors of Masculinity-Femininity in the MMPI-2 and MMPI-A Useful?

The Scale 5 factors related to masculinity-femininity, and especially the FM and A-FM scales, have incremental validity, in that they give information that is not provided by other MMPI-2 and MMPI-A scales. The non-masculinity-femininity factors of MMPI-2 Scale 5 (i.e., Hypersensitivity/Anxiety, Low Cynicism, and Restraint Factors) are not as useful, because they tap constructs that have already been measured better by other MMPI-2 scales. The same can be said of the Adolescent-Low Cynicism and the Adolescent-Restraint scales developed for the MMPI-A.

Our claim that the FM scale captures unique variance is consistent with factor analytic studies done in the past (Dahlstrom, Welsh, & Dahlstrom, 1975; Johnson, Null, Butcher, & Johnson, 1984) and is supported in our work by the pattern of correlations that this scale shows with external criteria. As expected, FM correlated highly with gender, with measures of gender identity, and with other measures of masculinity-femininity, and it had low correlations with scales that measure other well-known dimensions of personality. But the question remains: Is this unique information captured by FM useful? Or perhaps a more sophisticated question is: In what contexts is the information captured by the FM scale likely to be useful to researchers, clinicians, and clients? Further research should address this and many other questions that remain in this intriguing area of personality. The factors and markers developed in our studies may be useful in furthering that research. It should be noted, however, that clinical use of these factors is not recommended until further research has confirmed their utility. We are reminded of Scale 5's history of misuse and argue that irresponsible or premature applications of directions suggested by our work in this book should be avoided.

Directions for Future Research

In closing, it seems timely to offer our thoughts about next steps that could be profitable for research on masculinity-femininity and the MMPI. Before discussing specific projects, let us highlight two pitfalls that are important to avoid in future research. First, it is critical that any research use valid measures of masculinity-femininity. We noted in chapter 1 the enormous amount of research that has been done and continues to be done using the Bem Sex Role Inventory or the Personal Attributes Questionnaire, neither of which is a valid measure of masculinity-femininity. We understand that, to some extent, this practice is a result of the lack of a widely recognized, valid measure of masculinity-femininity. But the resulting confusion, not to mention waste of resources, is both damaging and disheartening. On the MMPI-2, FM and Gd and, on the MMPI-A, Adolescent-FM seem to be the best markers of masculinity-femininity available. Both FM scales have the advantage of assessing subcomponents within the construct of masculinity-femininity. We are hopeful that other valid measures will emerge, guided by accumulating scientific knowledge about masculinity-femininity.

Second, we caution against pursuing studies correlating the Scale 5 factors in existing MMPI data bases with numerous variables for which the links to masculinity-femininity are tenuous or ill-considered. This would be a repeat of the type of research that followed the publication of the Bem Sex Role Inventory. We believe that no further studies are needed of the relationship between masculinity-femininity and handedness, schizophrenia, or body shape.

With these two cautions, let us offer some ideas for future research. In general, psychological research on women has been neglected relative to that on men, and this neglect is clear in the area of masculinity-femininity. It is important that masculinity-femininity in women be studied to understand any differences between males and females that may exist. Beyond the immediate advantages of assessing and understanding women better than we do (and per-haps aiding in those sometimes difficult relationships between the genders that are the topic of the humor cited in chapter 1), gender differences in develop-ment, manifestations, biological and social influences, and so on, could be help-ful in deepening our overall understanding of masculinity-femininity. One area in which current evidence suggests possible gender differences is the relation-ship of sexual orientation with masculinity-femininity. Our studies suggested a weaker relationship between sexual orientation and masculinity-femininity (and even gender identity) in females than in males. Even though this is not a new finding, it is intriguing and deserves closer scrutiny.

Gender identity has been recognized as a central aspect of gender differences, and, for some theoreticians, it is the only viable aspect of masculinity-femininity. Less attention has been paid to stereotypical masculine and feminine interests, although our work shows that they play a major role in masculinity-femininity. As discussed, stereotypical sex-typed interests have been surprisingly stable in the United States over a long period during which there has been substan-tial social change, and they appear to be highly stable in adulthood. Studies designed to understand how masculine and feminine interests develop and how they are maintained across the life span could further understanding of masculinity-femininity in general.

This also brings up the need to better understand how the core components of masculinity-femininity are themselves related. Is gender identity the central organizing variable, which then leads to the development of interests (and perhaps sexual orientation), or might these more distal variables also influence gender identity? For example, Finn remembers interviewing a four-year-old boy some years ago who exhibited a great deal of cross-gender behavior. The boy calmly explained to Finn that he "could not be a boy" because "boys like to play ball and are interested in cars and trucks" whereas he was not. As Finn asked more questions, it became clear that one source of the boy's cross-gender identity was his dissimilarity to other boys in terms of interests. It was as if, in the boy's mind, "Boys play ball, I don't play ball, therefore I am not a boy." It seems likely that similar challenges to masculine gender identity might exist in adolescent boys who begin to notice that their sexual attractions are primarily toward other boys and men. If sexual orientation influences gender identity (perhaps in addition to gender identity influencing sexual orientation), it would explain the finding by Freund, Nagler, Langevin, Zajac, and Steiner (1974) that gay men show much wider variance in gender identity than do heterosexual men. Such questions about unidirectional or bidirectional relationships between the components of masculinity-femininity could be addressed by path analyses conducted on large samples of subjects. Again, for such research to be valuable, it needs to use viable measures of the components of masculinity-femininity.

Other areas that hold promise for deeper understanding of masculinity-femininity are cultural, generational, and developmental aspects of the construct. Long-term longitudinal studies could address generational issues in masculinity-femininity (as well as changes over the life span). By studying a range of ages, the developmental course of masculinity-femininity could be better understood. What are the differences in masculinity-femininity between children, adolescents, adults, and the elderly? What part of Scale 5 serves an "inhibitory" function in adolescents? Is it masculinity-femininity or the restraint component?

Although our studies suggest that cultural differences are minimal, we have worked with limited data. The future exploration of masculinity-femininity in diverse populations could reveal insights into the nature of the trait, such as the stability of the components and the factors that influence those components. By studying a range of cultures, the expressions of and influences on masculinity-femininity could be compared. Thus, the social and biological influences on masculinity-femininity may become clearer.

The fact that the MMPI-2 has already been translated into many languages and is used in other countries and cultures presents a potential opportunity for further investigation of the dimensions identified in this study. We encourage the study of the Scale 5 factors in other normative MMPI data developed in diverse countries. This would be a good way to investigate cultural differences in masculinity-femininity without the confusion of other traits represented in a global Scale 5 score.

Another area of fruitful research on masculinity-femininity might involve estimating the heritability of masculinity-femininity and its components. This effort could go a long way in addressing the nature and nurture debate. Family studies, adoption studies, and twin studies, as well as more recent sophisticated techniques designed to estimate heritability, could deepen our understanding of the development of masculinity-femininity. Again, existing MMPI-2 databases could be utilized in such research.

We also think that further study of the connection between gender identity and psychopathology would be helpful. In our studies, these constructs separated into distinct orthogonal dimensions, suggesting that one is not substantially correlated with the other.

In chapters 1 and 2, we discussed the possibility that observational information (O-data) may enhance the assessment and understanding of masculinity-femininity. Research into movement and speech patterns might identify behaviors that lead to perceptions of masculinity or femininity, either by oneself or by others. Also, the relationship of O-data to self-report data (S-data) could be explored. It is possible that some aspects of masculinity-femininity show a greater convergence between S- and O-data than others, which could help us understand the development and structure of masculinity-femininity. This could also lead to multimethod assessment being applied to masculinity-femininity, as recommended by the Psychological Assessment Work Group of the American Psychological Association (Meyer, Finn, Eyde, Kay, Moreland, Dies, Eisman, Kubiszyn, & Reed, 2001).

It is important to note that most of these O-method studies (with the exception of Benoist & Butcher, 1977) are using homosexual-heterosexual differences to define masculinity-femininity. As we discussed previously, this is a dubious assumption and one that led to much confusion about the construct of masculinity-femininity. It is important that these O-methods be studied within gender and within sexual orientation groups, so that the constructs are not confounded with differences unrelated to masculinity-femininity.

In closing, we must acknowledge that the future of masculinity-femininity in psychological assessment remains uncertain. The dropping of Scale 5 from the MMPI-2-RF is just one event that appears to reflect how controversial and unvalued this area of assessment has become. We can certainly acknowledge how "slippery" the constructs of masculinity and femininity have been, how poorly conceived were many past research studies, and the damage that may have been done to individuals based on erroneous conclusions from psychological research. Nevertheless, we still believe that masculinity-femininity is an important area of research that can lead to greater understanding of human nature, of differences between men and women, and of individuals of different sexual orientations and gender identities. As we stated at the beginning of this book, the terms *masculinity* and *femininity* are routinely used comfortably by people of diverse cultures to parse their worlds. We believe that, with continued effort, science can catch up. And we hope that this book is a contribution to this effort.

Appendix A

The Sixty Items Comprising Scale 5 of the MMPI

(adapted from Colligan et al., 1983)

Items Keyed True

4	Like library work.[a]
25	Would like to be a singer.[a]
69	Attracted to people of my own sex.[b]
70	Liked Drop-the-Handkerchief.[a]
74	Wished I were member of opposite sex.[a]
77	Like romances.
78	Like poetry.[a]
87	Would like to be a florist.[a]
92	Would like being a nurse.[a]
126	Like theater.[a]
132	Like collecting plants.[a]
134	Thoughts have raced.
140	Like to cook.[a]
149	Kept a diary.[a]
179	Worry about sex matters.[b]
187	Hands not clumsy or awkward.
203	Would like to report theater news.[a]
204	Would like to be a journalist.[a]
217	Frequently worry.
226	Habits of some family members very irritating.
231	Like to talk about sex.[b]
239	Disappointed in love.

261   Would like to be an artist who draws flowers.[a]

278   Often strangers look at me critically.

282   Occasionally hate family members I love.

295   Liked "Alice in Wonderland."[a]

297   Bothered by sexual thoughts.[b]

299   Feel more intensely than most.

Items Keyed False

1   Like mechanics magazines.[a]

19   On a new job, find out who is important.

26   Keep quiet when in trouble.

28   Retaliate when wronged.

79   Feelings not hurt easily.

80   Tease animals.

81   Would like being a forest ranger.[a]

89   Hard to convince people of truth.

99   Like loud parties.

112   Often stand up for what is right.

115   Believe in eternity.

116   Betting enhances a race.

117   People honest because they don't want to be caught.

120   Table manners almost as good at home as when out.

133   Don't engage in unusual sex.[a]

144   Would like to be in military.[a]

176   Don't fear snakes.

198   Seldom daydream.

213   I avoid stepping on sidewalk cracks.

214   Never had worrisome skin rashes.

219   Would like to be a building contractor.[a]

221   Like science.[a]

223   Like hunting.[a]

229   Would like to be a member of clubs or lodges.

249   Believe in Hell.

254   Like being with people who play jokes on one another.

260   Had trouble learning in school.

262   Don't mind not being better looking.

264   Wholly self-confident.

280   People have friends because they are useful.

283   Would like to be a sports reporter.[a]

300   Never liked to play with dolls.[a]

[a] denotes items not part of the original MMPI item pool that were added during 1940–43; they appear to be adapted from the Terman and Miles (1938) AIAT.

[b] denotes items are keyed in the opposite direction as indicated for women.

Appendix B

Preferred Promax Factor Solution of Scale 5 in the MMPI-2 for Males in the Normative Sample

Factor 1:

(–) 063. Feelings not hurt easily.
(–) 184. Seldom daydream.
(–) 194. Never had worrisome skin rashes.
196. Frequently worry.
205. Habits of some family members very irritating.
219. Disappointed in love.
(–) 237. Don't mind not being better looking.
(–) 239. Wholly self-confident.
251. Often strangers look at me critically.
256. Occasionally hate family members I love.

Factor 2:

004. Like library work.
025. Would like to be a singer.
064. Like romances.
067. Like poetry.
112. Like theater.
187. Would like to report theater news.
191. Would like to be a journalist.
236. Would like to be an artist who draws flowers.

Factor 3:

026. Keep quiet when in trouble.
076. Hard to convince people of truth.
104. People honest because they don't want to be caught.
254. People have friends because they are useful.

Factor 4:

001. Like mechanics magazines.
069. Would like being a forest ranger.
197. Would like to be a building contractor.
199. Like science.

Factor 5:

086. Like loud parties.
133. Would like to be in military.
231. Like being with people who play jokes on one another.
257. Would like to be a sports reporter.

Factor 6:

None

Note. Test item numbers are included for each item along with the direction in which the item is scored (a minus sign in parentheses preceding the item number indicates that the item is scored when the response is "false"; the absence of a minus marker indicates that the item is scored when the response is "true").

Appendix C

Preferred Promax Factor Solution of Scale 5 of the MMPI-2 for Females in the Normative Sample

Factor 1:

  063. Feelings not hurt easily.
  184. Seldom daydream.
 (–) 196. Frequently worry.
 (–) 205. Habits of some family members very irritating.
  237. Don't mind not being better looking.
  239. Wholly self-confident.
 (–) 251. Often strangers look at me critically.
 (–) 256. Occasionally hate family members I love.

Factor 2:

  026. Keep quiet when in trouble.
  027. Retaliate when wronged.
  076. Hard to convince people of truth.
  104. People honest because they don't want to be caught.
 (–) 163. Don't fear snakes.
  193. I avoid stepping on sidewalk cracks.
  254. People have friends because they are useful.
  268. Bothered by sexual thoughts.

Factor 3:

  086. Like loud parties.
  112. Like theater.
  207. Would like to be a member of clubs.
  209. Like to talk about sex.

Factor 4:

  004. Like library work.
  074. Would like to be a florist.
  119. Like collecting plants.
  236. Would like to be an artist who draws flowers.

Factor 5:

001. Like mechanics magazines.
069. Would like being a forest ranger.
197. Would like to be a building contractor.
201. Like hunting.

Note. Test item numbers are included for each item along with the direction in which the item is scored (a minus sign in parentheses preceding the item number indicates that the item is scored when the response is "false"; the absence of a minus marker indicates that the item is scored when the response is "true").

Appendix D

Preferred Promax Factor Solution of Scale 5 in the MMPI-2 for the Combined Data in the Normative Sample

Factor 1: (alpha = .63)

    001. Like mechanics magazines.
    069. Would like being a forest ranger.
    197. Would like to be a building contractor.
    199. Like science.
    201. Like hunting.

Factor 2: (alpha = .66)

(–) 063. Feelings not hurt easily.
    166. Worry about sex.
(–) 184. Seldom daydream.
(–) 194. Never had worrisome skin rashes.
    196. Frequently worry.
    205. Habits of some family members very irritating.
(–) 237. Don't mind not being better looking.
(–) 239. Wholly self-confident.
    251. Often strangers look at me critically.
    256. Occasionally hate family members I love.

Factor 3: (alpha = .60)

    064. Like romances.
    074. Would like to be a florist.
    080. Would like being a nurse.
    119. Like collecting plants.
    236. Would like to be an artist who draws flowers.

Factor 4: (alpha = .48)

    026. Keep quiet when in trouble.
    076. Hard to convince people of truth.
    104. People honest because they don't want to be caught.
    193. I avoid stepping on sidewalk cracks.
    254. People have friends because they are useful.

Factor 5: (alpha = .40)

086. Like loud parties.
209. Like to talk about sex.
231. Like being with people who play jokes on one another.

Factor 6: (alpha = .55)

187. Would like to report theater news.
112. Like theater.
191. Would like to be a journalist.
067. Like poetry.

Note. Test item numbers are included for each item along with the direction in which the item is scored (a minus sign in parentheses preceding the item number indicates that the item is scored when the response is "false"; the absence of a minus marker indicates that the item is scored when the response is "true").

Appendix E

Items Not on Scale 5, GM, or GF Selected by Judges as Possibly Related to Masculinity and Femininity

   7. Like articles on crime.

  34. No trouble because of sexual activities.

134. Like to pick fights.

139. Would rather win than lose.

169. When bored, stir things up.

340. Love going to dances.

343. Like children.

344. Enjoy small stakes gambling.

371. Wished I were member of opposite sex.

422. When young liked excitement.

Factor Loadings for MMPI-2 Scale 5 Factors Intercorrelation Matrix Computed in the Combined Normative MMPI-2 Sample

	Components		
	Higher Order Factor #1	Higher Order Factor #2	Higher Order Factor #3
Feminine Gender Identity	.82		
Stereotypical Feminine Interests	.76		
Denial of Stereotypical Masculine Interests	.67		−.41
Restraint		.71	
Hypersensitivity/Anxiety		−.58	
Low Cynicism		.55	.57
Aesthetic Interests	.47		.57

Note. Three-factor principle components solution (Component matrix).

Appendix G

Intercorrelations of the Scale 5 Factors with Validity and Clinical Scales: Females Computed in the Normative Sample

	DSMI	H/A	SFI	LC	AE	FGI	Rt	FM	5
L	.01	−.40	−.02	.01	−.13	.01	.29	.01	−.11
F	−.04	.37	−.12	−.38	.01	−.11	−.18	−.12	−.11
K	−.07	−.52	−.04	.51	−.02	.00	.16	−.07	−.04
Fp	−.01	.13	−.03	−.38	.02	−.05	−.12	−.04	−.19
S	−.05	−.63	−.02	.53	−.08	−.02	.23	−.05	−.08
Hs	.07	.34	.02	−.35	.01	−.06	−.05	.04	.00
D	.15	.35	−.06	−.17	−.10	−.05	.13	.07	.11
Hy	.02	.03	−.11	.22	.05	−.06	.09	−.06	.08
Pd	.00	.45	−.08	−.21	.08	−.05	−.18	−.06	.00
Pa	−.01	.37	−.03	.04	.08	−.09	−.08	−.06	.15
Pt	.06	.65	.01	−.42	.04	−.04	−.18	.03	.09
Sc	.00	.60	−.04	−.44	.07	−.07	−.23	−.05	−.02
Ma	−.13	.31	.00	−.28	.24	−.01	−.38	−.11	−.06
Si	.15	.38	−.03	−.33	−.23	−.06	.27	.09	.10
A	.09	.63	.02	−.44	.02	−.00	−.16	.08	.09
R	.41	−.23	−.17	.09	−.31	−.02	.38	.21	−.02
Mt	.08	.60	−.02	−.42	.02	−.03	−.12	.04	.08

Note. DSMI = Denial of Stereotypical Masculine Interests; H/A = Hypersensitivity/ Anxiety; SFI = Stereotypical Feminine Interests; LC = Low Cynicism; AE = Aesthetic Interests; FGI = Feminine Gender Identity; Rt = Restraint; FM = FM Factor Scale; 5 = Scale 5.

Intercorrelations of the Scale 5 Factors with Validity and Clinical Scales: Males Computed in the Normative Sample

	DSMI	H/A	SFI	LC	AE	FGI	RT	FM	5
L	.06	−.41	.06	.07	−.11	−.07	.26	.05	−.17
F	−.05	.39	−.02	−.31	.00	.04	−.09	.04	.13
K	.13	−.50	.11	.54	−.01	.03	.23	.10	−.02
Fp	.03	.13	.08	−.28	.01	.05	−.08	.07	−.02
S	.08	−.62	−.02	.56	−.08	−.03	.26	.05	−.12
Hs	.01	.32	−.01	−.29	−.23	−.03	−.02	−.01	.04
D	.22	.30	.01	−.11	−.05	−.08	.18	.15	.19
Hy	.15	.01	.01	.37	.06	−.03	.14	.12	.22
Pd	.04	.46	−.01	−.15	.14	.04	−.10	.05	.24
Pa	.04	.28	.08	.15	.10	.06	−.01	.09	.30
Pt	.01	.65	.01	−.40	.06	.02	−.18	.02	.22
Sc	−.02	.62	.04	−.39	.10	.07	−.20	.03	.24
Ma	−.22	.27	.09	−.26	.21	.11	−.43	−.10	.07
Si	.17	.37	−.10	−.30	−.25	−.07	.32	.07	.08
A	.00	.64	.05	−.44	.08	.01	−.17	.03	.20
R	.53	−.20	−.13	.24	−.25	−.15	.48	.32	.09
Mt	.04	.61	−.02	−.42	.04	−.01	−.15	.02	.18

Note. DSMI = Denial of Stereotypical Masculine Interests; H/A = Hypersensitivity/Anxiety; SFI = Stereotypical Feminine Interests; LC = Low Cynicism; AE = Aesthetic Interests; FGI = Feminine Gender Identity; Rt = Restraint; FM = FM Factor Scale; 5 = Scale 5.

Appendix I

Intercorrelations of the Scale 5 Factors with the Content Scales for Females Computed in the Normative Sample

	DSMI	H/A	SFI	LC	AE	FGI	Rt	FM	5
ANX	.10	.62	−.01	−.34	.04	−.03	−.17	.06	.12
FRS	.30	.17	.08	−.34	−.04	.06	−.05	.29	.04
OBS	.07	.55	.05	−.40	.06	.04	−.18	.09	.09
DEP	.07	.56	−.02	−.40	.00	−.04	−.14	.03	.03
HEA	.03	.35	.03	−.32	.04	−.07	−.07	.02	.02
BIZ	−.07	.31	.03	−.41	.08	.01	−.24	−.04	−.11
ANG	.03	.49	−.04	−.32	.06	−.05	−.23	−.01	.02
CYN	.03	.28	.02	−.70	−.03	.03	−.15	.04	−.20
ASP	−.03	.28	−.01	−.64	−.01	.01	−.31	−.03	−.27
TPA	.05	.39	−.02	−.40	.04	−.03	−.20	.02	−.04
LSE	.11	.47	.03	−.40	−.06	−.01	−.05	.10	.04
SOD	.06	.29	−.05	−.21	−.18	−.10	.27	−.01	.10
FAM	.03	.56	−.06	−.35	.05	−.05	−.17	−.02	.07
WRK	.10	.54	.00	−.40	.00	−.01	−.12	.07	.06
TRT	.12	.44	.00	−.48	−.04	.00	−.09	.09	−.02

Note. DSMI = Denial of Stereotypical Masculine Interests; H/A = Hypersensitivity/ Anxiety; SFI = Stereotypical Feminine Interests; LC = Low Cynicism; AE = Aesthetic Interests; FGI = Feminine Gender Identity; Rt = Restraint; FM = FM Factor Scale; 5 = Scale 5.

Appendix J

Intercorrelations of the Scale 5 Factors with the Content Scales for Males Computed in the Normative Sample

	DSMI	H/A	SFI	LC	AE	FGI	Rt	FM	5
ANX	.03	.63	.02	−.33	.03	−.01	−.18	.03	.23
FRS	.08	.23	.06	−.33	.00	.00	−.09	.09	.02
OBS	−.03	.54	.06	−.43	.05	.00	−.16	.01	.13
DEP	.03	.54	.01	−.37	.08	.02	−.13	.04	.18
HEA	.02	.37	.05	−.24	.05	−.01	−.07	.04	.14
BIZ	−.12	.36	.14	−.34	.13	.11	−.23	.00	.09
ANG	−.18	.42	−.06	−.39	−.01	.00	−.26	−.18	00
CYN	−.10	.30	.03	−.73	.02	.02	−.21	−.07	−.14
ASP	−.17	.29	−.02	−.62	.05	.04	−.32	−.13	−.14
TPA	−.11	.39	−.02	−.50	.00	−.01	−.28	−.11	−.05
LSE	.01	.45	.03	−.36	−.01	−.01	−.08	.02	.08
SOD	.14	.28	−.10	−.17	−.20	−.06	.32	.04	.12
FAM	.02	.56	.01	−.37	.08	.06	−.19	.04	.19
WRK	.02	.57	.03	−.40	.05	.00	−.13	.03	.16
TRT	.01	.46	.02	−.45	.00	−.05	−.09	.00	.04

Note. DSMI = Denial of Stereotypical Masculine Interests; H/A = Hypersensitivity/ Anxiety; SFI = Stereotypical Feminine Interests; LC = Low Cynicism; AE = Aesthetic Interests; FGI = Feminine Gender Identity; Rt = Restraint; FM = FM Factor Scale; 5 = Scale 5.

Appendix K

Intercorrelations of the Scale 5 Factors with Restructured Clinical Scales for Females Computed in the Normative Sample

	DSMI	H/A	SFI	LC	AE	FGI	Rt	FM	5
RCd	.08	.58	−.02	−.35	.01	−.02	−.14	.04	.08
RC1	.05	.32	.03	−.33	.05	−.05	−.06	.03	.00
RC2	.12	.35	−.08	−.10	−.12	−.07	.19	.03	.14
RC3	.04	.27	.02	−.71	−.02	.03	−.15	.05	−.20
RC4	−.09	.36	−.08	−.23	.05	−.06	−.29	−.13	−.10
RC6	.00	.24	.00	−.40	.02	−.02	−.20	−.01	−.15
RC7	.09	.60	.05	−.44	.02	.01	−.17	.10	.10
RC8	−.09	.28	.00	−.38	.09	−.03	−.23	−.08	−.11
RC9	−.10	.38	.02	−.36	.21	.00	−.52	−.07	−.11

Note. DSMI = Denial of Stereotypical Masculine Interests; H/A = Hypersensitivity/ Anxiety; SFI = Stereotypical Feminine Interests; LC = Low Cynicism; AE = Aesthetic Interests; FGI = Feminine Gender Identity; Rt = Restraint; FM = FM Factor Scale; 5 = Scale 5; RCd = Demoralization; RC1 = Somatic Complaints; RC2 = Low Positive Emotions; RC3 = Cynicism; RC4 = Antisocial Behavior; RC6 = Ideas of Malevolence; RC7 = Dysfunctional Negative Emotions; RC8 = Aberrant Experiences; and RC9 = Hypomanic Activation.

Appendix L

Intercorrelations of the Scale 5 Factors with Restructured Clinical Scales for Males Computed in the Normative Sample

	DSMI	H/A	SFI	LC	AE	FGI	Rt	FM	5
RCd	.05	.60	.03	−.31	.09	.02	−.13	.07	.25
RC1	−.01	.27	.02	−.26	−.01	−.03	−.07	−.01	.03
RC2	.23	.32	−.06	−.04	−.10	−.07	.26	.14	.22
RC3	−.06	.29	.01	−.71	.00	.01	−.17	−.05	−.13
RC4	−.11	.34	−.03	−.19	.09	.10	−.24	−.06	.11
RC6	−.04	.26	.09	−.34	.08	.02	−.13	.01	.02
RC7	−.07	.58	.04	−.46	.02	.03	−.21	−.04	.12
RC8	−.12	.31	.12	−.29	.14	.02	−.23	−.01	.10
RC9	−.27	.38	.06	−.38	.16	.08	−.56	−.17	.01

Note. DSMI = Denial of Stereotypical Masculine Interests; H/A = Hypersensitivity/ Anxiety; SFI = Stereotypical Feminine Interests; LC = Low Cynicism; AE = Aesthetic Interests; FGI = Feminine Gender Identity; Rt = Restraint; FM = FM Factor Scale; 5 = Scale 5; RCd = Demoralization; RC1 = Somatic Complaints; RC2 = Low Positive Emotions; RC3 = Cynicism; RC4 = Antisocial Behavior; RC6 = Ideas of Malevolence; RC7 = Dysfunctional Negative Emotions; RC8 = Aberrant Experiences; and RC9 = Hypomanic Activation.

Appendix M

Intercorrelations of the Scale 5 Factors with the PSY-5 Scales for Females Computed in the Normative Sample

	DSMI	H/A	SFI	LC	AE	FGI	Rt	FM	5
AGG	−.10	.05	−.04	−.26	.17	−.01	−.28	−.11	−.19
PSY	−.04	.39	.02	−.48	.08	−.01	−.24	−.03	−.09
DISC	−.24	.16	−.10	−.08	.09	−.05	−.41	−.25	−.23
NEGE	.13	.65	−.01	−.37	.04	−.03	−.20	.08	.11
INTR	.12	.22	−.17	−.11	−.21	−.13	.39	−.04	.07

Note. DSMI = Denial of Stereotypical Masculine Interests; H/A = Hypersensitivity/ Anxiety; SFI = Stereotypical Feminine Interests; LC = Low Cynicism; AE = Aesthetic Interests; FGI = Feminine Gender Identity; Rt = Restraint; FM = FM Factor Scale; 5 = Scale 5; AGG = Aggression; PSY = Psychoticism; DISC = Disconstraint; NEGE = Negative Emotionality; INTR = Introversion (Low Positive Emotionality).

Appendix N

Intercorrelations of the Scale 5 Factors with the PSY-5 Scales for Males Computed in the Normative Sample

	DSMI	H/A	SFI	LC	AE	FGI	Rt	FM	5
AGG	−.21	.09	.01	−.36	.08	.01	−.37	−.17	−.16
PSY	−.07	.45	.10	−.42	.14	.07	−.21	.01	.11
DISC	−.27	.18	−.02	−.09	.14	.12	−.39	−.19	.03
NEGE	−.01	.63	.02	−.40	.03	−.02	−.20	−.01	.17
INTR	.30	.20	−.13	−.01	−.19	−.10	.49	.15	.21

Note. DSMI = Denial of Stereotypical Masculine Interests; H/A = Hypersensitivity/ Anxiety; SFI = Stereotypical Feminine Interests; LC = Low Cynicism; AE = Aesthetic Interests; FGI = Feminine Gender Identity; Rt = Restraint; FM = FM Factor Scale; 5 = Scale 5; AGG = Aggression; PSY = Psychoticism; DIS = Disconstraint; NEGE = Negative Emotionality; INTR = Introversion (Low Positive Emotionality).

Intercorrelations of the Scale 5 Factors with Other MMPI Measures of Masculinity-Femininity for Females Computed in the Normative Sample

	DSMI	H/A	SFI	LC	AE	FGI	Rt	FM	5
Ap	.08	.22	.06	.19	.05	.09	.07	.13	.30
Gd	.13	−.35	.29	.27	.11	.29	.01	.35	.22
Hsx	−.01	−.46	.15	.28	−.02	.01	.18	.08	.04
Mfp	.23	.45	.06	−.16	−.04	.02	.14	.21	.31

Note. DSMI = Denial of Stereotypical Masculine Interests; H/A = Hypersensitivity/ Anxiety; SFI = Stereotypical Feminine Interests; LC = Low Cynicism; AE = Aesthetic Interests; FGI = Feminine Gender Identity; Rt = Restraint; FM = FM Factor Scale; 5 = Scale 5.

Appendix P

Intercorrelations of the Scale 5 Factors with Other MMPI Measures of Masculinity-Femininity for Males Computed in the Normative Sample

	DSMI	H/A	SFI	LC	AE	FGI	Rt	FM	5
Ap	.16	.17	.08	.28	.10	.09	.14	.20	.30
Gd	.14	−.19	.33	.25	.25	.40	−.01	.42	.29
Hsx	.13	−.30	.18	.32	.06	.03	.21	.20	.14
Mfp	.21	.31	.07	.00	−.04	−.03	.26	.19	.26

Note. DSMI = Denial of Stereotypical Masculine Interests; H/A = Hypersensitivity/Anxiety; SFI = Stereotypical Feminine Interests; LC = Low Cynicism; AE = Aesthetic Interests; FGI = Feminine Gender Identity; Rt = Restraint; FM = FM Factor Scale; 5 = Scale 5.

Appendix Q

Intercorrelations of the Scale 5 Factors with MMPI-2-RF Interest Scales for Females Computed in the Normative Sample

	DSMI	H/A	SFI	LC	AE	FGI	Rt	FM	5
AES	−.16	.14	.48	.03	.90	.06	−.11	.16	.50
MEC	−.81	.05	.10	−.02	.10	−.12	−.15	−.60	−.24

Note. DSMI = Denial of Stereotypical Masculine Interests; H/A = Hypersensitivity/Anxiety; SFI = Stereotypical Feminine Interests; LC = Low Cynicism; AE = Aesthetic Interests; FGI = Feminine Gender Identity; Rt = Restraint; FM = FM Factor Scale; 5 = Scale 5; AES = Aesthetic/Literary Interests; MEC = Mechanical/Physical Interests.

Appendix R

Intercorrelations of the Scale 5 Factors with the MMPI-2-RF Interest Scales for Males Computed in the Normative Sample

	DSMI	H/A	SFI	LC	AE	FGI	Rt	FM	5
AES	−.01	.18	.50	.01	.95	.20	−.14	.30	.53
MEC	−.91	−.08	.08	−.15	−.01	.03	−.26	−.70	−.43

Note. DSMI = Denial of Stereotypical Masculine Interests; H/A = Hypersensitivity/Anxiety; SFI = Stereotypical Feminine Interests; LC = Low Cynicism; AE = Aesthetic Interests; FGI = Feminine Gender Identity; Rt = Restraint; FM = FM Factor Scale; 5 = Scale 5; AES = Aesthetic/Literary Interests; MEC = Mechanical/Physical Interests.

Gender Identity Scale for Females (GIF) (Finn, 1986a)

1. I often think I would rather be a man.

2. I am very masculine.

3. I would make a better husband than wife.

4. In many ways, I feel I am more similar to men than to women.

5. Several times I have dreamed I was a man.

6. At times, people in stores and restaurants have mistaken me for a man.

7. I have thought about the possibility of a sex change operation.

8. I don't feel very feminine.

9. I pride myself on being feminine.[a]

10. People think I should act more feminine than I like to.

11. As a child, I sometimes wanted to be a boy.

12. As a child, I rebelled against "girlish" things.

13. I preferred to play with girls when I was child.[a]

14. As a child, I was a tomboy.

15. I enjoy wearing jewelry.[a]

16. The idea of wearing makeup doesn't appeal to me.

17. Women are more beautiful without makeup.

18. I'm pretty fussy about the way I look in my clothes.

Note. [a] Keyed False. All other items keyed True.

Gender Identity Scale for Males (GIM) (Finn, 1986a)

1. I often wonder what it would be like to be a woman.

2. I have thought about the possibility of a sex change operation.

3. Several times I have dreamed I was a woman.

4. I have had sexual fantasies in which I was a woman.

5. I feel like part of me is male and part of me is female.

6. At times, people in stores and restaurants have mistaken me for a woman.

7. I pride myself on being feminine.

8. I don't feel very feminine.[a]

9. I feel more comfortable around women than men.

10. In many ways, I feel more similar to women than to men.

11. In general, I understand women better than men.

12. I'm very different from most other men.

13. People think I should act more masculine than I like to.

14. I feel like I am more "fatherly" than "motherly."[a]

15. I would make a better husband than wife.[a]

16. As a child, I sometimes wanted to be a girl.

17. My parents were hoping that I would be a girl.

18. I preferred to play with girls when I was a child.

Note. [a] Keyed False. All other items keyed True.

UT92 Sample versus MMPI-2 Normative Sample: Scale 5, GM, and GF Mean Scores

	UT92 SAMPLE (Mean/standard deviation)	NORMATIVE SAMPLE (MMPI Restandardization Committee, 1989) (Mean/standard deviation)	COLLEGE SAMPLE (Butcher, Graham, Dahlstrom, & Bowman, 1990) (Mean/standard deviation)
MALES			
Scale 5	25.41 / 5.58	26.0 / 5.1	25.4 / 5.0
GM	36.46 / 5.27	37.87 / 4.87	NA
GF	24.53 / 4.99	27.93 / 4.72	NA
FEMALES			
Scale 5	34.99 / 4.14	36.0 / 4.1	34.9 / 4.2
GM	27.56 / 6.08	28.83 / 6.51	NA
GF	34.45/4.44	37.68 / 3.88	NA

Note. UT92 sample based on 252 males and 139 females. Normative data is based on 1,138 males and 1,462 females. The college norms are based on 515 males and 797 females. NA = Not available.

UT92 Sample versus California Psychological Inventory Normative Sample: F/M, BMS, and BFM Mean Scores

	UT92 SAMPLE (Mean/standard deviation)	NORMATIVE SAMPLE (Gough, 1987) (Mean/standard deviation)	COLLEGE SAMPLE (Gough, 1987) (Mean/standard deviation)
MALES			
F/M	12.30 / 3.47	13.59 / 3.44	13.68 / 3.65
BMS	36.50 / 8.53	36.61 / 9.18	37.51 / 8.73
BFM	23.76 / 5.12	25.95 / 5.41	26.75 / 4.52
FEMALES			
F/M	18.63 / 3.32	20.0 / 3.12	19.93 / 3.09
BMS	30.83 / 8.83	30.68 / 9.74	32.94 / 8.31
BFM	29.83 / 4.62	31.54 / 4.97	33.00 / 3.68

Note. The UT92 sample is based on 252 males and 139 females. Normative data is based on 1,000 males and 1,000 females. The college norms are based on 3,236 males and 4,126 females.

Appendix W

UT92 Sample and the Personal Attributes Questionnaire Normative Sample: M+, F+, and M-F+ Means

	UT92 SAMPLE (Mean/standard deviation)	NORMATIVE DATA (Spence & Helmreich, 1986) (Mean/standard deviation)
M+ scores		
Males	22.07 / 4.23	22.31 / 4.60
Females	19.76 / 4.41	20.38 / 4.68
F+ scores		
Males	22.18 / 4.14	22.08 / 4.15
Females	24.25 / 3.80	24.54 / 3.78
M-F+ scores		
Males	16.99 / 4.08	16.61 / 4.06
Females	13.63 / 4.39	13.22 / 4.09

Note. UT92 sample is based on 138 females and 252 males. Normative data is based on a sample of 380 male and 540 female college students.

UT92 Sample and the Male-Female Relations Questionnaire Normative Sample: Social Interaction, Expressivity/Male Preference, and Marital Roles Means

	UT92 SAMPLE (Mean/standard deviation)	NORMATIVE DATA (Spence, Helmreich, & Sawin, 1980) (Mean/ standard deviation)
Males		
Social Interaction	28.77 / 9.75	33.40 / 10.56
Expressivity	6.96 / 3.01	7.08 / 3.27
Marital Roles	16.52 / 8.42	22.70 / 8.62
Females		
Social Interaction	24.53 / 9.68	29.00 / 10.00
Male Preference	10.70 / 2.86	11.78 / 2.76
Marital Roles	13.99 / 9.19	22.37 / 8.47

Note. UT92 sample is based on 144 females and 258 males. Normative data is based on a sample of 250 male and 258 female college students.

Appendix Y

1

One-Way Analyses of Variance and Scheffe's Tests of Significance

Scale 5 Score and Age in Males

Age Group	Count	Mean	Standard Deviation	Significance at the .01 level
18–19 years	16	47.50	8.72	None
20–29 years	257	49.70	13.51	None
30–39 years	307	51.41	10.56	None
40–49 years	163	48.70	9.68	None
50–59 years	135	49.54	10.92	None
60–69 years	122	47.93	11.37	None
70–79 years	49	46.61	13.27	None
80–84 years	7	47.14	5.40	None

2

Denial of Stereotypical Masculine Interests and Age in Males

Age Group	Count	Mean	Standard Deviation	Significance at the .01 level
18–19 years	18	49.72	12.15	None
20–29 years	268	48.58	9.60	None
30–39 years	324	50.37	9.73	None
40–49 years	174	48.06	9.91	None
50–59 years	142	51.09	9.85	None
60–69 years	133	51.54	10.47	None
70–79 years	54	53.56	9.77	None
80–84 years	8	49.88	4.55	None

3

Hypersensitivity/Anxiety and Age in Males

Age Group	Count	Mean	Standard Deviation	Significance at the .01 level
18–19 years	19	51.00	11.54	None
20–29 years	264	51.23	10.43	None
30–39 years	326	51.15	9.60	None
40–49 years	172	49.92	9.45	None
50–59 years	143	48.99	10.52	None
60–69 years	130	48.36	9.22	None
70–79 years	53	48.17	10.33	None
80–84 years	8	42.88	7.16	None

4

Stereotypical Feminine Interests and Age in Males

Age Group	Count	Mean	Standard Deviation	Significance at the .01 level
18–19 years	19	46.16	8.39	None
20–29 years	269	48.67	9.48	None
30–39 years	330	49.86	10.08	None
40–49 years	175	49.19	10.27	None
50–59 years	144	50.00	10.05	None
60–69 years	133	51.21	9.63	None
70–79 years	53	53.34	11.35	None
80–84 years	9	56.78	8.74	None

5

Low Cynicism and Age in Males

Age Group	Count	Mean	Standard Deviation	Significance at the .01 level
18–19 years	19	44.95	10.52	None
20–29 years	266	50.13	9.99	None
30–39 years	328	52.44	9.05	Different from 60–69 years and 70–79 years
40–49 years	177	49.87	10.36	None
50–59 years	142	49.99	9.85	None
60–69 years	132	46.88	10.59	Different from 30–39 years
70–79 years	50	44.94	10.11	Different from 30–39 years
80–84 years	9	40.44	6.80	None

6

Aesthetic Interests and Age in Males

Age Group	Count	Mean	Standard Deviation	Significance at the .01 level
18–19 years	19	48.05	9.19	None
20–29 years	269	50.33	10.46	None
30–39 years	330	49.89	9.78	None
40–49 years	177	49.94	9.71	None
50–59 years	143	49.12	10.12	None
60–69 years	132	51.03	10.34	None
70–79 years	55	47.87	8.87	None
80–84 years	8	49.13	8.13	None

Note. Between-component variance is negative. It was replaced by 0.0 in computing above Random Effects Measures.

7

Feminine Gender Identity and Age in Males

Age Group	Count	Mean	Standard Deviation	Significance at the .01 level
18–19 years	18	50.00	11.96	None
20–29 years	266	50.49	10.24	None
30–39 years	326	50.62	10.40	None
40–49 years	177	50.05	8.99	None
50–59 years	141	48.79	10.10	None
60–69 years	129	48.53	9.42	None
70–79 years	55	49.29	8.70	None
80–84 years	9	44.00	6.36	None

Note. Levene Test for Homogeneity of Variances: two-tailed Sig. .007.

8

Restraint and Age in Males

Age Group	Count	Mean	Standard Deviation	Significance at the .01 level
18–19 years	19	44.32	10.11	None
20–29 years	267	46.61	10.15	None
30–39 years	325	50.40	9.97	Different from 20–29 years
40–49 years	175	50.22	10.07	None
50–59 years	139	53.39	9.24	Different from 20–29 years
60–69 years	130	52.16	9.04	Different from 20–29 years
70–79 years	54	52.24	8.96	None
80–84 years	9	50.56	9.51	None

9

FM Score and Age in Males

Age Group	Count	Mean	Standard Deviation	Significance at the .01 level
18–19 years	17	50.52	10.61	None
20–29 years	265	53.14	10.21	None
30–39 years	319	55.19	9.88	None
40–49 years	172	52.81	8.96	None
50–59 years	140	55.21	8.81	None
60–69 years	127	56.24	9.19	None
70–79 years	52	58.79	8.99	None
80–84 years	8	54.38	5.78	None

Appendix Z

1

One-Way Analyses of Variance and Scheffe's Tests of Significance

Scale 5 Score and Age in Females

Age Group	Count	Mean	Standard Deviation	Significance at the .01 level
18–19 years	28	52.61	14.86	None
20–29 years	349	51.46	10.71	None
30–39 years	411	49.00	10.74	None
40–49 years	205	48.48	10.80	None
50–59 years	162	47.68	11.56	None
60–69 years	125	49.70	10.30	None
70–79 years	53	49.30	11.29	None
80–84 years	9	51.67	8.87	None

2

Denial of Stereotypical Masculine Interests and Age in Females

Age Group	Count	Mean	Standard Deviation	Significance at the .01 level
18–19 years	29	50.66	9.71	None
20–29 years	368	49.24	10.20	None
30–39 years	434	49.25	10.27	None
40–49 years	220	50.92	8.93	None
50–59 years	173	50.76	10.33	None
60–69 years	141	51.26	8.65	None
70–79 years	56	53.16	9.38	None
80–84 years	12	53.58	5.82	None

3

Hypersensitivity/Anxiety and Age in Females

Age Group	Count	Mean	Standard Deviation	Significance at the .01 level
18–19 years	29	58.31	10.16	Different from 50–59 years, 60–69 years, 70–79 years, 80–84 years
20–29 years	366	51.48	10.20	Different from 60–69 years, 70–79 years, 80–84 years
30–39 years	431	51.37	9.78	Different from 60–69 years, 70–79 years, 80–84 years
40–49 years	221	50.35	9.51	Different from 60–69 years, 80–84 years
50–59 years	175	47.75	9.32	Different from 18–19 years
60–69 years	135	45.51	9.55	Different from 18–19 years, 20–29 years, 30–39 years, 40–49 years
70–79 years	64	45.72	8.69	Different from 18–19 years, 20–29 years, 30–39 years
80–84 years	12	37.25	8.21	Different from 18–19 years, 20–29 years, 30–39 years, 40–49 years

4

Stereotypical Feminine Interests and Age in Females

Age Group	Count	Mean	Standard Deviation	Significance at the .01 level
18–19 years	29	49.00	11.23	None
20–29 years	371	48.38	9.49	None
30–39 years	437	49.78	9.83	None
40–49 years	222	50.67	10.28	None
50–59 years	178	51.79	9.03	None
60–69 years	143	51.30	9.39	None
70–79 years	64	52.28	9.58	None
80–84 years	12	51.92	11.73	None

5

Low Cynicism and Age in Females

Age Group	Count	Mean	Standard Deviation	Significance at the .01 level
18–19 years	29	43.03	10.80	Different from 30–39 years
20–29 years	365	50.20	10.18	None
30–39 years	434	51.38	8.91	Different from 18–19 years
40–49 years	221	50.26	9.71	None
50–59 years	175	49.08	10.59	None
60–69 years	141	47.93	10.57	None
70–79 years	62	47.27	9.52	None
80–84 years	12	48.00	6.89	None

Note. Levene Test for Homogeneity of Variances: two-tailed Sig. .001.

6

Aesthetic Interests and Age in Females

Age Group	Count	Mean	Standard Deviation	Significance at the .01 level
18–19 years	29	48.86	10.35	None
20–29 years	371	49.89	10.46	None
30–39 years	436	50.00	10.27	None
40–49 years	223	49.19	9.64	None
50–59 years	177	51.14	9.65	None
60–69 years	141	49.99	9.27	None
70–79 years	64	51.42	9.15	None
80–84 years	12	51.08	6.91	None

Note. Between-component variance is negative. It was replaced by 0.0 in computing above Random Effects Measures.

Note. Levene Test for Homogeneity of Variances two-tailed Sig. .039.

7

Feminine Gender Identity and Age in Females

Age Group	Count	Mean	Standard Deviation	Significance at the .01 level
18–19 years	28	47.18	10.52	None
20–29 years	373	49.07	10.53	None
30–39 years	438	49.62	10.08	None
40–49 years	224	50.37	9.71	None
50–59 years	179	50.42	10.46	None
60–69 years	142	49.72	9.79	None
70–79 years	65	50.74	8.01	None
80–84 years	12	54.25	4.97	None

Note. This Appendix is computed excluding no cases with missing items.

8

Restraint and Age in Females

Age Group	Count	Mean	Standard Deviation	Significance at the .01 level
18–19 years	29	39.41	10.99	Different from 30–39 years, 40–49 years, 50–59 years, 60–69 years, 70–79 years, 80–84 years
20–29 years	371	45.73	10.05	Different from 30–39 years, 40–49 years, 50–59 years, 60–69 years, 70–79 years
30–39 years	431	49.65	9.53	Different from 18–19 years, 20–29 years, 60–69 years
40–49 years	217	51.41	9.08	Different from 18–19 years, 20–29 years
50–59 years	171	53.01	9.48	Different from 18–19 years, 20–29 years
60–69 years	138	54.42	9.62	Different from 18–19 years, 20–29 years
70–79 years	60	53.83	8.84	Different from 18–19 years, 20–29 years, 30–39 years
80–84 years	10	58.40	6.38	Different from 18–19 years

9

FM Scale and Age in Females

Age Group	Count	Mean	Standard Deviation	Significance at the .01 level
18–19 years	28	51.11	5.54	None
20–29 years	373	50.55	8.66	None
30–39 years	438	51.33	9.21	None
40–49 years	224	52.97	7.93	None
50–59 years	179	53.30	9.00	None
60–69 years	142	53.47	8.30	None
70–79 years	65	54.59	7.73	None
80–84 years	12	56.50	7.32	None

Note. This Appendix is computed excluding no cases with missing items.

Appendix AA

1

One-Way Analyses of Variance and Scheffe's Tests of Significance

Scale 5 Score and Education in Males

Highest Education	Count	Mean	Standard Deviation	Significance at the .01 level
Part High School	56	43.29	11.83	Different from College Grad and Postgrad
High School Grad	226	44.99	10.22	Different from College Grad and Postgrad
Part College	256	48.03	11.62	Different from College Grad and Postgrad
College Grad	286	51.71	11.03	Different from Part High School, High School Grad, and Part College
Postgrad	232	54.88	10.13	Different from Part High School, High School Grad, and Part College

2

Denial of Stereotypical Masculine Interests and Education in Males

Highest Education	Count	Mean	Standard Deviation	Significance at the .01 level
Part High School	60	47.65	9.97	Different from Postgrad
High School Grad	240	47.44	9.66	Different from College Grad and Postgrad
Part College	270	48.54	9.37	Different from Postgrad
College Grad	302	50.76	9.86	Different from High School Grad
Postgrad	249	53.49	9.77	Different from Part High School, High School Grad, and Part College

3

Hypersensitivity/Anxiety and Education in Males

Highest Education	Count	Mean	Standard Deviation	Significance at the .01 level
Part High School	58	49.88	9.86	None
High School Grad	238	48.03	9.52	Different from Postgrad
Part College	269	50.58	10.57	None
College Grad	302	50.57	10.16	None
Postgrad	248	51.37	9.25	Different from High School Grad

4

Stereotypical Feminine Interests and Education in Males

Highest Education	Count	Mean	Standard Deviation	Significance at the .01 level
Part High School	60	49.00	9.50	None
High School Grad	241	49.39	10.76	None
Part College	270	48.99	9.51	None
College Grad	310	50.51	10.50	None
Postgrad	251	50.41	9.18	None

Note. Levene Test for Homogeneity of Variances: two-tailed Sig. .008.

5

Low Cynicism and Education in Males

Highest Education	Count	Mean	Standard Deviation	Significance at the .01 level
Part High School	59	42.24	9.81	None
High School Grad	240	46.73	10.43	None
Part College	270	48.95	9.25	Different from Part High School
College Grad	307	52.01	10.10	Different from Part High School, High School Grad, and Part College
Postgrad	247	53.53	8.33	Different from Part High School, High School Grad, and Part College

Note. Levene Test for Homogeneity of Variances: two-tailed Sig. .001.

6

Aesthetic Interests and Education in Males

Highest Education	Count	Mean	Standard Deviation	Significance at the .01 level
Part High School	59	47.58	10.22	Different from College Grad and Postgrad
High School Grad	242	48.00	9.20	Different from College Grad and Postgrad
Part College	271	48.13	9.66	None
College Grad	309	51.16	9.71	Different from Part High School and High School Grad
Postgrad	252	52.65	10.50	Different from Part High School and High School Grad

Note. Levene Test for Homogeneity of Variances: two-tailed Sig. .007.

7

Feminine Gender Identity and Education in Males

Highest Education	Count	Mean	Standard Deviation	Significance at the .01 level
Part High School	61	49.21	9.53	None
High School Grad	241	49.32	9.58	None
Part College	266	49.30	10.23	None
College Grad	305	50.57	10.23	None
Postgrad	248	50.45	9.69	None

8

Restraint and Education in Males

Highest Education	Count	Mean	Standard Deviation	Significance at the .01 level
Part High School	61	49.23	9.37	None
High School Grad	238	49.90	9.93	None
Part College	267	50.09	10.10	None
College Grad	306	48.96	10.31	None
Postgrad	246	51.62	9.78	None

9

FM Score and Education in Males

Highest Education	Count	Mean	Standard Deviation	Significance at the .01 level
Part High School	59	52.03	7.86	Different from Postgrad
High School Grad	239	52.12	9.31	Different from College Grad and Postgrad
Part College	63	52.75	9.28	Different from College Grad and Postgrad
College Grad	297	55.81	9.93	Different from High School Grad and Part College
Postgrad	242	57.93	9.29	Different from Part High School, High School Grad, and Part College

Appendix BB

1

One-Way Analyses of Variance and Scheffe's Tests of Significance

Scale 5 Score and Education in Females

Highest Education	Count	Mean	Standard Deviation	Significance at the .01 level
Part High School	54	53.85	13.35	Different from Postgrad
High School grad	367	51.14	10.46	Different from Postgrad
Part college	357	49.14	11.52	None
College grad	354	49.25	10.01	None
Postgrad	210	46.99	11.14	Different from Part High School, High School grad

2

Denial of Stereotypical Masculine Interests and Education in Females

Highest Education	Count	Mean	Standard Deviation	Significance at the .01 level
Part High School	65	52.06	11.12	None
High School grad	388	51.65	9.69	Different from Postgrad, and College grad
Part college	376	50.52	9.97	None
College grad	383	48.74	9.59	Different from High School Grad
Postgrad	221	48.46	9.64	Different from High School Grad

3

Hypersensitivity/Anxiety and Education in Females

Highest Education	Count	Mean	Standard Deviation	Significance at the .01 level
Part High School	65	48.83	10.87	None
High School grad	388	49.30	10.15	None
Part college	372	50.26	10.24	None
College grad	383	50.25	9.71	None
Postgrad	225	50.81	9.96	None

4

Stereotypical Feminine Interests and Education in Females

Highest Education	Count	Mean	Standard Deviation	Significance at the .01 level
Part High School	66	51.23	9.20	None
High School grad	396	50.47	9.96	None
Part college	380	50.79	9.74	None
College grad	389	49.59	9.89	None
Postgrad	225	48.63	9.30	None

5

Low Cynicism and Education in Females

Highest Education	Count	Mean	Standard Deviation	Significance at the .01 level
Part High School	65	42.80	9.11	Different from Part College, College grad, and Postgrad
High School grad	394	47.07	10.64	Different from College grad, Postgrad
Part college	376	49.48	9.63	Different from Part High School, Postgrad
College grad	383	51.73	8.79	Different from Part High School College grad, Postgrad
Postgrad	221	54.70	7.90	Different from Part High School, High School grad, Part college, and College grad

Note. Levene Test for Homogeneity of Variances: two-tailed Sig. .000.

6

Aesthetic Interests and Education in Females

Highest Education	Count	Mean	Standard Deviation	Significance at the .01 level
Part High School	64	47.53	10.15	Different from Part College, College Grad, and Postgrad
High School grad	396	47.84	9.62	None
Part college	379	50.55	10.28	Different from Part High School
College grad	388	50.72	9.78	Different from Part High School
Postgrad	226	52.54	9.61	Different from Part High School

7

Feminine Gender Identity and Education in Females

Highest Education	Count	Mean	Standard Deviation	Significance at the .01 level
Part High School	97	48.95	10.11	None
High School grad	397	50.60	9.49	None
Part college	371	49.62	9.67	None
College grad	381	49.90	9.92	None
Postgrad	215	48.46	11.78	None

Note. This Appendix is computed excluding no cases with missing items.

8

Restraint and Education in Females

Highest Education	Count	Mean	Standard Deviation	Significance at the .01 level
Part High School	63	50.33	11.36	None
High School grad	392	50.85	9.79	None
Part college	373	48.97	10.74	None
College grad	375	48.77	9.84	None
Postgrad	224	50.84	9.67	None

9

FM Scale and Education in Females

Highest Education	Count	Mean	Standard Deviation	Significance at the .01 level
Part High School	97	52.89	8.76	None
High School grad	397	53.42	8.59	Different from College grad, Postgrad
Part college	371	52.44	8.89	None
College grad	381	51.05	8.30	Different from High School grad
Postgrad	215	49.91	8.78	Different from High School grad.

Note. This Appendix is computed excluding no cases for missing items.

Appendix CC

1

One-Way Analyses of Variance and Scheffe's Tests of Significance

Scale 5 Score and Ethnicity in Males

Ethnic Group	Count	Mean	Standard Deviation	Significance at the .01 level
Asian	6	46.33	12.36	None
Black	111	49.84	8.42	None
Hispanic	32	45.94	11.76	None
Native American	35	43.03	15.65	None
White	872	50.03	11.55	None

Note. Levene Test for Homogeneity of Variances: two-tailed Sig. .008

2

Denial of Stereotypical Masculine Interests and Ethnicity in Males

Ethnic Group	Count	Mean	Standard Deviation	Significance at the .01 level
Asian	6	47.00	9.45	None
Black	125	51.99	11.11	None
Hispanic	33	47.79	10.69	None
Native American	38	46.13	10.25	None
White	919	49.93	9.67	None

3

Hypersensitivity/Anxiety and Ethnicity in Males

Ethnic Group	Count	Mean	Standard Deviation	Significance at the .01 level
Asian	6	54.33	7.71	None
Black	120	48.34	8.62	None
Hispanic	32	49.31	9.45	None
Native American	37	50.41	10.82	None
White	920	50.41	10.11	None

4

Stereotypical Feminine Interests and Ethnicity in Males

Ethnic Group	Count	Mean	Standard Deviation	Significance at the .01 level
Asian	6	56.33	11.78	None
Black	126	50.17	10.62	None
Hispanic	35	48.83	9.12	None
Native American	38	49.32	10.51	None
White	927	49.77	9.92	None

Note. Between-component variance is negative. It was replaced by 0.0 in computing above Random Effects Measures.

5

Low Cynicism and Ethnicity in Males

Ethnic Group	Count	Mean	Standard Deviation	Significance at the .01 level
Asian	6	38.50	9.65	None
Black	123	45.36	10.84	Different from White
Hispanic	34	44.68	10.90	Different from White
Native American	37	43.32	9.88	Different from White
White	923	51.12	9.56	Different from Black, Hispanic, and Native American

6

Aesthetic Interests and Ethnicity in Males

Ethnic Group	Count	Mean	Standard Deviation	Significance at the .01 level
Asian	6	45.67	7.06	None
Black	124	53.65	9.64	Different from White
Hispanic	35	51.14	10.68	None
Native American	38	46.95	11.26	None
White	930	49.51	9.85	Different from Black

7

Feminine Gender Identity and Ethnicity in Males

Ethnic Group	Count	Mean	Standard Deviation	Significance at the .01 level
Asian	5	52.40	10.26	None
Black	123	51.68	9.87	None
Hispanic	34	48.06	9.07	None
Native American	38	48.89	10.50	None
White	921	49.76	9.95	None

8

Restraint and Ethnicity in Males

Ethnic Group	Count	Mean	Standard Deviation	Significance at the .01 level
Asian	6	45.33	9.48	None
Black	123	49.82	10.55	None
Hispanic	35	46.14	9.33	None
Native American	38	50.89	9.18	None
White	916	50.20	10.02	None

9

FM Score and Ethnicity in Males

Ethnic Group	Count	Mean	Standard Deviation	Significance at the .01 level
Asian	5	57.80	10.59	None
Black	122	56.69	9.84	None
Hispanic	32	51.66	8.76	None
Native American	38	50.82	11.67	None
White	903	54.49	9.51	None

Appendix DD

1

One-Way Analyses of Variance and Scheffe's Tests of Significance

Scale 5 and Ethnicity in Females

Ethnic Group	Count	Mean	Standard Deviation	Significance at the .01 level
Asian	13	50.85	10.56	None
Black	168	53.13	11.43	Different from White
Hispanic	37	54.59	11.81	None
Native American	36	55.22	14.67	None
White	1088	48.65	10.53	Different from Black

2

Denial of Stereotypical Masculine Interests and Ethnicity in Females

Ethnic Group	Count	Mean	Standard Deviation	Significance at the .01 level
Asian	13	48.46	13.61	None
Black	184	51.79	9.25	None
Hispanic	37	50.49	12.41	None
Native American	38	51.92	11.63	None
White	1161	49.78	9.76	None

Note. Levene Test for Homogeneity of Variances: two-tailed Sig. .026.

3

Hypersensitivity/Anxiety and Ethnicity in Females

Ethnic Group	Count	Mean	Standard Deviation	Significance at the .01 level
Asian	13	46.62	8.71	None
Black	183	49.44	10.09	None
Hispanic	37	52.73	11.65	None
Native American	39	48.95	11.88	None
White	1161	50.10	9.95	None

4

Stereotypical Feminine Interests and Ethnicity in Females

Ethnic Group	Count	Mean	Standard Deviation	Significance at the .01 level
Asian	13	50.62	8.16	None
Black	187	48.66	9.88	None
Hispanic	38	47.16	10.76	None
Native American	39	50.08	9.97	None
White	1179	50.38	9.71	None

5

Low Cynicism and Ethnicity in Females

Ethnic Group	Count	Mean	Standard Deviation	Significance at the .01 level
Asian	13	46.15	8.72	None
Black	186	44.32	10.49	Different from White
Hispanic	38	44.58	13.63	Different from White
Native American	39	41.26	12.62	Different from White
White	1163	51.32	9.01	Different from Black, Hispanic, and Native American

Note. Levene Test for Homogeneity of Variances: two-tailed Sig. .000.

6

Aesthetic Interests and Ethnicity in Females

Ethnic Group	Count	Mean	Standard Deviation	Significance at the .01 level
Asian	13	47.23	6.15	None
Black	186	50.31	9.63	None
Hispanic	38	50.50	9.41	None
Native American	38	45.74	10.77	None
White	1178	50.15	10.04	None

7

Feminine Gender Identity and Ethnicity in Females

Ethnic Group	Count	Mean	Standard Deviation	Significance at the .01 level
Asian	13	50.23	9.57	None
Black	187	49.71	9.33	None
Hispanic	37	50.16	9.11	None
Native American	38	48.32	11.76	None
White	1184	49.79	10.16	None

Note. This Appendix is computed excluding no cases for missing items.

8

Restraint and Ethnicity in Females

Ethnic Group	Count	Mean	Standard Deviation	Significance at the .01 level
Asian	13	53.00	9.40	None
Black	182	49.47	10.13	None
Hispanic	38	44.50	10.43	None
Native American	39	47.26	11.27	None
White	1155	50.06	10.06	None

9

FM Scale and Ethnicity in Females

Ethnic Group	Count	Mean	Standard Deviation	Significance at the .01 level
Asian	13	51.54	8.11	None
Black	187	52.39	7.95	None
Hispanic	37	51.14	10.58	None
Native American	38	53.37	8.45	None
White	1184	51.95	8.79	None

Note. This Appendix is computed excluding no cases with missing items.

References

Aaronson, B. S. (1959). A comparison of two MMPI measures of masculinity-femininity. *Journal of Clinical Psychology, 15*, 48–50.

Aaronson, B. S., & Grumpelt, H. R. (1961). Homosexuality and some MMPI measures of masculinity-femininity. *Journal of Clinical Psychology, 17*, 245–247.

Adams, C. H., & Sherer, M. (1982). Sex-role orientation and psychological adjustment: Comparison of MMPI profiles among college women and housewives. *Journal of Personality Assessment, 46*, 607–613.

Althof, S. E., Lothstein, L. M., Jones, P., & Shen, J. (1983). An MMPI subscale (Gd): To identify males with gender identity conflicts. *Journal of Personality Assessment, 47*, 43–49.

Alumbaugh, R. V. (1987). Contrast of the gender–identity scale with Bem's sex-role measures and the Mf Scale of the MMPI. *Perceptual and Motor Skills, 64*, 136–138.

Ambady, N., Hallahan, M., & Conner, B. (1999). Accuracy of judgments of sexual orientation from thin slices of behavior. *Journal of Personality and Social Psychology, 77*, 538–547.

Antill, J. K., & Cunningham, J. D. (1979). Self-esteem as a function of masculinity in both sexes. *Journal of Consulting and Clinical Psychology, 47*, 783–785.

Arbisi P. A., Ben-Porath, Y. S., & McNulty, J. L. (2002). A comparison of MMPI-2 validity in African American and Caucasian psychiatric inpatients. *Psychological Assessment, 14*, 3–15.

Archer, R. P. (2005). *MMPI-A: Assessing adolescent psychopathology* (3rd ed.). Mahwah, NJ: Lawrence Erlbaum Associates.

Archer, R. P., & Klinefelter, D. (1991). MMPI factor analytic findings for adolescents: Item-correlates for adolescent inpatients. *Journal of Personality Assessment, 53,* 356–367.

Bailey, J. M. (2003). *The man who would be queen.* Washington, D.C.: Joseph Henry Press.

Bailey, J. M., Dunne, M. P., & Martin, N. G. (2000). Genetic and environmental influences on sexual orientation and its correlates in an Australian twin sample. *Journal of Personality and Social Psychology, 78,* 524–536.

Bailey, J. M., Finkel, E., Blackwelder, K., & Bailey, T. (1996). *Masculinity, femininity, and sexual orientation.* Unpublished manuscript, Northwestern University, available from the first author.

Bailey, J. M., Willerman, L., & Parks, C. (1991). A test of the maternal stress hypothesis for human male homosexuality. *Archives of Sexual Behavior, 20,* 277–293.

Bailey, J. M., & Zucker, K. J. (1995). Special Edition: Sexual orientation and human development. *Developmental Psychology, 31(1),* 43–55.

Barnett, R., & Rivers, C. (2004). *Same difference: How gender myths are hurting our relationships, our children, and our jobs.* New York: Basic Books.

Baucom, D. H. (1976). Independent masculinity and femininity scales on the California Psychological Inventory. *Journal of Consulting and Clinical Psychology, 44,* 876.

Baucom, D. H. (1980). Independent CPI masculinity-femininity scales: Psychological correlates and sex-role typology. *Journal of Personality Assessment, 44,* 262–271.

Bem, S. L. (1974). The measurement of psychological androgyny. *Journal of Consulting and Clinical Psychology, 42,* 155–162.

Bem, S. L. (1979). Theory and measurement of androgyny: A reply to the Pedhazur-Tetenbaum and Locksley-Colten critiques. *Journal of Personality and Social Psychology, 37,* 1047–1054.

Bem, S. L. (1981a). The BSRI and gender schema theory: A reply to Spence and Helmreich. *Psychological Review, 88,* 369–371.

Bem, S. L. (1981b). *Bem Sex Role Inventory: Professional manual.* Palo Alto, CA: Consulting Psychologists Press.

Benoist, I. R., & Butcher, J. N. (1977). Nonverbal cues to sex-role attitudes. *Journal of Research in Personality, 11,* 431–442.

Ben-Porath, Y. S. (2008, August 20). *Introducing the MMPI-2-RF (Restructured Form).* Webinar sponsored by Pearson.

Ben-Porath, Y. S., & Forbey, J. D. (2003). *Non-gendered norms for the MMPI-2.* Minneapolis: University of Minnesota Press.

Ben-Porath, Y. S., Hostetler, K., Butcher, J. N., & Graham, J. R. (1989). New subscales for the MMPI-2 Social Introversion (Si) scale. *Psychological Assessment, 1,* 169–174.

Ben-Porath, Y. S., & Tellegen, A. (2007, April). *Introducing the MMPI-2-RF (Restructured Form).* Paper presented at the 42nd Annual Symposium on Recent Research with the MMPI-2 and MMPI-A, Minneapolis.

Ben-Porath, Y. S., & Tellegen, A. (2008). *Minnesota Multiphasic Personality Inventory-2 Restructured Form (MMPI-2-RF): Manual for administration, scoring, and interpretation.* Minneapolis: University of Minnesota Press.

Blais, M. A. (1995). MCMI-II personality traits associated with the MMPI-2 Masculinity-Femininity scale. *Assessment, 2,* 131–136.

Blanchard, R. (1991). Clinical observations and systematic studies of autogynephilia. *Journal of Sex and Marital Therapy, 17,* 235–251.

Blanchard, R., & Freund, K. (1983). Measuring masculine gender identity in females. *Journal of Consulting and Clinical Psychology, 51,* 205–214.

Bossé, R., Ekerdt, D., & Silbert, J. (1984). The veterans administration normative aging study. In S. A. Mednick, M. Harway, & K. M. Finello (Eds.), *Handbook of longitudinal research: Vol. 2. Teenage and adult cohorts,* pp. 273–289. New York: Praeger.

Braunwald, E., Isselbacher, K. J., Petersdorf, R. G., Wilson, J. D., Martin, J. B., & Fauci, A. S. (Eds.). (1987). *Harrison's principles of internal medicine,* (11th ed.). New York: McGraw-Hill.

Brems, C., & Johnson, M. E. (1990). Reexamination of the Bem Sex-Role Inventory: The interpersonal BSRI. *Journal of Personality Assessment, 55,* 484–498.

Brunswik, E. (1956). *Perception and the representative design of psychological experiments.* Berkeley: University of California Press.

Burton, A. (1947). The use of the masculinity-femininity scale of the Minnesota Multiphasic Personality Inventory as an aid in the diagnosis of sexual inversion. *Journal of Psychology, 24,* 161–164.

Buss, D. M. (1989). Sex differences in human mate preferences: Evolutionary hypotheses tested in 37 cultures. *Behavior Brain Science, 12,* 1.

Buss, D. M. (1995). Psychological sex differences: Origins through sexual selection. *American Psychologist, 50,* 164–168.

Buss, D. M., & Schmidt, D. P. (1993). Sexual strategies theory: An evolutionary perspective on human mating. *Psychological Review, 100,* 204–232.

Bussey, K., & Bandura, A. (1999). Social cognitive theory of gender development and differentiation. *Psychological Review, 106,* 676–713.

Butcher, J. N. (1990). Education level and MMPI-2 measured psychopathology: A case of negligible influence. *MMPI-2 News and Profiles, 1,* 2.

Butcher, J. M., Aldwin, C. M., Levenson, M. R., Ben-Porath, Y. S., Spiro, A., & Bossé, R. (1991). Personality and aging: A study of the MMPI-2 among older men. *Psychology and Aging, 6,* 361–370.

Butcher, J. N., Dahlstrom, W. G., Graham, J. R., Tellegen, A., & Kaemmer, B. (MMPI Restandardization Committee). (1989). *Manual for administration and scoring: MMPI-2.* Minneapolis: University of Minnesota Press.

Butcher, J. N., Graham, J. R., Ben-Porath, Y. S., Tellegen, A., Dahlstrom, W. G., & Kaemmer, B. (2001). *MMPI-2: Manual for administration, scoring, and interpretation, revised edition.* Minneapolis: University of Minnesota Press.

Butcher, J. N., Graham, J. R., Dahlstrom, W. G., & Bowman, E. (1990). The MMPI-2 with college students. *Journal of Personality Assessment, 54,* 1–15.

Butcher, J. N., Williams, C. L., Graham, J. R., Archer, R. P., Tellegen, A., Ben-Porath, Y. S., & Kaemmer, B. (1992). *MMPI-A (Minnesota Multiphasic Personality Inventory-Adolescent): Manual for administration, scoring, and interpretation.* Minneapolis: University of Minnesota Press.

Caldwell, A. B. (1997). MMPI-2 data research file for clinical patients. Unpublished raw data.

Caligor, L. (1951). The determination of the individual's unconscious conception of his own masculinity-femininity identification. *Journal of Projective Techniques, 15,* 494–509.

Campbell, D. P. (1971). *Handbook for the Strong Vocational Interest Blank.* Stanford, CA: Stanford University Press.

Campbell, D. P., & Fiske, D. W. (1959). Convergent and discriminant validation by the multitrait-multimethod matrix. *Psychological Bulletin, 56,* 81–105.

Campbell, D. P., & Hanson, J. I. C. (1981). *Manual for the Strong-Campbell Interest Inventory* (3rd ed.). Stanford, CA: Stanford University Press.

Campbell, J. (1971). *The portable Jung.* Kingsport, TN: Kingsport Press.

Canul, G. D., & Cross, H. J. (1994). The influence of acculturation and racial identity attitudes on Mexican Americans' MMPI performance. *Journal of Clinical Psychology, 50,* 736–745.

Cashel, M. L., Rogers, R., Sewell, K. W., & Holliman, N. B. (1998). Preliminary validation of the MMPI-A for a male delinquent sample: An investigation of clinical correlates and discriminant validity. *Journal of Personality Assessment, 71,* 49–69.

Castlebury, F. D., & Durham, T. W. (1997). The MMPI-2 GM and GF scales as measures of psychological well-being. *Journal of Clinical Psychology, 53,* 879–893.

Cattell, R. B. (1950). *Manual for forms A and B: Sixteen Personality Factor Questionnaire.* Champaign, IL: Institute for Personality and Ability Testing.

Cattell, R. B., Eber, H. W., & Tatsuoka, M. M. (1970). *Handbook for the Sixteen Personality Factor Questionnaire.* Champaign, IL: Institute for Personality and Ability Testing.

Cellucci, T., Wilkerson, A, & Mandra, D. (1998). The MMPI-2 gender-role scales as measures of sex-typing. *Psychological Reports, 83,* 752–754.

Choi, N., & Fuqua, D. R. (2003). The structure of the BEM Sex Role Inventory: A summary report of 23 validation studies. *Educational and Psychological Measurement, 63,* 872–887.

Clark, J. H. (1953). The interpretation of the MMPI profiles of college students: A comparison by college major subject. *Journal of Clinical Psychology, 9,* 382–384.

Cleveland, H. H., Udry, J. R., & Chantala, K. (2001). Environmental and genetic influences on sex-typed behaviors and attitudes of male and female adolescents. *Personality and Social Psychology Bulletin, 27,* 1587–1598.

Coan, R. W. (1989). Dimensions of masculinity and femininity: A self-report inventory. *Journal of Personality Assessment, 53,* 816–826.

Cohen, J. (1988). *Statistical power analysis for the behavioral sciences* (2nd ed.). Hillsdale, NJ: Lawrence Erlbaum Associates.

Cole, S. S., Denny, D., Eyler, A. E., & Samons, S. L. (2000). Issues of transgender. In L. T. Szucuchman and F. Muscarella (Eds.), *Psychological perspectives on human sexuality* (pp. 149–195). New York: Wiley & Sons.

Colligan, R. C., Osborne, D., Swenson, W. M., & Offord, K. P. (1983). *The MMPI: A contemporary normative study.* New York: Praeger.

Comrey, A. L. (1970). *Manual for the Comrey Personality Scales.* San Diego, CA: Educational and Industrial Testing Service.

Constantinople, A. (1973). Masculinity-femininity: An exception to the famous dictum? *Psychological Bulletin, 80,* 389–407.

Corona, D. M., & Izquierdo, M. A. L. (2003). Inventario Mexicano de masculinidad y feminidad. Desarrollo Psicométrico y version preliminary. *Revista Mexicana di Psicología, 20,* 113–126.

Craig, R. J. (1999). *Interpreting personality tests: A clinical manual for the MMPI-2, MCMI-III, CPI-R, and 16PF.* New York: Wiley & Sons.

Cronbach, L. J. (1970). *Essentials of psychological testing* (3rd ed.). New York: Harper & Row.

Cronbach, L. J., & Meehl, P. E. (1955). Construct validity in psychological tests. *Psychological Bulletin, 52,* 281–302.

Dahlstrom, W. G., & Tellegen, A. K. (1993). *Socioeconomic status and the MMPI-2: The relation of MMPI-2 patterns to levels of education and occupation.* Minneapolis: University of Minnesota Press.

Dahlstrom, W. G., & Welsh, G. S. (1960). *An MMPI handbook: A guide to use in clinical practice and research.* Minneapolis: University of Minnesota Press.

Dahlstrom, W. G., Welsh, G. S., & Dahlstrom, L. E. (1972). *An MMPI handbook: Vol. I. Clinical interpretation.* Minneapolis: University of Minnesota Press.

Dahlstrom, W. G., Welsh, G. S., & Dahlstrom, L. E. (1975). *An MMPI handbook: Vol. II. Research applications.* Minneapolis: University of Minnesota Press.

Deaux, K. (1984). From individual differences to social categories: Analysis of a decade's research on gender. *American Psychologist, 39,* 105–116.

Deaux, K. (1999). An overview of research on gender: Four themes from 3 decades. In W. B. Swann, Jr., & J. H. Langlois (Eds.), *Sexism and stereotypes in modern society: The gender science of Janet Taylor Spence* (pp. 11–33). Washington, D. C.: American Psychological Association.

de Cillis, O. E., & Orbison, W. D. (1950). A comparison of the Terman-Miles M-F test and the Mf scale of the MMPI. *Journal of Applied Psychology, 34,* 338–342.

Derogatis, L. (1977). *SCL-90-R: Administration, scoring, and procedures manual-II for the revised version.* Towson, MD: Clinical Psychometric Research.

Diamond, M. (1982). Sexual identity, monozygotic twins reared in discordant sex roles and a BBC follow-up. *Archives of Sexual Behavior, 11,* 181–186.

Didato, S. V., & Kennedy, T. M. (1957). Masculinity-femininity and personal values. *Psychological Reports, 2,* 231.

Duckworth, J. (1984). *MMPI interpretation manual for counselors and clinicians.* Muncie, IN: Accelerated Development.

Eagly, A. H., & Wood, W. (1999). The origins of sex differences in human behavior: Evolved dispositions versus social roles. *American Psychologist, 54* (6), 408–423.

Engel, I. M. (1966). A factor-analytic study of items from five masculinity-femininity tests. *Journal of Consulting Psychology, 30,* 565.

Eugenides, J. (2002). *Middlesex.* New York: Picador.

Evans, R. G., & Dinning, W. D. (1982). MMPI correlates of the Bem Sex Role Inventory and Extended Personal Attributes Questionnaire in a male psychiatric sample. *Journal of Clinical Psychology, 38,* 811–815.

Eysenck, H. J., Eysenck, S. B. G., & Barrett, P. (1995). Personality differences according to gender. *Psychological Reports, 76,* 711–716.

Feingold, A. (1994). Gender differences in personality: A meta-analysis. *Psychological Bulletin, 116,* 429–456.

Finlay, S. W., & Kapes, J. T. (2000). Scale 5 of the MMPI and MMPI-A: Evidence of disparity. *Assessment, 7,* 97–101.

Finn, S. E. (1986a). *The structure of masculinity-femininity self-ratings.* Unpublished manuscript, The University of Texas at Austin, available from the author at 4310 Medical Parkway, Suite 101, Austin, TX, 78756.

Finn, S. E. (1986b). Stability of personality ratings over 30 years: Evidence for an age/cohort interaction. *Journal of Personality and Social Psychology, 50,* 813–818.

Foerstner, S. B. (1986). *The factor structure and stability of selected Minnesota Multiphasic Personality Inventory (MMPI) subscales: Harris and Lingoes subscales, Wiggins content scales, Wiener subscales, and Serkownek subscales.* Unpublished doctoral dissertation, University of Akron, Akron, OH.

Fraas, L. A. (1970). Sex of figure drawing in identifying practicing male homosexuals. *Psychological Reports, 27,* 172–174.

Frable, D. E. S. (1989). Sex typing and gender ideology: Two facets of the individual's gender psychology that go together. *Journal of Personality and Social Psychology, 56,* 95–108.

Franck, K., & Rosen, E. (1949). A projective test of masculinity-femininity. *Journal of Consulting Psychology, 13,* 247–256.

Freund, K., Nagler, E., Langevin, R., Zajac, A., & Steiner, B. (1974). Measuring feminine gender identity in homosexual males. *Archives of Sexual Behavior, 3,* 249–260.

Friberg, R. R. (1967). Measures of homosexuality: Cross-validation of two MMPI scales and implications for usage. *Journal of Consulting Psychology, 31,* 88–91.

Friedman, A. F., Lewak, R., Nichols, D. S., & Webb, J. T. (2001). *Psychological assessment with the MMPI-2.* Mahwah, N. J.: Lawrence Erlbaum Associates.

Fry, F. D. (1949). A study of the personality traits of college students and of state prison inmates as measured by the MMPI. *Journal of Psychology, 28,* 439–449.

Gangestad, S. W., Bailey, J. M., & Martin, N. G. (2000). Taxometric analysis of sexual orientation and gender identity. *Journal of Personality and Social Psychology, 78,* 1109–1121.

Gaudreau, P. (1977). Factor analysis of the Bem Sex-Role Inventory. *Journal of Consulting and Clinical Psychology, 45,* 299–302.

Goen, J. Y., & Lansky, L. M. (1968). Masculinity, femininity, and masculinity-femininity: A phenomenological study of the Mf scale of the MMPI. *Psychological Reports, 23,* 183–194.

Goodenough, F. L. (1946). Semantic choice and personality structure. *Science, 104,* 151–156.

Goodstein, L. D. (1954). Regional differences in MMPI responses among male college students. *Journal of Consulting Psychology, 18,* 437–441.

Gough, H. G. (1947). Simulated patterns of the MMPI. *Journal of Abnormal Psychology, 42,* 215–225.

Gough, H. G. (1952). Identifying psychological femininity. *Educational and Psychological Measurement, 12,* 427–439.

Gough, H. G. (1964). *California Psychological Inventory Manual.* Palo Alto, CA: Consulting Psychologists Press.

Gough, H. G. (1966). A cross-cultural analysis of the CPI Femininity scale. *Journal of Consulting Psychology, 30,* 136–141.

Gough, H. G. (1987). *California Psychological Inventory: Administrator's guide.* Palo Alto, CA: Consulting Psychologists Press.

Gough, H. G., McKee, M. G., & Yandell, R. J. (1955). *Adjective checklist analyses of a number of selected psychometric and assessment variables.* Officer Education Research Laboratory (Technical Memorandum No. OERL-TM-55-10).

Graham, J. R. (1977). *The MMPI: A practical guide.* New York: Oxford University Press.

Graham, J. R. (1987). *The MMPI: A practical guide* (2nd ed.). New York: Oxford University Press.

Graham, J. R. (1990). *MMPI-2: Assessing personality and psychopathology.* New York: Oxford University Press.

Graham, J. R. (2000). *MMPI-2: Assessing personality and psychopathology* (3rd ed.). New York: Oxford University Press.

Graham, J. R., Schroeder, H. E., & Lilly, R. S. (1971). Factor analysis of items on the Social Introversion and Masculinity-Femininity scales of the MMPI. *Journal of Clinical Psychology, 27,* 367–370.

Granick, S., & Smith, L. J. (1953). Sex sequence in the Draw-a-Person Test and its relation to the MMPI Masculinity-Femininity Scale. *Journal of Consulting Psychology, 17,* 71–73.

Gray, J. (1992). *Men are from Mars, women are from Venus: A practical guide for improving communication and getting what you want in relationships.* New York: Harper Collins.

Gray, J. (1997). *Mars and Venus on a date: A guide for navigating the 5 stages of dating to create a loving and lasting relationship.* New York: Harper Perennial.

Green, R. (1987). *The "Sissy boy syndrome" and the development of homosexuality.* New Haven, CT: Yale University Press.

Greene, K. S., & Gynther, M. D. (1994). Another femininity scale? *Psychological Reports, 75,* 163–170.

Greene, R. L. (1980). *The MMPI: An interpretive manual.* New York: Grune & Stratton.

Greene, R. L. (2000). *The MMPI-2: An interpretive manual* (2nd ed.). New York: Grune & Stratton.

Gruber, K. J., & Powers, W. A. (1982). Factor and discriminant analysis of the Bem Sex-Role Inventory. *Journal of Personality Assessment, 46,* 291–294.

Guilford, J. P., & Guilford, R. B. (1936). Personality factors S, E, and M and their measurement. *Journal of Psychology, 2,* 109–127.

Guilford, J. P., & Zimmerman, W. S. (1949). *The Guilford-Zimmerman Temperament Survey: Manual of instructions and interpretation.* Beverly Hills, CA: Sheridan Supply Company.

Guilford, J. P., & Zimmerman, W. S. (1956). Fourteen dimensions of temperament. *Psychological Monographs, 70*(10), 26.

Guilford, J. S., Zimmerman, W. S., & Guilford, J. P. (1976). *Guilford-Zimmerman temperament survey handbook: Twenty-five years of research and application.* San Diego, CA: Edits Publishers.

Hare-Mustin, R. T., & Marecek, J. (1990). *Making a difference: Psychology and the construction of gender.* New Haven, CT: Yale University Press.

Harkness, A. R., McNulty, J. L., & Ben-Porath, Y. S. (1995). The personality psychopathology five (PSY5): Constructs and the MMPI-2 scales. *Psychological Assessment, 7,* 104–114.

Harkness, A. R., Tellegen, A., & Waller, N. (1995). Differential convergence of self-report and informant data for Multidimensional Personality Questionnaire traits: Implications for construct of negative emotionality. *Journal of Personality Assessment, 64,* 185–204.

Harris, R., & Lingoes, J. (1955/1968). *Subscales for the Minnesota Multiphasic Personality Inventory.* Unpublished manuscript, The Langley Porter Neuropsychiatric Institute, San Francisco, CA.

Haslam, N. (1997). Evidence that male sexual orientation is a matter of degree. *Journal of Personality and Social Psychology, 73,* 862–870.

Hathaway, S. R. (1956). Scales 5 (Masculinity-Femininity), 6 (Paranoia), and 8 (Schizophrenia). In W. G. Dahlstrom & L. E. Dahlstrom (Eds.), *Basic readings on the MMPI* (pp. 104–111). Minneapolis: University of Minnesota Press.

Hathaway, S. R., & Briggs, P. F. (1957). Some normative data on new MMPI scales. *Journal of Clinical Psychology, 13,* 364–368.

Hathaway, S. R., & McKinley, J. C. (1942). A multiphasic personality schedule (Minnesota): Construction of the schedule. *Journal of Psychology, 10,* 249–254.

Hathaway, S. R., & McKinley, J. C. (1943). *Minnesota Multiphasic Personality Inventory manual.* New York: Psychological Corporation.

Hathaway, S. R., & Meehl, P. E. (1951). *An atlas for the clinical use of the MMPI.* Minneapolis: University of Minnesota Press.

Hathaway, S. R., & Meehl, P. E. (1957). *Adjective checklist correlates of MMPI scores.* Unpublished manuscript, University of Minnesota. (Cited in Dahlstrom, Welsh, & Dahlstrom, 1972).

Hathaway, S. R., & Monachesi, E. D. (1957). The personalities of predelinquent boys. *Journal of Criminal Law & Criminology, 48,* 149–163.

Hathaway, S. R., & Monachesi, E. D. (1963). *Adolescent personality and behavior: MMPI patterns of normal, delinquent, dropout, and other outcomes.* Minneapolis: University of Minnesota Press.

Hefner, R., Rebecca, M. & Oleshansky, B. (1975). Development of sex role transcendence. *Human Development, 18,* 143–158.

Helgeson, V. S. (1994). Prototype and dimensions of masculinity and femininity. *Sex Roles, 31,* 653–682.

Helmreich, R. L., Spence, J. T., & Wilhelm, J. A. (1981). A psychometric analysis of the Personal Attributes Questionnaire. *Sex Roles, 7,* 1097–1108.

Helmstadter, G. C. (1964). *Principles of psychological measurement.* NY: Appleton-Century-Crofts.

Heston, J. C. (1948). A comparison of four masculinity-femininity scales. *Educational and Psychological Measurement, 8,* 375–387.

Hiatt, D., & Hargrave, G. E. (1994). Psychological assessment of gay and lesbian law enforcement applicants. *Journal of Personality Assessment, 63,* 80–88.

Hoffman, R. M. (2001). The measurement of masculinity and femininity: Historical perspective and implications for counseling. *Journal of Counseling and Development, 79,* 472–485.

Hoffman, R. M., & Borders, L. D. (2001). Twenty-five years after the Bem Sex-Role Inventory: A reassessment and new issues regarding classification variability. *Measurement and Evaluation in Counseling and Development, 34,* 39–55.

Horstman, W. R. (1975). MMPI responses of homosexual and heterosexual male college students. *Homosexual Counseling Journal, 2,* 66–75.

Huston, A. C. (1984a). Sex-typing. In E. M. Hetherington (Ed.), *Personality and Social Development.* New York: Wiley.

Huston, A. C. (1984b). Children's comprehension of televised formal features with masculine and feminine connotations. *Developmental Psychology, 20,* 707–716.

Hyde, J. S. (2005). The gender similarities hypothesis. *American Psychologist, 60,* 581–592.

Imperato-McGinley, J., Peterson, R. E., Gautier, T., & Sturla, E. (1979). Androgens and the evolution of male-gender identity among male pseudohermaphrodites with 5alpha-reductase deficiency. *The New England Journal of Medicine, 300,* 1233–1237.

Jackson, D. N. (1967). *Personality Research Form manual.* Goshen, NY: Research Psychologists Press.

Jackson, D. N. (1971). The dynamics of structured personality tests: 1971. *Psychological Review, 78,* 229–248.

Johnson, J. H., Null, C., Butcher, J. N., & Johnson, K. N. (1984). Replicated item level factor analysis of the full MMPI. *Journal of Personality and Social Psychology, 47,* 105–114.

Johnson, M. E., Jones, G., & Brems, C. (1996). Concurrent validity of the MMPI-2 Feminine Gender Role (GF) and Masculine Gender Role (GM) scales. *Journal of Personality Assessment, 66,* 153–168.

Jung, C. G. (1951). Aion: Researches into the phenomenology of the self. Collected works, Vol. 9, 1–42. In Campbell, J. (1971). *The portable Jung.* Kingsport, TN: Kingsport Press.

Jung, E. (1972). *Animus and anima.* Zurich, Switzerland: Spring Publications.

Keisling, B. L., Gynther, M. D., Greene, K. S., & Owen, D. L. (1993). A behavioral self-report of masculinity: An alternative to trait, attitudinal, and "behavioral" questionnaires. *Psychological Reports, 72,* 835–842.

Kimura, D. (1999). *Sex and cognition.* Cambridge, MA: The MIT Press.

King, G. D., & Kelley, C. K. (1977). MMPI behavioral correlates of spike-5 and two-point code types with Scale 5 as one elevation. *Journal of Clinical Psychology, 33,* 180–185.

Krippner, S. (1964a). The identification of male homosexuality with the MMPI. *Journal of Clinical Psychology, 20,* 159–161.

Krippner, S. (1964b). The relationship between MMPI and WAIS masculinity-femininity scores. *Personnel and Guidance Journal, 42,* 695–698.

Leaper, C. (1995). The use of masculine and feminine to describe women's and men's behavior. *Journal of Social Psychology, 135,* 359–369.

Lewin, M. (1984). Rather worse than folly?: Psychology measures femininity and masculinity, 1. In M. Lewin (Ed.), *In the shadow of the past: Psychology portrays the sexes* (pp. 179–204). New York: Columbia University Press.

Lippa, R. (1991). Some psychometric characteristics of gender diagnosticity measures: Reliability, validity, consistency across domains and relationship to the big five. *Journal of Personality and Social Psychology, 61,* 1000–1011.

Lippa, R. (1998). The nonverbal display and judgment of extraversion, masculinity, femininity, and gender diagnosticity: A lens model analysis. *Journal of Research in Personality, 32,* 80–107.

Lippa, R. (2002). Gender-related traits of heterosexual and homosexual men and women. *Archives of Sexual Behavior, 31,* 83–98.

Lippa, R., & Hershberger, S. (1999). Genetic and environmental influences on individual differences in masculinity, femininity, and gender diagnosticity: Analyzing data from a classic twin study. *Journal of Personality, 67,* 127–155.

Littlejohn, M. T. (1967). Creativity and masculinity-femininity in ninth graders. *Perceptual and Motor Skills, 25,* 737–743.

Loehlin, J. C., Jonsson, E. G., Gustavsson, J. P., Stallings, M. C., Gillespie, N. A., Wright, M. J., & Martin, N. G. (2005). Psychological masculinity-femininity via the gender diagnosticity approach: Heritability and consistency across ages and populations. *Journal of Personality, 73,* 1295–1319.

Long, K. A., & Graham, J. R. (1991). The Masculinity-Femininity scale of the MMPI-2: Is it useful with normal men? *Journal of Personality Assessment, 57,* 46–51.

Lowe, P. A., Mayfield, J. W. & Reynolds, C. R. (2003). Gender differences in memory test performance among children and adolescents. *Archives of Clinical Neuropsychology, 18,* 865–878.

Lubinski, D., Tellegen, A., & Butcher, J. N. (1981). The relationship between androgyny and subjective indicators of emotional well-being. *Journal of Personality and Social Psychology, 40,* 722–730.

Lucio, E., Ampudia, A., Duran, C., Leon, I., & Butcher, J.N. (2001). Comparison of the Mexican and American norms of the MMPI-2. *Journal of Clinical Psychology, 57,* 1459–1468.

Lueptow, L. B., Garovich-Szabo, L., & Lueptow, M. B. (2001). Social change and the persistence of sex typing: 1974–1997. *Social Forces, 80,* 1–36.

Lunneborg, P. W. (1972). Dimensionality of MF. *Journal of Clinical Psychology, 28,* 313–317.

Lunneborg, P. W., & Lunneborg, C. E. (1970). Factor structure of MF scales and items. *Journal of Clinical Psychology, 25*, 360–366.

Lutz, D. J., Roback, H. B., & Hart, M. (1984). Feminine gender identity and psychological adjustment of male transsexuals and male homosexuals. *Journal of Sex Research, 20*, 350–362.

Manosevitz, M. (1970). Item analyses of the MMPI MF scale using homosexual and heterosexual males. *Journal of Consulting and Clinical Psychology, 35*, 395–399.

Manosevitz, M. (1971). Education and MMPI Mf scores in homosexual and heterosexual males. *Journal of Consulting and Clinical Psychology, 36*, 395–399.

Marks, P. A., & Briggs, P. F. (1972). Adolescent norm tables for the MMPI. In W. G. Dahlstrom, G. S. Welsh, & L. E. Dahlstrom (Eds.), *An MMPI handbook: Volume I. Clinical interpretation* (Rev. ed., pp. 388–399). Minneapolis: University of Minnesota Press.

Marsh, H. W. (1985). The structure of masculinity/femininity: An application of confirmatory factor analysis to higher-order factor structures and factorial invariance. *Multivariate Behavioral Research, 20*, 427–449.

Marsh, J. T., Hilliard, J., & Liechti, R. (1955). A sexual deviation scale for the MMPI. *Journal of Consulting Psychology, 19*, 55–59.

Martin, C. L. (1999). A developmental perspective on gender effects and gender concepts. In W. B. Swann, Jr., J. H. Langlois, & L. A. Gilbert (Eds.), *Sexism and stereotypes in modern society: The gender science of Janet Taylor Spence*. Washington, D.C.: American Psychological Association.

Martin, E. H. (1991). *Subscales for Scale 5 of the Minnesota Multiphasic Personality Inventory-2*. Unpublished master's thesis, University of Texas at Austin, Austin, TX.

Martin, E. H. (1993). *Masculinity-Femininity and the Minnesota Multiphasic Personality Inventory-2*. Dissertation, University of Texas at Austin, Austin, TX.

McCormick, C. M., & Witelson, S. F. (1994). Functional cerebral asymmetry and sexual orientation in men and women. *Behavioral Neuroscience, 108*, 525–531.

McCrae, R. R., & Costa, P. T. (1987). Validation of the five-factor model of personality across instruments and observers. *Journal of Personality and Social Psychology, 52*, 81–90.

McCrae, R. R., Martin, T. A., & Costa, P. T. (2005). Age trends and age norms for the NEO Personality Inventory-3 in adolescents and adults. *Assessment, 12*, 363–373.

McFadden, D. (2002). The auditory system as a window onto human prenatal development and sexual differentiation. Invited address American Psychological Society, available from the author, University of Texas.

McGrath, R. E., Sapareto, E., & Pogge, D. L. (1998). A new perspective on gender orientation measurement with the MMPI-2: Development of the Masculine-Feminine Pathology Scale. *Journal of Personality Assessment, 70,* 551–563.

Meyer, G. J., Finn, S. E., Eyde, L. D., Kay, G. G., Moreland, K. L., Dies, R. R., Eisman, E. J., Kubiszyn, T. W., & Reed, G. M. (2001). Psychological testing and psychological assessment: A review of evidence and issues. *American Psychologist, 56,* 128–165.

Millon, T. (1987). *Millon Clinical Multiaxial Inventory-II manual* (2nd ed.). Minneapolis: National Computer Systems.

Money, J., & Ehrhardt, A. A. (1972). *Man & woman, boy & girl: The differentiation and dimorphism of gender identity from conception to maturity.* Baltimore, MD: Johns Hopkins University Press.

Moreland, J. R., Gulanick, M., Montague, E. K., & Harren, V. A. (1978). Some psychometric properties of the Bem Sex-Role Inventory. *Applied Psychological Measurement, 2,* 249–256.

Moreland, K. L. (1985). *Test-retest reliability of 80 MMPI scales.* Unpublished materials available from Pearson Assessments. Minneapolis, MN.

Morton, T. L., Farris, K. L., & Brenowitz, L. H. (2002). MMPI-A scores and high points of male juvenile delinquents: Scales 4, 5, and 6 as markers of juvenile delinquency. *Psychological Assessment, 14,* 311–319.

Munley, P. H., Morris, J. R., & Murray, D. A. (2001). A comparison of African-American and white American veteran MMPI-2 profiles. *Assessment, 8,* 1–10.

Murphy, C. (1997). Can an infant's sex be changed? Researchers report that boy raised as a girl was miserable until learning his true identity. *The Washington Post,* March 18, 1997, Final Edition.

Murray, J. B. (1963a). The Mf scale of the MMPI for college students. *Journal of Educational Research, 19,* 113–115.

Murray, J. B. (1963b). Correlational study of the MMPI and GZTS. *Journal of General Psychology, 69,* 267–273.

Murray, J. B. (1985). Borderline manifestations in the Rorschachs of male transsexuals. *Journal of Personality Assessment, 49,* 454–466.

Nichols, D. S. (1980). *Notes on the Nichols corrected Acceptance of Passivity scale.* Unpublished manuscript, available from the author, 5107 NE Couch St., Portland, OR, 97213-3021.

Nichols, D. S. (2001). *Essentials of MMPI-2 assessment.* New York: Wiley & Sons.

O'Heron, C. A., & Orlofsky, J. L. (1990). Stereotypic and nonstereotypic sex role trait and behavior orientations, gender identity, and psychological adjustment. *Journal of Personality and Social Psychology, 58,* 134–143.

O'Neil, J. M., & Egan, J. (1992). Men's and women's gender role journeys: A metaphor a healing, transition, and transformation. In B. Wainrib (Ed.), *Gender issues across the life cycle.* New York: Springer.

O'Neil, J. M., Egan, J., Owen, S. V., & Murry, V. M. (1993). The gender role journey measure: Scale development and psychometric evaluation. *Sex Roles, 28,* 167–185.

O'Neil, J. M., & Fishman, D. M. (1986). Adult men's career transitions and gender role themes. In Z. Leibowitz & D. Lea (Eds.), *Adult career development: Concepts, issues, and practices.* Alexandria, VA: American Association for Counseling and Development.

Orlofsky, J. L. (1981). Relationship between sex role attitudes and personality traits and the Sex Role Behavior Scale-1: A new measure of masculine and feminine role behaviors and interests. *Journal of Personality and Social Psychology, 40,* 927–940.

Orlofsky, J. L., & O'Heron, C. A. (1987). Development of a short form Sex-Role Behavior Scale. *Journal of Personality Assessment, 51,* 267–277.

Orlofsky, J. L., Ramsden, M. W., & Cohen, R. S. (1982). Development of the revised Sex-Role Behavior Scale. *Journal of Personality Assessment, 46,* 632–638.

Ozer, D. J. (1989). Construct validity in personality assessment. In D. M. Buss & N. Cantor (Eds.), *Personality psychology: Recent trends and emerging directions* (pp. 224–234). New York: Springer.

Panton, J. H. (1960). A new MMPI scale for the identification of homosexuality. *Journal of Clinical Psychology, 16,* 17–21.

Pedhazur, E. J., & Tetenbaum, T. J. (1979). Bem Sex-Role Inventory: A theoretical and methodological critique. *Journal of Personality and Social Psychology, 37,* 996–1016.

Peña, L. M., Megargee, E. I., & Brody, E. (1996). MMPI-A patterns of male juvenile delinquents. *Psychological Assessment, 8,* 388–397.

Pepper, L. J., & Strong, P. N. (1958). *Judgmental subscales for the Mf scale of the MMPI.* Unpublished manuscript, Hawaii Department of Health, Honolulu, HI.

Peterson, C. D. (1991). *Masculinity and femininity in independent dimensions on the MMPI.* Unpublished doctoral dissertation, University of North Carolina, Chapel Hill.

Peterson, C. D., & Dahlstrom, W. G. (1992). The derivation of gender-role scales *GM* and *GF* for MMPI-2 and their relationship to Scale 5 *(Mf)*. *Journal of Personality Assessment, 59,* 486–499.

Plomin, R, Willerman, L., & Loehlin, J. C. (1976). Resemblance in appearance and the equal environments assumption in twin studies of personality traits. *Behavior Genetics, 6,* 43–52.

Ratliff, E. S., & Conley, J. (1981). The structure of masculinity-femininity: Multidimensionality and gender differences. *Social Behavior and Personality, 9,* 41–47.

Reece, M. (1964). Masculinity and femininity: A factor analytical study. *Psychological Reports, 14,* 123–139.

Reynolds, C. R. & Bigter, E. D. (1944). Test of Memory and Learning. Austin, TX: Pro-ed.

Rhoads, S. E. (2004). *Taking sex differences seriously.* San Francisco, CA: Encounter Books.

Roid, G. H., & Fitts, W. H. (1991). *Tennessee Self-Concept Scale, revised manual.* Los Angeles, CA: Western Psychological Services.

Ross, M. W., Burnard, D., & Campbell, I. M. (1988). Utility of the *Gd* scale for the measurement of gender dysphoria in males. *Psychological Reports, 63,* 87–90.

Ruble, D. N., & Martin, C. L. (1998). Gender development. In W. Damon (Series Ed.) & N. Eisenberg (Vol. Ed.), *Handbook of child psychology. Vol. 3: Social, emotional and personality development* (5th ed., pp. 933–1016). New York: Wiley & Sons.

Ruch, L. O. (1984). Dimensionality of the Bem Sex-Role Inventory: A multidimensional analysis. *Sex Roles, 10,* 99–117.

Schatzberg, A. F., Westfall, M. P., Blumetti, A. B., & Birk, C. L. (1975). Effeminacy. I. A. quantitative rating scale. *Archives of Sexual Behavior, 4,* 31–41.

Schinka, J. A., & LaLone, L. (1997). MMPI-2 norms: Comparisons with a census-matched subsample. *Psychological Assessment, 9,* 307–311.

Schuerger, J. M., Foerstner, S. B., Serkownek, K., & Ritz, G. (1987). History and validities of the Serkownek subscales for MMPI scales 5 and 0. *Psychological Reports, 61,* 227–235.

Scott, R. L., & Pampa, W. M. (2000). The MMPI-2 in Peru: a normative study. *Journal of Personality Assessment, 74,* 95–105.

Serkownek, K. (1975). *Subscales for Scales 5 and 0 of the Minnesota Multiphasic Personality Inventory.* Unpublished materials.

Shepler, B. F. (1951). A comparison of masculinity-femininity measures. *Journal of Consulting Psychology, 15,* 484–486.

Sines, J. O. (1977). M-F: Bipolar and probably multidimensional. *Journal of Clinical Psychology, 33,* 1038–1041.

Singer, M. I. (1970). Comparison of indicators of homosexuality on the MMPI. *Journal of Consulting and Clinical Psychology, 34,* 15–18.

Slaby, R. G., & Frey, K. S. (1975). Development of gender constancy and selective attention to same-sex models. *Child Development, 46,* 849–856.

Sopchak, A. L. (1952). College students' norms for the MMPI. *Journal of Consulting Psychology, 16,* 445–448.

Spence, J. T. (1984). Masculinity, femininity, and gender-related traits: A conceptual analysis and critique of current research. *Progress in Experimental Personality Research, 13,* 1–97.

Spence, J. T. (1985). Gender identity and its implications for concepts of masculinity and femininity. In T. B. Sondregger (Ed.), *Nebraska symposium on motivation: Psychology of gender* (pp. 59–96). Lincoln: University of Nebraska Press.

Spence, J. T. (1993). Gender-related traits and gender ideology: Evidence for a multifactorial Theory. *Journal of Personality and Social Psychology, 64,* 642–635.

Spence, J. T., & Buckner, C. (1995). Masculinity and femininity: Defining the undefinable. In P. Kalbfleisch & M. Cody (Eds.), *Gender, power and communication in interpersonal relationships* (pp. 105–138). Hillsdale, NJ: Lawrence Erlbaum Associates.

Spence, J. T., & Helmreich, R. (1981). Androgyny versus gender schema: A comment on Bem's gender schema theory. *Psychological Review, 88,* 365–368.

Spence, J. T., & Helmreich, R. (1986). *Personal Attributes Questionnaire (PAQ).* Unpublished manuscript, University of Texas at Austin.

Spence, J. T., Helmreich, R., & Holahan, C. K. (1979). Negative and positive components of psychological masculinity and femininity and their relationship to self-reports of neurotic and acting out behaviors. *Journal of Personality and Social Psychology, 37,* 1673–1682.

Spence, J. T., Helmreich, R. L., & Sawin, L. L. (1980). The Male-Female Relations Questionnaire: A self-report inventory of sex role behaviors and preferences and its relationships to masculine and feminine personality traits, sex role attitudes, and other measures. *JSAS Selected Documents in Psychology, 10,* 87 (Ms. 916).

Spence, J. T., Helmreich, R., & Stapp, J. (1974). The Personal Attributes Questionnaire: A measure of sex-role stereotypes and masculinity-femininity. *JSAS Catalog of Selected Documents in Psychology, 4,* 43–44.

Spence, J. T., Helmreich, R., and Stapp, J. (1975). Ratings of self and peers on self-role attributes and their relations to self-esteem and conceptions of masculinity-femininity. *Journal of Personality and Social Psychology, 32,* 29–39.

Spence, J. T., & Sawin, L. L. (1985). Images of masculinity and femininity: A reconceptualization. In V. O'Leary, R. Unger, & B. Wallston (Eds.), *Sex, gender, and social psychology* (pp. 35–66). Hillsdale, N. J: Lawrence Erlbaum Associates.

Storms, M. D. (1979). Sex role identity and its relationship to sex role attributes and sex role stereotypes. *Journal of Personality and Social Psychology, 37,* 1779–1789.

Strong, E. K. (1943). *The vocational interests of men and women.* Stanford, CA: Stanford University Press.

Swaab, D. F., Chung, W. C. J., Kruijver, F. P. M., Hofman, M. A., & Ishunina, T. A. (2001). Structural and functional sex differences in the human hypothalamus. *Hormones and Behavior, 40,* 93–98.

Tannen, D. (1990). *You just don't understand: Men and women in conversation.* New York: Ballantine Books.

Tanner, B. A. (1990). Composite descriptions associated with rare MMPI two-point codetypes: Codes that involve Scale 5. *Journal of Clinical Psychology, 46,* 425–431.

Tellegen, A. (1982). *Brief manual for the Differential Personality Questionnaire.* Minneapolis: University of Minnesota Press.

Tellegen, A. (1991). Personality traits: Issues of definition, evidence, and assessment. In D. Cicchetti & W. Grove (Eds.), *Thinking clearly about psychology: Essays in honor of Paul Everett Meehl, 2,* 10–35. Minneapolis: University of Minnesota Press.

Tellegen, A., & Ben-Porath, Y. S. (2008). *Minnesota Multiphasic Personality Inventory-2 Restructured Form (MMPI-2-RF): Technical manual.* Minneapolis: University of Minnesota Press.

Tellegen, A., Ben-Porath, Y. S., McNulty, J. L., Arbisi, P. A., Graham, J. R., & Kaemmer, B. (2003). *The MMPI-2 restructured clinical (RC) scales: Development, validation and interpretation.* Minneapolis: University of Minnesota Press.

Tellegen, A., Butcher, J. N., & Hoeglund, T. (1993, June). Are unisex norms for the MMPI-2 needed? Would they work? *News and Profiles, 4,* 4–5.

Tellegen, A., & Lubinski, D. (1983). Some methodological comments on label, traits, interaction and types in the study of "femininity" and "masculinity": Reply to Spence. *Journal of Personality and Social Psychology, 44,* 447–455.

Tellegen, A., & Waller, N. G. (2008). Exploring personality through test construction: Development of the Multidimensional Personality Questionnaire. In G. J. Boyle, G. Matthews, and D. H. Saklofske (Eds.), *Handbook of personality theory and testing: Vol. II.* Personality measurement and assessment (pp. 254–285). London: Sage.

Terman, L. M., & Miles, C. C. (1936). *Sex and personality: Studies in masculinity and femininity.* New York: McGraw-Hill.

Terman, L. M., & Miles, C. C. (1938). *Manual of information and directions for use of Attitude-Interest Analysis Test.* New York: McGraw-Hill.

Todd, A. L., & Gynther, M. D. (1988). Have MMPI Mf scale correlates changed in the past 30 years? *Journal of Clinical Psychology, 44,* 505–510.

Tonsager, M. E., & Finn, S. E. (1992, May). *MMPI-2 Content and Clinical Scale correlations: Implications for interpretation.* Paper presented at the 27th Symposium on the MMPI, Minneapolis, MN.

Trivers, R. L. (1972). Parental Investment and Sexual Selection. In B. G. Campbell (Ed.), *Sexual Selection and the Descent of Man, 1871–1971* (pp. 136–179). Chicago: Aldine.

Twenge, J. M. (1999). Mapping gender: The multifactorial approach and the organization of gender-related attributes. *Psychology of Women Quarterly, 23,* 485–502.

Udry, J. R. (2000). Biological limits of gender construction. *American Sociological Review, 65,* 443–457.

Udry, J. R., & Chantala, K. (2004). Masculinity-femininity guides sexual union formation in adolescents. *Personality and Social Psychology Bulletin, 30,* 44–55.

Udry, J. R., & Chantala, K. (2006). Masculinity femininity predicts sexual orientation in men but not in women. *Journal of Biosocial Science, 38,* 797–809.

Vatican Information Services (2004). *Letter to the bishops of the Catholic church on the collaboration of men and women in the church and the world.* Holy See Press Office, Cardinal Joseph Ratzinger, Prefect, Angelo Amato, SDB, Titular Archbishop of Sila, Secretary.

Volentine, S. Z. (1981). The assessment of masculinity and femininity: Scale 5 of the MMPI compared with the BSRI and PAQ. *Journal of Clinical Psychology, 37,* 367–374.

Wainer, H. (1976). Estimating coefficients of linear models: It don't make no nevermind. *Psychological Bulletin, 83,* 213–217.

Wakefield, J. A., Sasek, J., Friedman, A. F., & Bowden, J. D. (1976). Androgyny and other measures of masculinity-femininity. *Journal of Consulting and Clinical Psychology, 44,* 766–770.

Ward, L. C., & Dillon, E. A. (1990). Psychiatric symptom correlates of the Minnesota Multiphasic Personality Inventory (MMPI) masculinity-femininity scale. *Psychological Assessment, 2,* 286–288.

Waters, C. W., Waters, L. K., & Pincus, S. (1977). Factor analysis of masculine and feminine sex-typed items from the Bem Sex-Role Inventory. *Psychological Reports, 40,* 567–570.

Whetton, C., & Swindells, T. (1977). A factor analysis of the Bem Sex-Role Inventory. *Journal of Clinical Psychology, 33,* 150–153.

Wiggins, J. S., & Holzmuller, A. (1978). Psychological androgyny and interpersonal behavior. *Journal of Consulting and Clinical Psychology, 46,* 40–52.

Willemsen, T. M., & Fischer, A. H. (1999). Assessing multiple facets of gender identity: The Gender Identity Questionnaire. *Psychological Reports, 84,* 561–562.

Willerman, L. (1991). Sex differences, psychological. *Encyclopedia of Human Biology, 6,* 855–863.

Williams, C. L., & Butcher, J. N. (1989). An MMPI study of adolescents: I. Empirical validity of the standard scales. *Psychological Assessment, 1,* 251–259.

Williams, J. E., & Best, D. L. (1990). *Measuring sex stereotypes: A multination study.* Newbury Park, CA: Sage.

Wilson, J. D. (2000). Androgens, androgen receptors and male gender role behavior. *Hormones and Behavior, 40,* 358–366.

Winfield, D. (1953). The relationship between I.Q. scores and Minnesota Multiphasic Personality Inventory scores. *Journal of Social Psychology, 38,* 299–300.

Witelson, S. F. (1991). Neural sexual mosaicism: Sexual differentiation of the human temporo-parietal region for functional asymmetry. *Psychoneuroendrocrinology, 16,* 131–153.

Wong, M. R. (1984). MMPI Scale Five: Its meaning or lack thereof. *Journal of Personality Assessment, 48,* 279–284.

Woo, M., & Tian, P. S. O. (2006). The MMPI-2 Gender-Masculine and Gender-Feminine scales: Gender roles as predictors of psychological health in clinical patients. *International Journal of Psychology, 41,* 413–422.

Woo, M., & Tian, P. S. O. (2008). Empirical investigations of the MMPI-2 Gender-Masculine and Gender-Feminine Scales. *Journal of Individual Differences, 29,* 1–10.

Index

Aaronson, B. S., 68

Acceptance of Passivity (Ap) scale, 67, 68, 136

Adolescent-Denial of Stereotypical Masculine Interests factor, 172, 173 (table), 176 (table), 179, 187, 184, 196; correlations, 187–192; described, 174–175; distribution of scores on, 184 (fig.); summary of, 192 (table)

Adolescent Femininity-Masculinity factor (A-FM), 182, 182 (table), 183–184, 186 (fig.) , 187, 192, 196, 213, 214; bimodal distribution of, 186; correlations, 187–192; masculinity-femininity and, 215; parameters of in MMPI-A normative sample, 183 (table); summary of, 192 (table); variance explained by, 183 (table)

Adolescent-Hypersensitivity/Anxiety factor, 173 (table), 176 (table), 192, 193, 196; correlations, 187–192; described, 175–176;

distribution of scores on, 185 (fig.); gender differences in, 184; summary of, 192 (table)

Adolescent-Low Cynicism factor, 173 (table), 176 (table), 192, 193, 196, 214; correlations, 187–192; CYN Content scale and, 187; described, 175–176; distribution of scores on, 185 (fig.); male-female scores on, 186; summary of, 192 (table)

Adolescent-Restraint factor, 173 (table), 176, 176 (table), 193, 196, 214; correlations, 188–192; CON content scale and, 192; described, 175–176; distribution of scores on, 186, 186 (fig.); summary of 192 (table)

Adolescent-Stereotypical Femininity factor, 172, 173 (table), 175, 179, 187, 196; correlations, 187–192; described, 174–175; differential endorsement rates between males/females on, 174 (table);

distribution of scores on, 185 (fig.); gender differences in, 184, 186; summary of, 192 (table)

AES. *See* Aesthetic-Literary Interests

Aesthetic Interests factor, 96, 97, 98, 100, 102, 108, 132, 150–151, 153 (table), 155, 166, 196, 199, 200, 202; adolescents and, 173; AES and, 138; age and, 250, 255; Black/White males and, 210; correlations with, 137; described, 141, 143; distribution of scores on, 118 (fig.), 119; education and, 158, 159, 260, 264; ethnicity and, 161, 268, 272; factor structure of, 121–122 (table); Gd and, 136; gender difference and, 144; MPQP and, 144, 145, 151, 152; PSY-5 Scales and, 135; Stereotypical Feminine Interests and, 101, 107, 138, 207; test-retest coefficient for, 120; Validity/Clinical/Supplementary scales and, 130

Aesthetic-Literary Interests (AES), 84, 85, 90, 97, 200, 213; Aesthetic Interests and, 138; constraint and, 89; correlations in *MMPI-2-RF Technical Manual* with, 86–88 (table); Feminine Gender Identity and, 138, 139

A-FM. *See* Adolescent Femininity-Masculinity

Age, 51, 166, 212; Aesthetic Interests and, 250, 255; Denial of Stereotypical Masculine Interests and, 248, 253; Feminine Gender Identity and, 251, 256; FM Scale and, 252, 257; gender differences

and, 22, 27; Hypersensitivity/Anxiety and, 155, 249, 254; Low Cynicism and, 155, 250, 255; men and, 153–154; Restraint and, 155–156, 251, 256; Scale 5 factors and, 152–162, 253; Stereotypical Feminine Interests and, 249, 254

AIAT. *See* Attitude-Interest Analysis Test

Aldwin, C. M., 154

Althof, S. E., 68, 136, 137

Amato, Angelo, 4

Ambady, N., 42

Androgens, 8, 9, 10, 40, 44, 46, 71–72, 74, 57, 75, 77, 161

Androgyny theory, 44, 46, 71–72, 74, 161

Antill, J. K., 28

Ap scale. *See* Acceptance of Passivity scale

Arbisi, P. A., 91, 110, 133, 160, 200, 205

Archer, R. P., 67, 69

Attitude-Interest Analysis Test (AIAT), 34, 61, 62, 63, 69; contents of, 35–38; drawings from, 36 (fig.)

Augmented factors MMPI-2, 110–112, 126, 139; intercorrelations of/normative sample, 115 (table); variance explained by, 114 (table)

Augmented factors MMPI-A, 174–176, 176 (table); variance explained by, 183 (table)

Bailey, J. M., 17, 42, 53, 140, 146

Bandura, A., 13, 15

Barnett, Rosalind, 3, 211

Barrett, P., 26

(O'Neil, Egan, Owen, and Murry), 50

Gender roles, 14, 15, 16, 49, 56, 83; defined, 7 (table); developmental changes for, 50

Genetics, 10, 12; environmental factors and, 10; hormones and, 9, 11

GF scale. *See* Feminine Gender Role scale

GIF. *See* Gender Identity Scale for Females

GIM. *See* Gender Identity Scale for Males

GIS. *See* Gender Identity Scale

GM scale. *See* Masculine Gender Role scale

Gough, H. G., 40, 64, 66

Graham, J. R., 39, 47, 65, 67, 70, 77, 78, 91, 98, 110, 133, 146, 162, 200, 205

Green, R., 24

Greene, K. S., 49, 61, 74, 116, 152, 154–155, 158, 160

Guilford, J. P.: GTZS and, 39–40

Guilford, J. S.: GTZS and, 39–40

Guilford-Zimmerman Temperament Survey (GZTS), 34, 39–40, 65

Hallahan, M., 42

Handedness, 215

Hare-Mustin, R. T., 5

Hargrave, G. E., 64–65

Harkness, A. R., 23, 24, 134

Harris, R., 69, 136

Haslam, N., 79

Hathaway, S. R., 39, 60, 63, 72; homosexuality and, 62, 64; on item selection, 61; Scale 5 and,

61, 64, 66–67, 82, 192; scale for women by, 63–64

Hefner, R. M., 49

Helgeson, V. S., 19, 204

Helmreich, R., 20, 28, 46, 47, 71, 77

Hershberger, S., 10

Hiatt, D., 64–65

Hilliard, J., 67

Hoeglund, T., 80

Hoffman, R. M., 45, 51

Hoffman Gender Scale, 51

Holliman, N. B., 82

Holzmuller, A., 45, 206

Homosexual Concern-Passivity, 47

Homosexuality: heterosexuality and, 19, 20, 32, 64–65; incomplete masculinity and, 9, 17; scales identifying, 67; transsexualism and, 199

Homosexuals, 16, 19, 61, 113; femininity in, 52, 62; neuroanatomical/neurochemical differences for, 17; psyche of, 91

Hormones, 7, 25; behavior and, 8–9; genetics and, 9, 11; prenatal, 8–9; sexual orientation and, 17

Hyde, J. S., 22

Hypersensitivity/Anxiety factor, 95, 97, 98, 100, 102, 107, 108, 116, 126, 153 (table), 154–155, 165, 166, 172, 182, 199, 200, 202, 209, 214; age and, 155, 249, 254; Content Scales and, 132; described, 141, 150; distribution of scores on, 117, 117 (fig.); education and, 157, 159, 259, 263; ethnicity and, 161, 267, 271; factor structure of, 121 (table); Gd scale and, 136; gender identity

Hale Martin, Ph.D., earned his doctorate in clinical psychology from the University of Texas at Austin. He completed his internship at Michael Reese Hospital in Chicago and a postdoctoral fellowship at the University of Texas Health Science Center at San Antonio. After this training, he served as the associate director of the Center for Therapeutic Assessment in Austin until 1996, when he returned to Denver to teach at the University of Colorado and start a private practice. In 2001, he joined the core faculty of the Graduate School of Professional Psychology at the University of Denver, where he teaches and supervises assessment as well as oversees assessment training in the associated community clinic. He is director of the Colorado Center for Therapeutic Assessment, and he founded the Colorado Assessment Society.

Stephen E. Finn, Ph.D., is the founder of the Center for Therapeutic Assessment in Austin, Texas, and an adjunct clinical assistant professor of psychology at the University of Texas at Austin. He is author of *In Our Clients' Shoes: Theory and Techniques of Therapeutic Assessment, A Manual for Using the MMPI-2 as a Therapeutic Intervention* (Minnesota, 1996) and many articles and chapters on psychological assessment and psychodiagnosis. He obtained his Ph.D. in clinical psychology from the University of Minnesota and is a fellow of the American Psychological Association (Clinical Psychology) and of the Society of Personality Assessment, for which he served as president in 2002–2004. He lectures frequently around the world on psychological assessment.